# Breaking the Circle of One

T0346429

# Studies in the
# Postmodern Theory of Education

Joe L. Kincheloe and Shirley R. Steinberg
*General Editors*

Vol. 55

PETER LANG
New York • Washington, D.C./Baltimore • Boston
Bern • Frankfurt am Main • Berlin • Vienna • Paris

# Breaking the Circle of One

## Redefining Mentorship in the Lives and Writings of Educators

Carol A. Mullen, Senior Editor

Maggie D. Cox, Cindy K. Boettcher,
and Diane S. Adoue, Editors

PETER LANG
New York • Washington, D.C./Baltimore • Boston
Bern • Frankfurt am Main • Berlin • Vienna • Paris

**Library of Congress Cataloging-in-Publication Data**

Breaking the circle of one: redefining mentorship in the lives
and writings of educators / Carol A. Mullen ... [et al.] (editors).
p. cm. — (Counterpoints; vol. 55)
Includes bibliographical references (p. ).
1. Mentoring in education—United States. 2. Teachers—Training of—United States.
3. College-school cooperation—United States. 4. Interpersonal relations—United
States. I. Mullen, Carol A. II. Series: Counterpoints (New York, N.Y.); vol. 55.
LB1731.4.B74   370'.71—dc21   96-50060
ISBN 0-8204-3758-1
ISSN 1058-1634


**Die Deutsche Bibliothek-CIP-Einheitsaufnahme**

Breaking the circle of one: redefining mentorship in the lives
and writings of educators / Carol A. Mullen ... (ed.). –New York;
Washington, D.C./Baltimore; Boston; Bern; Frankfurt am Main;
Berlin; Vienna; Paris: Lang.
(Counterpoints; Vol. 55)
ISBN 0-8204-3758-1
NE: Mullen, Carol A. [Hrsg.]; GT

Cover design by William A. Kealy and Carol A. Mullen.


The paper in this book meets the guidelines for permanence and durability
of the Committee on Production Guidelines for Book Longevity
of the Council of Library Resources.

© 1997, 2000 Peter Lang Publishing, Inc., New York

Printed in the United States of America.

To the mentors and teachers throughout our lives and careers, and to the students who have helped to educate us. We, the writers, are inspired by the special mentoring relationships and opportunities that have served as nurturing forces over time. For our readers who are similarly inspired by their own stories of mentorship, we also thank you for contributing to the "breaking of the circle of one" in people's lives.

# Contents

# Figures and Tables

# Foreword

## Joe L. Kincheloe
## and Shirley R. Steinberg

If we are guessing correctly, most of you who read this book are teachers in one capacity or another. We hope you are all mentors. If not, perhaps this book will aid in your attempts to break into circles and begin to mentor and be mentored. If our first assumption is correct, that is, most of the readers are teachers, then we will make a second assumption: teachers who love to teach have often been mentored by other teachers who love to teach. In other words, we are in the classroom for different reasons, but one reason does prevail: someone influenced our lives, someone helped us become teachers. Unfortunately, we cannot always assume that "someone" was always a positive influence—only that someone was a strong influence. Who influenced our decision to be in the classroom? Were they positive mentors/teachers? or negative?

In our own lives, we cannot write or teach a word without an acknowledgment to those who have mentored and taught us. Joe often speaks of Gene Razor at Emory and Henry College and Clint Allison at the University of Tennessee. Both men saw potential and fervor that had gone unrecognized or condemned by other teachers. Joe teaches because others taught him.

Shirley writes of Mrs. G., her ninth grade English teacher. Mrs. G. made the difference in guiding an awkward, talkative female toward career choices that were commensurate with her character traits (flaws in the eyes of other teachers). Kathleen Berry was Shirley's university mentor. She exemplified in undergraduate teacher education the model for Shirley's teaching career. Kathy was/is the personification of critical pedagogy and holistic education; she infused much more than methods in every class session.  Kathy's mentor was Dorothy Heathcote–Dorothy changed the face of drama and education not only in Kathy's mind but in the English-speaking world.  As our mentors and mentoring continue, we enlarge our circle by returning to our students what was given so unselfishly to us.

Sometimes we remember with thanks the negative mentoring we received and observed.  We remember the positivists, the punitive blowhards, the quasi-intellectuals, the macho-mean men and women who stood in front of our classes and reinforced our unlearning— through them we silently vowed to change education, to pay them back. We thank those who were such bad teachers, such nonmentors, for in their examples we find who we are not. Unfortunately, much to our chagrin, they will not be reading this book.

# Preface

# Breaking the Circle of One through Mentorship

## Carol A. Mullen
## with Maggie D. Cox

*Breaking the Circle of One: Redefining Mentorship in the Lives and Writings of Educators* grew out of a self-study writing group that consisted of graduate students and professors who gathered primarily to provide and receive support from one another within our traditional university setting. Among ourselves we were simply known as the "*Circle.*"

In an effort to combat feelings of isolation, competition, and abandonment, we met to break through our circles of one. We also wanted to continue the learning experiences from our interconnected doctoral courses and supervisory relationships. We had yet to discover the strength of our community for developing innovative forms of academic expression. While stretching ourselves to engage in cocreated perspectives on research and teaching, we simultaneously found ourselves interacting within another circle. This other circle represented, in our minds, social control and power dynamics at the university level. Although our relationship to this broader circle had definitely played a role in the formation of the group, we nonetheless had to continue to make allowances for it as a pervasive dynamic in our work and within our circle.

The group met for one academic year. Individuals negotiated varying degrees of comfort with the project and its overlapping circles from within and without. A core group of educator-writers became established through this process. Others joined us later, celebrating our project and helping to turn it into a book. The *Circle* has continued other, often related, work in both formal and informal mentoring contexts.

Clearly, we had not met with a fully articulated agenda, purpose, or mission. Just the opposite. The stimulation, encouragement, and mentorship that we each had been experiencing with one or more of the others became central to our need to formally gather. We had already known one another from academic courses, through corridor conversations, and from other contexts and places. It was out of this web of support that we had already engaged in transformative learning. We came together as collegial friends, both recent and more established, feeling connected beyond our institutional mentoring roles. However, even in this warm context we did not wish to function exclusively as a circle of one. Invitations were sent to others in our college to participate in a new group.

Our purpose was shaped over time—but we had to struggle, cope with feelings of frustration, and listen very carefully to each another. Notes were taken and several sessions were taped. At each meeting we brought up the issue of what our focus might be, or come to be. We sometimes avoided asking this question, but mostly encouraged one another to this end. We openly valued engaging in genuine inquiry while looking past the need for a "perfect circle of consensus" (Grumet, 1995, p. 15). The rough edges of our search coincided with the need to talk, offer advice, and share a fresh perspective through stories of mentoring. These stories of mentorship at first represented our effort to engage in more talk, but at the level of textual conversation. In the meantime, my fellow contributors mentored one another as we all searched for a commonly shared focus. Dynamic, everyday shifts occurred within our *Circle* as individuals met in pairs and small groupings, the essence of which were reported to the rest of us. Weary but patient, we were doing the work of doing the work. In other words, we had shaped a process of comentorship while trying to discover our purpose and intentions. After realizing our progress, we became committed to delivering our conversations to a broader forum in an effort to help others break through their own circle of one.

One of the many writing circles that our group overlaps is Shirley Steinberg and Joe Kincheloe's. Their guiding voices echo throughout our own attempts at a "critical system of meaning ... that rests on the critical teachers' willingness to reveal their allegiances, to admit their solidarities and value structures, and to encourage analysis of the ways such orientations affect their teaching" (Kincheloe & Steinberg, 1995, p. 6).

An open-ended but guided structure has been devised for the chapters that would honor our personal voice and story, and permit the reader entry. Our *Circle* created a structure that has been implicit in our narrative–critical incidents, questions to ponder, retrospectives, and musings for mentors. This narrative structure has been adapted to reflect the idiosyncratic quality of each chapter and each writer's vision. Personal metaphors further communicate the unique elements of each story. Educational and literary metaphors energize our individual stories. They also help to convey the value of transformation in our writings and lives.

Our book celebrates diverse perspectives on mentoring in the lives of students, teachers, and teacher educators. This collection of stories illustrates mentoring relationships in public and private schools and in higher education. We present narratives of the role of mentorship in our own student teaching, public and private school teaching, graduate education, and work with preservice teachers and research participants. Our *Circle* consists of doctoral students who are also experienced former public and private school teachers, beginning professors of education, and experienced tenured professors. Those contributors who were not members of our group nonetheless participated in many overlapping circles within the same university. We also have in common many of the same mentoring issues and concerns as well as goals and dreams. Our *Circle* widened still further with the inclusion of textual mentors whose voices have influenced the field of teacher education and research. Maxine Greene, for example, shows that the mentoring experience may, at its finest, combine poetry and politics in the participation of a democracy for all.

It is when spaces open among them, when their diverse perspectives are granted integrity that something they can hold in common may begin to emerge. It requires imagination ... , the identification of deficiencies in the world around

... and a shared effort in some manner to repair. It is when this occurs that values are created, that persons with diverse backgrounds can come together. (1995, p. 312)

As students and educators, our voices communicate diversity across subject areas, throughout the various levels of education, and within our own lives and educational experiences. We also portray diversity through our cultural identity and background, experiences, gender, age, professional role, point of view, and sense of humor. But each chapter shares, at its center, the need for reciprocal and caring mentoring relationships that can serve as structures to nurture individuals and groups. Such mentoring relationships can also gradually transform forces of repression that operate within restrictive educational settings. Breaking the circle of one by forming circles of many represents our solution to the isolation, competition, and exploitation faced by many in education.

The four sections of this book were organized organically, after the chapters were completed. These parts represent the four dimensions of mentorship in education that best define our project and its redefinition of mentoring. These dimensions are focused on innovative approaches to mentoring student teachers within established university systems, the role of mentorship in the graduate assistantship teaching of preservice students, effective school-university programs aimed at mentoring preservice teachers, and the search for new patterns of mentoring within higher education circles.

These sections are artificial in the sense that contributors share numerous, overlapping mentoring contexts. To varying degrees, most or even all of these dimensions have a role to play in our stories. Also vital are those biographic situations and incidents that are central to the development of each writer's stories of mentorship. This book, then, could have alternatively been organized according to themes of biographic development in education. Instead, the emphasis is on our individual and collective redefinition of mentorship within educational arenas.

In part I, the first chapter, "My Emerging Destiny: Mentoring from an African-American Perspective" (Webb-Johnson), explores the "culture of power" commonly experienced by students and faculty of color in higher education. Benefits are derived from efforts at "communal mentoring" at the programmatic level. The experience of culturally diverse education majors in a teacher preparation program is provided along with demographics on enrollment and completion. A five-tiered mentoring model, currently in operation in a predominately white university, is reviewed for its influence on this traditional system. Chapter 2, "The Unbroken Circle: Teachers Mentoring Students Mentoring Teachers" (Kemp), reveals from a feminist point of view the writer's struggles in obtaining a doctorate within a traditional graduate school program. She highlights alternatives to the hierarchical mentoring model by sharing personal journal entries from preservice students.

Chapter 3, "Four Recipes (Scenarios) on Mentoring: Or, How I Became an E-Mail MaMa" (Zellner), a kaleidoscopic account is provided of a doctoral student/former teacher's experience of mentoring preservice teachers. Through an electronic mail system, a community of learners is established and comentoring forms of support are made available. On a meta-level, the Internet is presented not only as a vital communication system and tool for teaching and learning, it is also a vital means for increasing and deepening contact among multiple circles of students and teachers.

In part II, chapter 4, "Mentoring: The Magical Wand in Education" (Boettcher), is shaped as a Cinderella story with fairy-godmothers serving as mentoring figures throughout this former teacher's elementary school career. Parallels are drawn to her current doctoral program and experiences with several mentoring figures. The next chapter, "Walking the Tightrope: The Role of Mentoring in Developing Educators as Professionals" (Cox), also illustrates the growth of the developing teacher educator. The author seeks answers to questions regarding the transition from a public school teacher offering professional mentoring to fellow teachers to a teacher educator working primarily with preservice teachers. The vision of successful mentoring relationships offered enables professionals to alternately walk the tightrope and hold the net.

Next, part III, chapter 6, "Mentoring Preservice Science Teachers: The Professional Development School" (Adoue), provides a close-up of mentoring among student teachers. Featured is a professional development school and its faculty and associates (doctoral students and professors). In this account, conflicting views from professors of education within a graduate school environment expose issues resulting from university-public school partnerships. In chapter 7, "Creating a Circle of Many: Mentoring and the Preservice Teacher" (Hughey), the author presents an exciting tension between mentoring as a circle of one and mentoring as a circle of many. The former metaphor captures a traditional mentoring practice whereas the latter envelops the wider and current realities of the preservice teacher context. A positive view of the mentoring benefits for teachers, students, and professors is articulated in this evaluation of a thriving school-university collaboration.

Finally, part IV ends this collection with the intent of beginning new conversations with other teacher educators and professionals. The eighth chapter, "Mentors and Mentoring: Reflections of a Circle with/in Circles" (Stansell), provides an account for understanding how mentors and neophytes might journey together in a climate of mutual empowerment. A retrospective on the author's personal experience of getting his doctorate among multiple mentoring figures is advanced. Herein, individual circles of one are joined together in larger circles across lines of gender, rank, and experience.

Chapter 9, "Post-Sharkdom: An Alternative Form of Mentoring for Teacher Educators" (Mullen), brings into view the shark like, competitive, and lonely training involved in getting a doctorate and having your dissertation published. A new metaphorical language is used to expose the gap between institutional voices and voices of diversity. Interviews with Hispanic preservice teachers give an added textured quality to this search for new patterns of mentoring with higher education. Participation in communities of comentors, without human cost, is put forth as a model of post-sharkdom in the academy.

Chapter 10, "Full Circle: Insights on Mentoring from My Mentor's Heroes" (Kealy), tells the story of an ongoing relationship between a professor and his mentor from graduate school and their shared interest in the lives of legendary naval leaders. The author discusses how in the course of their dialogue about naval leaders he discovered the leaders that inspired his mentor's mentorship practice. The traits of these leaders are brought forth at the end of the chapter as suggested characteristics that can contribute to successful mentoring.

Finally, chapter 11, "Patterns of Mentoring: Weaving Teacher Educators' Career Stories" (Wiseman), presents a focused reflection on those dynamics that shaped our *Circle* and the process by which professional growth had taken place. Reflections on our project as a conversational tapestry woven from personal and professional stories of critical events and incidents are offered in this account. The author asserts that our stories expose the process of becoming a teacher educator, ultimately providing relevant insights into our profession.

We hope that our working model helps to redefine the traditional process of mentorship within school and college systems. Each of the authors has lived, learned, and taught in settings that have had pieces of this model in operation. Our mentorship model (see *Figure 1: Mentoring as Life: A Circular Model of Education*) views mentoring as a lifelong process that brings mentors and the mentored close together at times, and further away at other times. The tighter, textured circle (on top) represents the intensity of contact in mentoring relationships. As the mentoring contact increases through structured activities (e.g., student teaching, dissertation writing, and coauthorship on publications), the outline of the circle thickens. The circle also thickens when living in the middle of sticky political or bureaucratic issues that seem beyond our control. Each chapter shows what can happen as the circle thickens, contact intensifies, and inner and outer circles merge or become entangled.

The larger circle illustrates an ebb and flow in these relationships as they change with life and the specific needs of mentors and those who are mentored. Little research has been undertaken on how mentoring relationships develop, endure, die, or change over time or on the impact of past mentoring on the actual relationships between mentors and neophytes (Kealy & Mullen, 1996). However, in some recent public school restructuring efforts there is a move toward including elements of effective mentoring: teacher networks, enriched professional roles, and collegial work (Darling-Hammond, 1996), as well as peer coaching (Showers & Joyce, 1996). A three-strand braid in our model connotes the interaction of the mentored with multiple mentoring figures. Temporary broken lines of contact or even severed periods of communication and work can characterize these lifelong phases of mentoring relationships. The shadow coils contained within the larger circle convey the dense layers of mentoring stories that are often a part of educators' and students' lives. Dense layers of mentoring stories are conveyed through our writers' voices and experiences as we engage the private encounter of mentoring, but in broader contexts. These dense layers are evident in our multiple reflections as developing teacher educators engaged in reciprocal teaching and learning situations.

Judith Little (1989) acknowledged trust and reciprocity as essential elements of care in traditional relationships shared by teachers and advisors. Our mentoring model of multiple, intertwining circles emphasizes these and other elements necessary for the professional

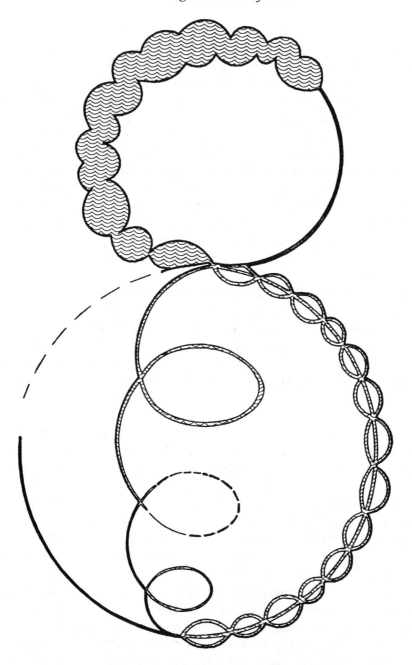

*Figure 1. Mentoring as Life: A Circular Model of Education*
*(group effort)*

and personal growth of teachers and teacher educators. These "elements" of mentorship were spontaneously shared by the *Circle* during our last formal meeting. We spoke in verse form, overlapping voices beginning and completing each other's poetic thoughts:

Picture a life filled with caring and supportive relationships
with mutual trust and respect
where there is time and space to talk,
to grow,
to share meaning
to co-create text
to be
a real person
whether or not "real" personal
where lines blur
and mentors and mentees become one
cycling in and out of each other's lives
cycling back, checking in
sharing the real stuff of life
a relationship that looks different
depending on where you stand.

This invitation to share meaning and cocreate text about "the real stuff of [a mentoring] life" now includes our readers. While becoming familiar with the stories in this collection, readers will probably make connections with personal mentoring experiences. We hope to inspire others' stories of mentoring to be told and for our own ideas to be revisited, critiqued, or expanded. Finally, we challenge our readers to break the circle of one to improve mentoring conditions for the professional development of educators and students.

# Acknowledgments

Many educator-writers have contributed to this book. First and foremost, we, the four editors, wish to thank the contributors. Without the efforts of these mentor-writers, this book would have remained a manuscript only. *Breaking the Circle of One* had its origins in a self-study writing group nicknamed the *Circle*. Professors and graduate students gathered for the purpose of working beyond the isolation, competition, and struggle that sometimes affect daily and lifelong work. The chapters presented here grew to include contributions from other teacher educators who knew of our self-study group and who showed interest in issues and experiences of mentorship.

We, the editors, appreciate the responsiveness of the contributors to our feedback. Carol A. Mullen provided conceptual and editorial feedback on all chapters. She also designed the framework of the book and its parts. Co-editors Maggie D. Cox, Cindy K. Boettcher, and Diane S. Adoue responded to chapters provided by the core writing group.

We also send deep thanks to Joe L. Kincheloe and Shirley R. Steinberg, Penn State University, for preparing the Foreword to this collection. We appreciate being a part of their continuing dialogue on the postmodern in education in their series "Counterpoints." Special acknowledgment goes to Shirley Steinberg, who further assisted at critical junctures to ensure that writers were honored and that the project was successfully completed.

Christopher S. Myers, Managing Director of Peter Lang Publishing, kindly offered advice and ensured smooth transition throughout the various stages of feedback and production. Jacqueline Pavlovic, Production Supervisor, gave special attention to formatting details and reviewed the final copy.

Finally, our thanks go to William A. Kealy, Associate Professor at Florida State University, for sharing his technological know-how and for providing technical direction on graphics.

# Part I

# Innovative Approaches to Mentoring Student Teachers within Established University Systems

**Gwendolyn Webb-Johnson**

**April Whatley Kemp**

**Luana Zellner**

# Chapter 1

# My Emerging Destiny: Mentoring from an African-American Perspective

## Gwendolyn Webb-Johnson

### Musings for Mentors

My voice has emerged and continues to emerge from my African-American cultural center. It is a voice that has always existed, but has only recently been bridged toward the development of personal understanding. The definitions of this voice develop on a daily basis. I only began to recognize my voice, from a cultural center, in the last 12 years. As a teacher of youths who demonstrate behavior disorders, I began to realize that I had a voice that was silenced by standards of status quo mores expected from home, community, and a Eurocentric society. As I observed and taught those who others chose not to teach because of their behavioral representations, I began to admire their resilience, verve, persistence, and zest for life from a survivor perspective. Even though many of their choices in school caused these young people to be ostracized and ridiculed by teachers, administrators, and peers, they maintained an integrity of character. Even in their quest for survival they responded to challenges of care.

When more was expected from these vibrant individuals, as it related to their academic and social skill performance, they clearly demonstrated all the predictable behavior asserted in the research. Such inappropriate behavior often compels those in authority to terminate any degree of care or concern for student progress. Yet, when an authority figure shattered the predictable, by not lowering standards, they often emerged as critical thinkers who took the risk of again trying to fit into a school society that had systematically attempted to silence their voices.

I learned so much from their strength that my own voice began to emerge from the shadows of ignorance and cowardice. This chapter explores my emerging voice by describing my cultural birth and educational quest to make a difference in the lives of African-American children who historically have been silenced within a public school context because of institutional racism designed to dehumanize African-American existence and experience. While that premise may not be the intent of many well-meaning educators, it is often the impact of historical practices that initially denied, then segregated and remediated, and finally shortchanged masses of African-American school-aged children. This chapter explores also the emergence of mentoring as a way of life. While few of my early life experiences were defined by having a mentor per se, I can honestly reflect on the dynamic interactions with my family and schooling to see those positive and negative mentors who helped mold me into the being I am still to become.

**Looking Back on My Story**

At the age of four, I began kindergarten. I remember vividly my excitement. I wanted nothing more than to attend school to learn everything under the sun. My mother and father graduated from high school. Education was always important in their early lives in rural Mississippi. When they migrated to the north, they freely continued to buy into the American Dream. While my father was an enlisted man in the army, stationed at various locations throughout the United States and Europe, my mother chose to stay in Chicago to raise our growing family. By the time I reached my kindergarten classroom, I knew how to write my name and draw. I had always been an avid talker. In fact, my family literally could not convince me that there was ever any good time not to talk.

**Negative Mentoring**

My first day of school was no exception. I literally talked from the time I walked through the door until the noon bell rang to dismiss the class. I do not remember my first teacher's name, though I can still visualize her physical and emotional presence. She was a rather short European-American woman, probably in her forties, with short brown hair and glasses. She wore a white, short-sleeved blouse, and a beige skirt. She consistently told me to be quiet. I continued to talk to her, to my peers, to myself. My excitement was overwhelming. I wanted to know everything that was to happen in this place called school. By mid-morning, I sat in a corner with my mouth plastered in off-white masking tape. I still see and feel the tears that streamed down my stinging cheeks. I did not remove the tape. I merely sat and watched as kindergarten progressed without me. I talked to myself about what school would be like the next day. When the bell rang, I was to walk home with a neighbor from my public housing complex. I decided not to join her. Instead, I remained on the playground and returned to my kindergarten classroom for the afternoon session. By the time my teacher realized I had returned and prepared to call my home, my mother appeared at the door very concerned that something had happened to me. With much protest, I was taken home.

I remember the names of every one of my elementary school teachers except my kindergarten teacher. I only see her face. At the age of 41, I have yet to feel any hate for her deed. I imagine I am numb to those feelings because I continue to remember scenarios from my kindergarten days. I remember the joy of learning, of drawing queens, of helping my cousin put on his snowsuit because he could not. I remember the teacher screaming throughout the year in efforts to terminate my perceived excessive chatter. I remember also my persistence in talking. I talked of learning and every wonderful experience of acquiring new knowledge. I never disrespected my teacher, in fact, I never said a mean word to or about her. She was a messenger of power. She represented learning, and I wanted every morsel available. My conduct grades were deplorable, while my academic grades were superior.

For many children, such an experience could have been traumatic in many nonproductive ways. However, that kindergarten teacher was a negative mentor who attempted to, and succeeded in, silencing the persistence and resilience of my voice, instead of molding it. Yet, that teacher did not and could not silence my spirit. I had a mother who loved and cherished me. My mother never said I must do well in school. There was always a tacit expectation that said nothing less was acceptable. My teacher was my mentor of sorrow because her continued insistence that I not talk so much continued to remind me that she was wrong to tape my mouth. I am sure that she did not feel this way. She wanted to teach her class without my constant interruptions. Yet, the tape could not terminate that which was incapable of being sealed away. That experience served as a backdrop in my educational experience. My kindergarten teacher became a constant reminder that one should have better ways of motivating students not to talk during class. Even though my mother continued to tell me to not talk during class, it did not happen during elementary school. What did happen was that I had other teachers who found ways of motivating my talk to meet the demands of the learning environment. I was slowly exposed to positive mentors who paved another tenet in my educational development.

**Emerging Positive Mentoring**

I attended a culturally diverse elementary school. Haines School was located in Chinatown, not far from downtown Chicago. My peers were African-American, Chinese-American, and Hispanic-American. I remember peers like Winston Williams, Arthur Moy, and Roberto Gonzalez. I remember my teachers–Mr. Moy, Miss Cooper, Mr. Williams, Ms. Luckett, and Mr. Gaynor. I kept my reputation as a talker, but I always maintained high grades.

Mr. Gaynor, my fifth grade teacher, was my mentor of hope and challenge. He loved me and told me so on a daily basis, seldom articulating the actual words. He taught me to dream beyond tomorrow. He taught me also how to shape those dreams into reality. He spoke of a world beyond Chinatown. Mr. Gaynor showed me a world removed from and beyond the projects (my public housing complex). He taught me never to be ashamed of my dwelling but also what happened behind many of the closed doors of our dwellings. We never knew that many considered us poor. My classmates and I ate every day. Our family situations offered us all that we needed and some of what we wanted. However, we often teased one another about the pests that also dwelled in the projects. It was not unheard of for us to taunt one another about "roaches." Having them in our homes carried with it the stigma of somehow being dirty. We learned that some people did not have to detest the roaches that crawled through their apartment. In fact, some people ate chocolate covered roaches and ants. We learned that insects were good sources of protein and that the United States was one of the few countries where people did not consume these pests. Mr. Gaynor offered us the opportunity to taste these "delicacies." (I did not sample the roaches, but I did taste the ants. They tasted like chocolate covered raisins.) He brought water from open springs in Colorado and we dined on turtle soup.

Every Thursday was dress-up day. Girls wore dresses and boys wore ties. While this may have been perceived as gender bias or restrictive by today's standards, 30 years ago it was appropriate. The practice reinforced a standard. Mr. Gaynor kept grooming items that were freely used by those who neglected to brush or comb their hair. Most important, on each Thursday in fifth grade, we did presentations centered on our educational experiences from the past week. He demonstrated to us the importance of studying and then sharing the results of our efforts. By the end of our fifth grade year, Mr. Gaynor no longer had to encourage students to dress up on each Thursday. In fact, he no longer had to stress the importance of systematically demonstrating our commitment to educational excellence on a daily basis. It became as natural as breathing.

Those experiences stayed with me as I progressed through school. Yet, my cultural voice was still silent. No one talked openly about being an African-American, and what it meant in the context of this nation. While I knew that Mr. Gaynor was a proud African-American teacher, we never talked about the meaning of race and culture in a race-conscious society. I was deeply committed to the music of Paul Revere and the Raiders and the Monkees, while the Civil Rights Movement in the 1960s and the 1970s occurred in the periphery of my immediate life. I was culturally deprived. While I knew of the Supremes, the Temptations, and Martin Luther King, I knew nothing of their value to my development and the development of this country. Even as my community exploded with the racist murder of Fred Hampton (a member of the Black Panther Party and resident of my Chicago suburban community), I was detached. While the national guard was posted outside my high school as a result of the rioting within my high school, I remained in history class playing hangman. My brother, along with at least 500 other African-Americans walked out of school in protest as I sat idly by, thinking how disappointed my mother would be if I left school.

In a small midwestern liberal arts college, I continued to lead a sheltered life that mentored me into protection from the evil forces of the 1970s even as racial strife further tore the African-American and mainstream society apart.    There were approximately 60 African-American students on a campus of 1,200 students.  It was here that I began to realize consciously that somehow I was different from the rest of the world.  This experience in higher education was a continuation of my journey toward cultural realization and affirmation.  Because I was enrolled in the comprehensive rather than the college preparatory track in high school, I was not prepared for the rigor expected in college writing.  When I entered college, the only research or term paper I had ever written was the result of the one I typed from my text in typing class.  I was never required to write more than a two to three page essay in four years of high school.

By my junior year in college I encountered the impact of instructional racism when an English professor stressed my inability and ineptness because I chose to champion John Milton himself as the hero of the epic "Paradise Lost."  The poem quite frankly overwhelmed me and I had little idea what was going on, much less who could or should be deemed the hero.   I therefore read about the life of John Milton and then attempted to demonstrate how he used each of his characters to somehow exemplify an aspect of his own troubled life.  My professor questioned my license to make such assertions with no scholarly support for my contention.  This professor joined my kindergarten teacher as a negative mentor who chose to only see his perceived limitations.  He wondered how I could possibly be a junior in college with such poor writing skills.  I was never taught to write in a scholarly fashion, and I had no idea that my literary premises should be supported by the established literary rhetoric.  That experience clearly began my journey and commitment to facilitate for students a reality-based understanding of the world of academe while affirming foremost the creative strength that all students bring to any setting. That journey has continued.

**Early Career Mentoring**

While I had initial plans of taking Broadway by storm, the reality of my age and very zealous ambitions led me to pursue a career in education by default. It was merely a tool to rest upon if theatrical plans fell short. While the college writing dilemma continued to plague me, my double major of English and theatre became a major in theatre and a minor in English. I graduated from college and returned to my high school alma mater as a speech, drama, and English teacher.

I was so excited about returning to the place where I received my high school education. I loved my students and believed that I had what it took to educate them. Little did I know that my limited education as to who I was as an African-American in a race-conscious society prevented me from embracing the demands of effectively educating students. While I knew I must never be my kindergarten teacher or college professor, it was unclear to me why I needed to do more than affirm my students.

The demographics of my high school had changed significantly during my four-year absence. The African-American population had grown from 25% to approximately 40%. Most of my classroom challenges involved interactions with African-American students. I did not know how to be their teacher; I knew only how to be their friend.

School officials expected me to control my classes. They persisted in reprimanding me on every issue I did not know how to orchestrate. "Why did that student have his feet on your desk during the observation?" "Why did you overlook that student misspelling 'writing' on two occasions when you graded her essay?" "Why are you eating lunch in the student cafeteria?" Yet, they provided me little guidance as to how to meet the academic needs of these students. I was consumed by my attempts to do a good job. However, I did not know how. I taught five classes daily, often with three preparations. I coached the cheerleaders, I coached the forensics team, and I directed musical and theatrical productions. I arrived at school at 7:00 A.M. and left at 7:00 P.M. In the final analysis, none of this mattered. I was not in control. I was asked to leave my first teaching assignment after three years.

School officials held expectations that I did not know how to meet. My preservice program taught me to teach the way I was taught in high school. I was to provide the information, and the students would rise to the occasion. While I believe that my students had good experiences as a result of my being their teacher, I know now that I have few guarantees that their educational outcomes were improved as a result of being in my class. Did I assist them in being better cultural beings with improved academic outcomes? Mr. Gaynor, in retrospect, did that for me. I had little idea that Mr. Gaynor's methods were culturally responsive and affirming. I had no one to talk to to assist me in conquering this raging frustration. I cried often. Mr. Gaynor's guidance failed me because I had no building blocks to assist in using this experience as a means to an end. I had no knowledge of how to break the cycle of failure that was slowly consuming my life of presumed success. I did not know who I was as a cultural being who had chosen teaching as a profession. Yet, I began to realize that I must assist and develop an ideology to mentor students, most specifically African-Americans, who were facing a more subtle racist school system in kindergarten through higher education settings. In all the limitations I began to uncover, I also began to realize that the students I taught were not receiving the kind of education I received. They were not from the inner city from where I had emerged and they were not poor, yet they were dropping out of school, being referred to alternative settings, and not going on to college. What could I do to influence this situation? How could I become a better teacher? I talked to students; I taught them from the designated curriculum guides. I shared my experiences, but was I mentoring them from an empowerment paradigm (Young, 1994)?

**Molded Mentoring**

I returned to school to earn a master's degree. While beginning a program in speech and communication during my first years as a teacher, I was plagued with a need to become a better disciplinarian. After yet another year of unsuccessful classroom management in yet another school district, I knew I needed to get more training. While jobless, yet needing to work, I began my initial journey into the world of special education. I began to substitute-teach and discovered that making myself available for special education guaranteed my receiving assignments on a daily basis. It then dawned on me, "Learn to teach the ones most consider impossible to teach and never again will they say I'm not a good teacher!" I enrolled in a master's program for teachers of adolescent youth with behavior disorders. Ironically, I fell in love. This love stemmed from one perceived need, but emerged as a continuation of my journey into self-discovery in critical pedagogical practices that challenged the status quo of school service delivery. While I believed that I was going to learn how to modify the behavior of children, I began to learn how to challenge the behavior of teachers and of schools.

I learned behavior modification techniques and how to collect data to aid in making decisions. I eagerly tried some of these methods with my new disorder students. "This stuff was working!" Little did I realize then, the methods worked not because they were best for students but because brilliant students were quite accustomed to the routine procedures of teachers modifying systematically their behavior.

I therefore immediately submerged myself in the implementation of some of my newfound strategies. I was the one who experienced a transformation. My students taught me more than I could ever have taught them. While we developed a reciprocal relationship, I did what I knew how best to do; I loved them unconditionally. They in turn taught me that all of those behavior modification methods meant nothing without some sustenance of character and self-knowledge building. These young people knew who they were through the school's defined measures. Their parents, in their trust that schools knew best how to educate their children, supported the methods.

My students' behaviors were being modified on a daily basis. My students demonstrated that these methods could indeed influence and manipulate their actions, but those methods were incapable of influencing their spirits and their souls. In fact, the more management techniques I succeeded in teaching, the further behind my students continued to be academically. Many of them demonstrated an acute disbelief in their worth and ability as learners. They demonstrated little faith in their reading and math abilities. They coined themselves "nonlearners." Many teachers agreed with that assessment. However, their persistent spirit taught me differently. While they often gave up on academic assignments, they never gave up on demonstrating their protest of injustice. While they may have earned three days suspension, they persisted in letting me know, "you won't kill my spirit while controlling my behavior."

Over the years I taught students who threatened suicide, committed crimes, sold and consumed drugs, and persisted in surviving. I discovered through them that my greatest responsibility to them was to never stop believing in them. That belief system was necessary as a standard for them, not as a substitute for their believing in themselves. I slowly learned that I could teach some of those standards through teaching them who they were as cultural beings. I began to share with them examples of others who faced ridicule, strife, and struggle. Many of my students did not believe they could emerge from their differences in an unfair society. When I shared with them Frederick Douglass, who taught himself to read, or Mary McLeod Bethune, who began a school with $1.50, they immediately wanted to know more. These historical African-American figures looked like them, but overcame fantastic obstacles. While some said, "But they are dead, they cannot teach me," I then shared with them Ben Carson (a living African-American doctor), who while in high school almost killed someone, but emerged as one of the leading neurosurgeons in the world. I gained the attention of dissenters. As I also became caught in the web of history, I realized how much I did not know about who I was as a cultural being. Nine years of teaching adolescents who demonstrated behavior disorders resulted in students and a teacher being more aware and grounded in the history and brilliance of African-Americans as cultural beings.

Over these years, as my role as mentor set itself in a mold of wonder and promise, I began to realize that there was more to teaching than merely controlling students. Teachers have a responsibility to assist students in their development as cultural beings who exercise their existence on at least three realms. Du Bois (1903/1996) identified the phenomenon as a double consciousness. He asserted that African-Americans, in their efforts to negotiate the responsibilities of citizenship in the United States, had to learn and orchestrate what it meant to be "Negro, and American." Almost a decade later, there are researchers who identify this phenomenon as having progressed to that of a triple quandary (Boykins, 1983, 1994), or three warring souls (Townsend & Patton, 1995). Individuals of African-American descent are charged with the responsibility of negotiating the waters of existence as a cultural being, as a member of mainstream society, and in reference to their sameness and/or differences within the first two realms (i.e., being female, gifted and talented, behaviorally disordered, learning disabled, poor).

## Mentoring Responsibilities in the 21st Century

With a desire to be an effective mentor, I have recently become a teacher educator. My journey taught me that my impact could extend beyond the 25 to 30 students that I taught in general education classes and the 10 to 15 often found in the special education classes. I have found that teacher impact can be multiplied through teacher education. I am committed to mentoring all preservice teachers. A strong compelling force demands that I assist them in overcoming obstacles that functioned as oppressors during my early teaching experiences. Those experiences also prompt me to be especially committed to assisting African-American preservice teachers. Culturally diverse individuals presently comprise less that 8% of the United States teaching force. Approximately 5% of those teachers are African-American. African-American school-aged students comprise 16.5% of the school aged population (U.S. Department of Education, 1995). While there is a compelling need to prepare effective teachers for all students, there is an equally compelling need to increase the number of African- American teachers to assist public education in transforming classrooms to meet the unique needs of African-American learners. The responsibility requires collaborative efforts from all those interested in providing effective services.

During my doctoral journey I finally began to envision how my past, present, and future could pave a path for social action (Banks, 1996). Along with another doctoral student, I created and implemented a retention program for culturally diverse preservice teachers at a midwestern university within the College of Education. Over a three-year period programs were institutionalized to increase the number of African-American and Hispanic-American preservice graduates. This university of over 23,000 students produced more teachers than any other college or university in that state. In fact, the university began as a normal school in 1857. Ironically, the number of African-American graduates from the program averaged approximately nine per semester over a five year period prior to the implementation of the program. Preliminary data gathering revealed that recruitment was not the real challenge. The university experienced great success, as do many other institutions, in attracting African-Americans. In fact, during the time we were gathering information, we discovered that over 100 culturally diverse students had identified education as a major, yet less than 25% of them had been officially accepted into the teacher education program. Through interviews and program evaluation, students shared that their incomplete matriculation involved a sense of alienation commonly experienced by students of color at predominantly European-American colleges and universities.

Students were not always aware of the culture of power (Delpit, 1988) that often operates at such institutions. Finally, preliminary and subsequent inquiry revealed that communal mentoring assisted students of color in negotiating the waters of college life, information gathering, strategic academic planning, and eventually, completion of the teacher preparation program (Young, 1994). By the end of the third year of the program the average number of African-American graduates had grown to 12 per semester with an estimated average of 15 per semester targeted to complete the program over the next three years.

This retention program developed a three-tiered mentoring model (Webb-Johnson & Young, 1992). Freshmen and sophomores were mentored by juniors and seniors while juniors and seniors were mentored by graduate students and faculty members. This mentoring model, developed conceptually with the philosophical foundations of the dimensions of African-American culture (Boykin, 1983), stressed mentoring as a way of life. As individuals are mentored, they are also being mentored. This philosophy is based on spirituality, movement, rhythm, harmony, verve, individual expression, communalism, oral tradition, and social time perspective (Table 1).

Over the past few years, this model has evolved to include five tiers. The research demonstrates that the retention of African-Americans in higher education is failing to meet the market's demands when professions like teaching examine the outcomes of program efforts. As a way of life, mentoring offers the challenge of individuals reaching beyond individual desires to contribute to a given profession. In a five-tiered mentoring model currently in use by participants involved in the Office of Culturally Diverse Student Services and Research at a large southern university, several additions to the original three-tiered model exist. Senior faculty mentor junior faculty and graduate level students. Junior faculty and graduate level students mentor junior and senior level education majors. They in turn mentor freshmen and sophomores, who then mentor K–12 students of color in local public schools. This program, along with various other initiatives, is part of the college's overall goal to increase the number of culturally diverse preservice and education majors. Since the office's inception in the fall of 1992, the culturally diverse enrollment has grown from 5% to 12.5% in 1996, with a goal for culturally diverse representation of 20% by 2005.

*Table 1.  Dimensions of African-American Culture*

| | |
|---|---|
| Spirituality | Approach to life vitalistic, non-material forces influence life. |
| Harmony | Fate interrelated with other elements/schemes, humankind and nature harmonically conjoined. |
| Movement | Emphasis on interweaving of movement, rhythm, percussion, music, dance; central to psychological health. |
| Verve | Propensity for high levels of stimulation, energetic and lively action. |
| Affect | Emphasis on emotions and feelings; sensitivity to emotional cues, tendency to be emotionally expressive. |
| Communalism | Commitment to social connectedness; social bonds and responsibility transcend individual privileges. |
| Expressive Individualism | Cultivation of distinctive personality and a proclivity for spontaneous, genuine personal expression. |
| Oral Tradition | Preference for oral/aural modes of communication; speaking and listening treated as performances. |
| Social Time Perspective | Orientation in which time is treated as passing through social space; recurring, personal and phenomenological. (Boykin, 1983) |

The challenge of influencing a traditional system that must presently respond to the ramifications of the recent Hopwood decision and even more traditional tenets in preparing teachers, is monumental, but nonetheless compelling. (The Hopwood court decision prohibits any institution of higher learning in the state of Texas to include race as a factor for admission. The court case is currently being interpreted as a rationale to also prohibit the use of race as a factor in the awarding of scholarships as well.) Mentoring African-American preservice students presents one of the greatest challenges for the present director. Currently, approximately 65 African-American students are enrolled in the teacher preparation program at the university. Only 23 seek to participate in at least three of seven programs currently available through the office. Since it is a relatively new program, college leadership realizes that growth and results will take time. As the director of this program, my mentoring journey continues.

**Questions to Ponder**

As a mentor and a teacher educator, I learn daily of the increased challenge of making a difference in the lives of African-American preservice teachers and African-American K–12 students. As a member of the faculty at a predominantly European-American university, the challenge of dealing with misperceptions and reeducation is ever before me. Can one person really make a difference? While I might answer a resounding "yes," are there ears to listen and eyes to see the slow but steady progress? Is there the patience to realize that if mentoring efforts help but one African-American student enter and complete the teacher preparation as a more fulfilled and fulfilling cultural being able to negotiate the three warring souls, the program can be seen as successful? Will such efforts assist those who lack awareness and understanding to embrace the fact that the impact of one better informed and prepared teacher will have a positive influence on every student and colleague encountered along the journey? Will the efforts of my continued journey provide a model for the college, demonstrating that the responsibility in transforming our education program belongs to each and every one of us? Will my efforts to meet the demands and rigor of tenure and promotion be compromised by my mentoring efforts? Will collaborative efforts beyond me as an individual provide a model for all those interested in improving public education? The more I learn, the more I question. That I believe is important. Education has become my way of life. The challenge and struggle continue and the demands increase.

## Final Musings for Mentors

Such questions presently challenge me with hope and vision. My journey and the powerful mentors of hope I have encountered in my recent past demonstrate to me on a daily basis that mentoring is indeed a way of life. It is the tenet that literally paved the way for the survival and emerging nature of African-Americans through the horrors of the middle passage, the injustices of slavery, the glory and demise of reconstruction, the victory and struggle in the continued quest for civil rights, and the emerging hope for triumph and continued survival in the aftermath of the repercussions of all that remains to be done in the quest for life as we approach a new millennium.

My Emerging Destiny: Confronting the Circle of One

I began for some as one of many,
Some saw me as an eyesore, an inconvenience
a bother in the educational arena
because of my differences.

I was on the outside of the circle
vibrantly shining, but not knowing the way
or the culture of power that dictated a course.

I continued and learned to comply
though my essence
was untapped and my star of hope
uncherished and unknown.
I knew not that I stood on the shoulders of a vibrant past,
yet I was balanced and steadied in my course
by those who had lived generations making a way out of no way.

I was on the outside of the circle
vibrantly shining but not knowing the way
or the culture of power that dictated a course.

Slowly, but steadily my "I" emerged as "we."
We are but beacons and tools
living the present, but carving the future
I have an obligation grounded in choice
to make a difference
to strengthen my shoulders, providing
continued foundations for footsteps
of the future.

I was on the outside of the circle
vibrantly shining but not knowing the way
or the culture of power that dictated a course.

I now break the circle
sitting comfortably within the
depth and the breadth of
its circumference
traveling boldly on its revolving
radius of discovery.

I sit with many of
my brothers and sisters of color
my present sisters in a cause
readied for more
and charged to enthrall the children
of our future.

I was on the outside of the circle
vibrantly shining but not knowing the way
or the culture of power that dictated a course.

We are the circle
it is no longer closed to undesirables
It is ours for the breaking, for the molding
for the merger.

I am now the circle,
an extension of inclusion.

I vibrantly shine still not knowing the way,
but clearly knowing the culture of power
and dictating a collaborative course.

The circle embodies who I am,
what we must become,
and where we must go
to transform the lives of our future.

If the present circle chooses not
to hold the vibrant manifestations of my
peoplehood
we won't ask for permission, inclusion
or acceptance.

If it chooses not to break
we will redefine and create
a new circle
one that demonstrates how
life will be embraced
inviting dissenter to join
but not waiting.

Our children deserve our ultimate
and for that we can't wait
I was on the outside of the circle
but I am the circle
still vibrantly shining for change.

# Chapter 2

---

# The Unbroken Circle:
# Teachers Mentoring Students
# Mentoring Teachers

## April Whatley Kemp

I have a clear image of myself sitting in my attorney's office a few weeks before my divorce was final, feeling like there was no other place in the world where I could be and still be functional. In fact, I remember asking him if I could come and just sit in that chair every day until I felt like myself again. I was 30 years old and my entire world had collapsed. I had no job, no home, no promise of a future spent with my husband. Everything I had counted on and taken for granted in life had suddenly disappeared, and I was left with the prospect of caring for myself and my child alone. In spite of all this, I had a storehouse of resources upon which to draw: not one, but two, college degrees; a small savings, and tremendous support from family and friends. Yet at that moment, in that office, I felt entirely alone. I felt victimized, not only by my husband, but by a legal and economic system that is antagonistic toward women. I thought about other women who had been through similar experiences and those who would be facing such hardships without sufficient resources. I privately acknowledged that I wanted to use this event in my life as a means of reaching out to other women who needed support. It would be my way of turning personal, legalistic devastation into triumph.

At that time, I really didn't know how I might go about making these changes or what I would do next. I had obviously reached what Walker and Mehr (1992) call a "critical choice point" (p. 43) in my life. Critical choice points are defined as "pivotal moments" in women's lives when they have an opportunity to make a decision that will determine the direction of their future. In their study of women in the academic profession, *Women of Academe: Outsiders in the Sacred Grove*, Aisenberg and Harrington (1988) found that many of the women they interviewed reached a point in their personal development when they were no longer willing for their lives to remain static. These same women were able to make decisions that led to significant personal change. Conversely, such transformations in the lives of these women were often precipitated by a traumatic event such as a divorce or the death of a loved one, as was mine. Walker and Mehr uncovered the same findings about transformational experiences in their study of women who had been identified as exceptional students and who were graduates of New York City's Hunter School for Girls. Sometimes these critical choice points precipitate a major change in a woman's life, and sometimes they are precipitated by a significant life event. The results of these critical choices are frequently called crystallizing experiences.

Getting a doctorate has been a dream of mine since I was an undergraduate, one that I had hoped to begin pursuing the year of my divorce. Due to the drastically changed circumstances of my life that year, I thought graduate study would have to be postponed indefinitely, possibly permanently. Then one night, after a fruitless day of searching for jobs and apartments, my mother sat me down. She told me that she and my aunt had talked, and they decided that if going back to school was what I really wanted they would help to make my dream possible. Suddenly, returning to graduate school seemed like exactly what I needed to do! Although it would be difficult, if I could just make it through the next few years until the degree was completed, then I would have options that seemed virtually limitless. I have always enjoyed school and excelled in academic work. Graduate study would force me to stay focused–at a time when my attention span rarely lasted beyond two minutes–on learning and on a positive future outlook. My mother did not want my former husband to take away any more of my dreams. The only thing that really stood in the way of me returning to school was money, and my mother and aunt had just offered to help me overcome that obstacle. My critical choice had become to obtain a doctorate on the path to becoming a teacher educator.

And so my doctoral journey began. The focus I knew my studies would require became a reality, and, thankfully, I was able to meet this challenge. I soon became caught up in classes, in research, in single parenthood, and, yes, even in dating and, later, a second marriage. My thoughts of reaching out to other women never left me though. I began to wonder if my chosen career goal to be a university professor, a teacher educator, would allow me that kind of outreach, the kind of intimate connection I needed to establish. I realized that few of my own future students' lives would revolve entirely around school. Even now, as a graduate student, mine did not.

As an undergraduate, my formal studies had actually been only a minor part of my college experience. Indeed, my life at that time had revolved around my future, and now former, husband! I almost convinced myself that I could establish more personal, authentic relationships with students by working in some other aspect of college life, like student advisement. In this capacity, I would be on more even footing with students. While I still might be able to share my experiences with them in a way from which they might benefit, I thought that more comfortable sharing might occur if I was other than a "professor," an often intimidating and authoritarian figure. Then, several things happened at once to change my perspective.

## Critical Incidents

Last fall, our curriculum and instruction department and entire College of Education underwent a number of major changes, including changes in leadership. I felt uneasy with the rapid return to very traditional ways of doing bureaucracy that came along with these administrative changes. Some of us in graduate school had recently been exposed to the concepts of personal, practical knowledge and narrative inquiry (Carter & Doyle, 1996; Connelly & Clandinin, 1990). We expressed interest in pursuing this type of research even though it is not commonly practiced in our department. We also began to question the objective stance and impersonal voice of academic discourse and an authoritarian structure of teaching, and we were able to identify faculty members who would be open to these questions. In fact, these were professors with whom we had already established relationships as mentors and students. This group of faculty members and doctoral students began to meet to offer support and sustenance for its members. To my delight, we expanded to establish a forum for exploring ideas, research, and stories. Finally, the group meetings evolved into a self-study of teaching and learning that led to the writing of this book!

As the group continued to meet, we found that each of us took on the role of mentor at different times. In other words, it was not always the professors who acted as mentors and the students who were mentored. Instead, what was happening personally or professionally to a particular group member at a particular time became the basis for who needed nurturing and who became the nurturer. To paraphrase Nel Noddings (1984), we each had the opportunity to be the one who is caring and the one who is cared for. I was mentored by individual professors with whom I share common points of interest or experience, as well as other doctoral students; in return, there were opportunities for me to share my knowledge and concern with group members in a mentoring capacity. I agree with David Hunt's (1994) description of the doctoral journey: "There is something about meeting with others who are at different stages in their journey yet who have common destinations which can be very powerful. It also acknowledges how much travellers learn from one another" (p. 97). Each member of our group is a "traveler" on his or her journey as a teacher educator, and we each have stories that contribute to the learning of others.

That same semester, I was working on a pilot study for my dissertation. My study is modeled closely after Catherine Bateson's (1990) study of women in creative careers, *Composing a Life*. I read this book near the beginning of my doctoral study, and it strongly influenced me. I am fascinated by Bateson's finding that the women she studied "composed" their lives around significant life events, often involving caring for others, rather than in a linear progression of goal attainment. This concept has emerged over and over again in conversations with the women in my self-study group and is the impetus for my dissertation. My qualitative study focuses on the life experiences of women as they have made the transition from teacher to teacher educator.

In preparation for my study, I had the opportunity to interview four women who have all been mentors to me at various stages of my education and career. One theme that emerged from these interviews with women who have all achieved levels of leadership and esteem in their careers as teacher educators is that they see themselves as *teachers* first. All of them expressed the importance of being able to act as mentors to their students and establish caring relationships with them. These women find their roles as teachers and teacher educators so fulfilling precisely because they are allowed to be nurturing. Noddings (1992) argues that the "first job of the schools is to care for our children" (p. xiv). The women I interviewed seem to embody that belief in their roles as teachers regardless of the age or educational level of their students. Certainly, I have been a recipient of the care and nurturing of each of these women. I have enjoyed, and still do, personal and intimate relationships with them that began when I was a student in each of their graduate classes.

A third experience I had as a doctoral student last semester was taking my first course in women's studies. One of my mentors, Donna Wiseman, mentioned to me when I was just beginning my doctoral program that women's studies might be an area I would want to explore. Like me, Donna had never thought much about women's studies as a formal discipline area before that point. At our highly traditional university, it is a newly emerging program. But my vision of myself in that chair in my attorney's office was still with me, and I was motivated by Donna's newfound interest, so I decided to follow her suggestion. I hoped that women's studies might offer me a way to understand and transform my own life experiences and possibly share them with other women facing critical choice points. Since then, I have discovered many connections between women's studies and education.

I have come to realize, more from women's studies than from any class I have ever taken in education, that there are alternatives to the image of the teacher or professor as authority or expert. In fact, my recent experiences with women's studies have caused me to rethink many of my long-held assumptions about teachers, students, and curriculum. This fresh perspective has completely reinvigorated my interest in education and the way I think about the entire teaching and learning processes.

Most importantly, last fall I had the opportunity to teach. After 16 months in my doctoral program, I began teaching children's literature to future teachers. I was delighted by the prospect for two reasons: I have a passion for children's books and teaching this class would help me to decide if I wanted to continue moving in the same direction on my career path. The mentoring relationships that developed between me and my students definitely did influence that decision. Initially, the mentoring process began without my recognition. One by one, students began coming to me to ask questions and to talk, first about the class and later about their lives.

Tina came first, in fact, the very first day of class. She asked if she could make an appointment to talk with me about her struggles with college study. She quietly, sometimes falteringly, explained to me that she had been an undergraduate for six years. She was finally classified as a senior, although her expected graduation date was as yet unknown. She spoke to me of her test anxiety, and I agreed to work with her in whatever way I could. As a result of that conversation, I gave all my students the option of taking a written final exam or developing a final project. Tina made a beautiful scrapbook about the experiences that led her to choose teaching as a career. She included pictures, letters, and poems about the people who had influenced and supported her decision, and she wrote eloquently and lovingly about the meaningful educational experiences in her life. I felt honored that she shared such a personal creation with me, and I urged her to share it with her future students as an incentive to share the same kinds of creative projects about themselves.

Leslie came next. Early in the semester, she mentioned to me that she and her parents were receiving counseling about some family problems. I tried to communicate to her that I would be willing to listen to whatever she wanted to tell me. She didn't respond immediately. As we studied modern fantasy, a genre not well liked by the majority of the class, Leslie asked me if I would read some of her writing. She brought me three beautifully written science fiction stories in which she had created highly detailed new worlds. I noticed, to my delight, that each story was told from a distinctly feminist perspective–women were always the rulers of the kingdoms–but I did not comment on this to Leslie. However, I did communicate to her how impressed I was with her talent. Shortly after this, Leslie told me that she and her mother had decided that it would be all right for her to tell me that the family problem about which she was receiving counseling was a date rape that had occurred the previous semester. Every now and then, orally or in writing, she would reveal how this experience was influencing every aspect of her life. At the end of the semester, she wrote a touching note thanking me for listening to her. I was overwhelmed that she had felt comfortable enough to share such a personal and devastating experience with me. Listening seemed such a small contribution to have made, and I wished I could have done more.

Caroline also came to me. Caroline always makes an effort to introduce herself to her instructors, not in an ingratiating way, but rather out of genuine need to connect and express enthusiasm for the process of schooling. Early in the semester, she began talking to me about books from her childhood, about her love for children, and about her desire to be a teacher. Soon, she began to bring in books to share with me, both old favorites and newly discovered treasures. She also told me of her plans to marry in a few months and showed me pictures of the man she loved. Then, one night, she called to tell me she wouldn't be in class the next day because she was having surgery. When she returned, she tearfully told me of the "female" health problems from which she had suffered for years and the endometriosis the surgery had hopefully curbed. A short time later, she gave me the devastating report from her doctor that her chances for having children were very slim. I could understand so well how she felt! I had desperately wanted children when I was her age, and I had shared many anecdotes about my son, Tommy, with the class. What I had not shared with the class, as a whole, but what I shared with Caroline now, privately, was my own debilitating battle with infertility and the miracle of receiving my son through adoption. My story probably did not take away her pain, but our conversation gave her hope, and for this I am thankful.

**Questions to Ponder**

What factors led to the development of such intimate relationships between my students and myself? What steps can teacher educators take in order to establish caring relationships with their students? By looking back at my experience of teaching children's literature to preservice teachers, I am aware of several activities that helped me to connect with my students. None of them is particularly unique or original. First, I was teaching a course for which I felt genuine enthusiasm. The subject matter had a significant influence in my own life. Such enthusiasm and concern for content, I believe, cannot be imitated. Second, I came to know each of my students personally through writing in dialogue journals. This form of written communication allowed us to express thoughts and feelings that we would not be comfortable sharing with the entire class. I was also able to communicate with my students through written feedback on their other class assignments, a practice they appreciated. Third, through the medium of children's literature, and especially through reading aloud, my students and I were able to share our own stories with each other and to reflect on the stories of others that had touched our lives. By examining each of these activities more closely, it is apparent how a reciprocal mentoring relationship evolved between myself and my students.

## Looking Back on My Story

I know the subject I was teaching made a difference in my relationships with my students. Reading has been my main source of learning, pleasure, and escape since I was a young child. Many of the characters of children's books are like old friends to me; knowledge of them has made a significant imprint on my life. Having the opportunity to share these friends with my students also allowed me to share parts of myself: memories, both painful and joyous, evoked by images within my favorite books. Sharing my own stories and those found in literature gave me an instant connection to my undergraduate students, just as it always had with my students in elementary school.

Obviously, my genuine enthusiasm for what I was teaching came across to my students even more than I realized. Several of them commented on it in their course evaluations: "April was excited about this course. She turned a lecture course into a fun, interesting, motivating class." And, "Her love for books is contagious, and her love of the topic showed through." Also, "April's love of books just poured over into the class. It made such a difference to have a positive outlook on the information we were learning" (December 5, 1995). My feelings about what I was teaching made the entire semester more fulfilling for me; apparently it also did for my students.

My experiences as a *student* that semester (taking graduate classes at the same time I was teaching children's literature) reminded me of the importance of having a teacher respond in writing to my ideas. For the first time, I was introduced to the concept of discovery writing. I was amazed that I could actually learn new things about myself by putting them in writing. This process was enhanced even further for me by the extensive and thoughtful written feedback provided by my professor, Carol Mullen, one of the comentors of this writing group and book. I wanted to model this process for my students, all future teachers, in hopes that they would provide written comments for their own students. My students' comments about this written communication on their final course evaluations indicate that written responses from teachers are equally as important to them: "The written feedback was the best part of this class." And, "April always took the time to give positive, thoughtful response to our work." Also, "She gave great suggestions and feedback on all of our assignments. She was very understanding and caring about what I was doing" (journal entries, September 5, 1995). Obviously, my written feedback communicated care to my students, exactly the message I had hoped to convey.

I also responded to my students through writing by having them keep dialogue journals. All of my students that semester were female except for one. Joanne Cooper (1991) says that journal writing is a familiar medium of communication for most girls and women. Although keeping a journal that is to be read by a teacher as an assignment does not necessarily allow for the same type of reflection as a private journal kept by choice, I do believe my students' journals offered them a means to tell their own stories of teaching and learning. Jo Anne Pagano (1994) argues that in thinking about women as teachers, women as students, and especially about women teaching women, we must pay close attention to the impact of gender on their lives. I tried to be very conscious of this advice while teaching children's literature and to give my students opportunities to think and write about their educational experiences in relation to gender.

During each class period, I asked my students to respond to a question or thought I posed about the literature we were studying. Although responding in writing to all of their journal entries was quite a time-consuming task, it was the single most effective method I found for getting to know each student individually. In responding to questions about their favorite books, my students revealed childhood experiences, why they chose to become teachers, and most significantly, aspects of their personalities that they might not publicly share. One student, Carrie, wrote about always having felt "different" from her peers or like "an outsider." Consequently, she has deep compassion for students who appear different from the norm, and this is one of the reasons she chose to become a teacher. She also experienced a "connection" with characters from literature she met as a child, such as Meg from *A Wrinkle in Time* (L'Engle, 1962) and Kit from *The Witch of Blackbird Pond* (Speare, 1958). I, too, have experienced these same feelings of "differentness" all of my life, and I reduced that sense of isolation through reading. Meg and Kit were two of my favorite characters as well. I was able to communicate our shared experiences privately, in writing, in responding to Carrie's journal.

Another student, Vicki, wrote about how much she had been influenced by the character of Charlotte from *Charlotte's Web* (White, 1952): "She was so gentle and quiet in spirit, yet so friendly and smart. She is a great example of what a true friend should be" (journal entry, September 5, 1995). As I came to know Vicki better, I realized that she had, in her description of Charlotte, described herself perfectly. In her journal, I pointed out how her own "gentle and quiet spirit" would be a gift to her future students.

Darby wrote this early in the semester:

> One of my favorite characters from children's literature is the engine in the book, *The Little Engine That Could* (Piper, 1990). For a little girl who needed a lot of reassurance it was a great story. In everything I did, I had to have people reassure me that I could. This story helped me to see that I could do anything if I set my mind to it. (journal, September 1995)

Through writing, I became aware that quiet Darby might need a little extra reassurance from me to express some of her insights to the class. These journal entries not only allowed me to know my students better but also convinced me of the importance of stories in their lives, just as stories have always been important in mine.

Like many other reading teachers, I believe that the value of reading aloud to students cannot be underestimated. For me, this activity provided another means for establishing personal relationships with my students. I took a risk last semester and read aloud to my class a children's novel that I had never read before. I was familiar with the author and read several reviews of the book, so I hoped that the experience of reading a brand new book together would be a positive one. The book I chose was *Baby* (1993) by Patricia MacLachlan, which surpassed all of my expectations. MacLachlan is a master storyteller and has a gift for figurative language. In fact, the beauty of language is a theme of the book. Virtually all of my students wrote in their journals about MacLachlan's use of words and the emotions they evoked, as well as the experience of reading aloud: "I really enjoyed this book, especially because it was read aloud to me. That is something I have missed." And, "I loved this book. It's been a long time since a teacher read aloud to me. I thought I was too old for it, but I found myself getting to class early just to find out what would happen next!" Also, "I had a hard time not crying in class the last day. I *really* loved this book. I already bought it to add to my collection" (December 1995). The number of students who mentioned their plans to purchase and reread the book thrilled me. I commented in all of their journals my belief that we are never too old for reading aloud and that containing my emotions while reading was also difficult. One journal entry was particularly moving:

> I can especially relate to this book because I lost my baby brother at an early age. I remember how much my family struggled with talking (or not talking) about him. I can recall my mother's struggle with losing a son and how hard it was on my father. The book was *wonderful*! Thanks for sharing it with us! (December 1995)

Even though I took a chance on reading an unfamiliar book aloud, I feel that the experience brought our entire class closer together.

## Musings for Mentors

I firmly believe that sharing some of my stories with my students and allowing them to share theirs with me contributed to some of them choosing me as a mentor. I never expected to have so many connecting encounters in one semester! I cannot say I am glad I had all of them because some of them were experiences of pain, of loss, and of violence that I wish had not occurred. Still, they were real-life experiences that undoubtedly have an impact on the school experiences of the students involved. These encounters confirmed for me beyond a doubt that I could make a difference in the lives of my students.

Other students whose stories were less dramatic touched me, nevertheless, and reminded me of why I chose to be a teacher in the first place. When I gave them opportunities to share their stories, or simply made myself open to listen, almost all my students responded. These experiences allayed my doubts about whether or not I, as a teacher, could establish relationships of reciprocal care with my students. I was also reminded of the joy I have always received from being a colearner with my students.

As a teacher educator, I can model for my students the kinds of practices I hope they will consider using with their future students. No other career offers me these opportunities; this lesson was taught to me by my students. By choosing me as their mentor, my students mentored me. In our class, mentoring became a reciprocal process between myself and my students. The idea of an unbroken circle, with no beginning and no end, represents for me the kind of mentoring relationship I experienced the last semester I taught children's literature.

The experience of being chosen as a mentor by undergraduate students also reminds me of two lessons taught to me by my own mentor, Donna Wiseman. One is that, as teachers or teacher educators, we never know whom we influence or what kind of impact we have in the lives of particular students. A second lesson Donna shared with me, as she told me the story of her own first year as an elementary teacher, is of the importance of being yourself when teaching. A letter I received last semester brought both of these lessons into clear focus for me. Tracy, one of my quietest but most gifted students, wrote:

> Thank you so much for the wonderful semester! I never knew so much about books and about myself. This class was exactly what I needed before student teaching. You have been a wonderful role model–as a teacher, wife and mother. I have learned so much by listening to and watching you each week. Thanks for all the creative ideas and activities. This class has been great! (December 1995)

I realized from this letter that Tracy had been watching me all semester, paying attention to what I said and how well it matched what I did in the classroom. I had made a conscious choice to articulate my own crystallizing experiences for my students as they related to my personal knowledge of teaching, learning, and children's literature. Sally Reis (1995) suggests that all female students should be told throughout their educational experiences that they will face critical choice points in balancing professional and personal, and public and private lives. I hope that sharing my stories with these young women will make them more aware of their own choices. Tracy's letter indicates to me that this possibility exists.

In a recent graduate class on instructional theory each student described his or her perception of characteristics belonging to teachers and students. One student, an experienced high school and college math teacher, said that he could not understand when he first began teaching why students were so affected by the death of a family member or the divorce of parents. It wasn't until after he had been teaching a few years that he realized that students were field dependent and therefore could not separate their experiences in school from their experiences at home. He commented that he, as a teacher, who was more mature than his students, was field independent and therefore able to prevent his personal experiences from influencing his teaching. This separation from the other is impossible for me to do. Nor do I believe I would want to if I could.

Like Nel Noddings, I believe that the first job of teachers is to care for their students. I don't believe we can communicate that kind of care unless we share ourselves, our lives and stories, with our students and allow them to share theirs with us. All of my mentors, my teachers, my colleagues, and especially my students, have modeled this ethic of caring for me.

# Chapter 3

# Four Recipes (Scenarios) on Mentoring: Or, How I Became an E-Mail MaMa

## Luana Zellner

The words *mentor* and *mentoring* are interesting words that conjure up different visions and definitions. Webster defines *mentor* as teacher; counselor. The words *teacher* and *counselor* best describe the role that a mentor plays in this chapter. I find it hard to separate the two. A mentor can be a sister, brother, dad, mother, friend, a saint, a have-to-be or a want-to-be. The role of mentor is often viewed as a blessing; seldom a curse. You may train to be a teacher, but seldom does a day go by that teacher does not become counselor, and vice versa. The two words were born to be together! I was fortunate to have a variety of extended family relationships upon which to learn and gather information on the art of mentoring. Stepmothers, stepfathers, mothers, fathers, stepgrandparents, grandparents, friendly nuns, teachers, children, next door neighbors, a wonderful husband, and two great sons were my support system. My family network was richly filled with a variety of wonderful supportive individuals. It helps!

## The Circle

I thought I knew what mentor meant. Being a baby boomer ready to boom in her forties, I was ready to live my dream of pursuing my doctorate in curriculum and instruction with an emphasis in reading. I had arrived! After all, the kids were grown, my family life was pretty mellow. I could now focus on developing my career. At my age and with my experience, surely I knew what mentoring meant and who it was for. Through my contacts with the *Circle,* I realized how all of us need to be a mentor or need to be mentored at some points in our lives. The *circle* of friendships that evolved from our research group at the university broadened my concept of what a mentor is and could be. Before joining the *Circle,* I pretty much had the message that I was on my own in deciding on my research areas, planning my coursework for my doctoral studies, etc.

I had the utmost respect for the members of the *Circle.* I felt privileged to know and work with each participating graduate student and professor. They were talented, creative, and very supportive of each other. Our conversations helped me reflect on the opportunities where being a mentor took place. I was fortunate to have had friends and family members that served as mentors in the ups and downs of my life. What I didn't realize until I returned to college as a graduate student and instructor, was that one never forgets those who take the time to listen, share and be a part of your life.

## Need a Recipe on How-to–?? How about a Scenario

A mentor is one that has a different recipe for every situation. Sometimes you don't even recognize it when you see it, but the ingredients when blended together make a difference in your life. Through our conversations, the *Circle* helped me realize this.

### *Recipe (Scenario) Number 1:*
### *Recipe for Trailblazing from a Grandmother Who Dared!*

Upon entering college, I knew immediately that I wanted to be a teacher. The role seemed all too familiar. There were no teachers in my family; however, my grandmother had modeled the role for me throughout my life. She *was* a mentor! Grandma Jenny was a groundbreaker during the turn of the century by being the first female court recorder in Sioux City, Iowa. She was a career-oriented young women who was active in a variety of civic activities and community theater. At the age of 40, when health interfered with her ability to hold employment, she married. A housewife and mother she became, but the skills she had perfected while single were unselfishly passed on to her daughter and granddaughter. She had an uncanny knack for sewing without a pattern, playing piano without written music, making pie crust without a recipe, and crocheting intricate patterns in doilies (she made lots of these and we never seemed to have enough places to put them, and they were so useful too). She wasn't bad at building a tent out of chairs and bedspreads in the living room either. Her patience and genuine interest mentored me into a field that I knew from the start was what I wanted to do: teach. If there was something I wanted to learn, she taught it.

Growing up as an only child constantly on the move from location to location in California (9 schools in 10 years) created a situation where friendships were short-lived and fleeting. My education was a patchwork alternating between old and new materials. I was either catching up or bored to tears, depending upon where my mother and I moved. However, no matter what my living situation, my grandmother was always there. She was the root system, the tree, the main support in my life. No matter what time, day, or place, she was there, in letters, in person, and in spirit. The important ingredients in her recipe for mentorship were patience, listening, and being available. They were lessons that I wanted to mimic and model later in life. I always tried to remember the ingredients that made her such a remarkable person. She was definitely a teacher, counselor, and mentor.

My point with this scenario is that a mentor may be an extended family member. Many of our children in school have such a relationship with someone other than Mom and Dad who serve as mentors. The classroom teacher may be that unintentional extended family member who mentors a child. We just need to be aware of when that happens and open our hearts, heads, and hands.

### *Recipe (Scenario) Number 2: Recipe from a Not-So-Wicked Stepmother*

Much blame is often placed on parents for not mentoring or creating opportunities for their children; however, I am convinced that no matter how neglected you are as a child, all you need is one person to show an interest, to care, or to support and encourage you to make a difference. That person may or may not be your parent. That person may just be your friend or teacher. Parents don't get lessons or preparation for their job as parent. Much of what they do is on a wing and a prayer. As children, we don't come with a set of instructions; we just come with a set of obligations and responsibilities for others.

In Recipe number 2, the ingredients are unusual. So many stories we read about wicked stepmothers and fathers come from the myths and stories of the past. In my situation, the character cast as my wicked stepmother was actually one of the most likable, sensitive people I know. She opened worlds that I had little experience with. Art, music, dance, culture, and the importance of education were the ingredients in her recipe for mentoring. She was truly a lifelong learner. She had training in being a gourmet cook, an interior decorator, a pen and ink painter, a teacher of French; the list goes on. She was an educational inspiration. I never dreamed that I would be seeking a doctorate until I met her. She encouraged and stressed the importance of study and reflection.

While in her forties, she received her baccalaureate and master's degrees from San Francisco State University. She was single and almost destitute at the time. English, as her second language, placed another obstacle in her pursuit for education. However, with persistence she graduated with honors and a 4.0 GPA. When I announced that I would be pursuing my Ph.D. in my forties, she was delighted and has followed my progress ever since.

One of the nicest gifts I ever received was her recipe for self-confidence. From this scenario, I learned how mentoring can come from sources you never imagined. She was an excellent role model and cheerleader.

### *Recipe (Scenario) Number 3: The Come-Back Kids!*

For several years I taught children in special education classrooms called *resource* classrooms–resource meaning that you, the teacher, were the school resource to all teachers, all students, all parents, and were definitely *all knowing*. Well, maybe that is an exaggeration. It really meant that you, the teacher, worked with children who had emotional, social, intellectual, physical, or other problems that no one wanted to deal with. Whatever the meaning of my teaching position, I loved it! I loved working with these unusual kids. They were fun and challenging. I honestly loved every day. What I didn't realize was that when you love doing something, others may also love you for it. I was first made aware of this six years after I left the classroom to work as a lecturer at the university.

One day while sitting in my office, a tall polite young man knocked on my office door. He was nicely dressed and looked vaguely familiar. Politely he introduced himself. "Hello Mrs. Z. Do you remember me?" I really couldn't recall where or when I knew this young man, so I finally admitted that I was humbly sorry, but I just couldn't place the face. "I'm Daniel! Daniel Chowsky from your first grade class. Remember me?"

As this young man introduced himself to me, my life experience as a first grade resource teacher flashed before me! In horror I remembered Daniel Chowsky, but not as this nice tall young man standing before me. Instead of Daniel Chowsky, I remembered *Danny the Biter*! He was the terror of the school, the most feared six-year-old on the campus!

My preliminary introduction to Danny was first through vivid verbal tales of horror from the school nurse, former teachers, and classmates. This kid was a legend in his own time! I knew that eventually he would be placed in my classroom and that I would probably need help in handling him. Before he passed through my doorway, I imagined him to be six feet tall, with a muscular jaw, a growl in his voice, and a personality similar to the sinister Dr. Lector in *Silence of the Lambs*. Needless to say, I was disappointed when the day came, and my new student, Danny, was actually less than four feet tall, rather thin, quiet and very loving. At that time his reputation far exceeded his actual persona. He was a troubled child who evidently bit anyone who displayed authority or aggression toward him. He was such an abused case, that both he and his sister were placed in and out of foster care throughout their school life.

Danny and I had a very good working relationship. I found him to be an average boy with good academic ability. Academically, he was a star in my class and, as his home situation stabilized, so did his behavior. His outbursts of anger subsided and gradually he made his way back into the regular classroom. Danny had really had a series of wonderful, supportive teachers and counselors who helped him survive his school years. What meant so very much to me was that he remembered his experience in my classroom as a positive one. Seeing this relaxed, friendly person before me reminded me that it is sometimes the little daily experiences that make a difference in your life and in the lives of others. It was obvious that Danny didn't want to be remembered as *Danny the Biter*, but as Daniel Chowsky, the confident, cool person before me.

We continued our conversation as long lost friends, never referring to past bad experiences. It was obvious that Daniel Chowsky only wanted to remember the good times–the popcorn parties, the story times, field trips, classroom plays, heart-to-heart conversations, hugs, class awards, and stickers.

Over the years, I have run into former students and their parents. They didn't discuss reading, math, or other academic activities that took place in the classroom. Their recollections of my classroom were about being a friend, a supporter, a mentor. I never would have guessed that those were the things that they remembered about their former teacher. However, that was exactly what I remembered about my teachers, grandmother, stepmother, and others in my life who mentored me. I have often wondered if these selected mentors ever realized how those day-to-day experiences remained fondly in my memory and molded my choices in life.

### *Recipe (Scenario) Number 4: Becoming an E-Mail Mama*

In fulfilling my doctoral duties as a research assistant, I was assigned to teach two undergraduate classes. Each class had 50-plus students. The classes consisted of sophomores, juniors, and seniors majoring in one or more areas in education. Most had an emphasis in elementary education. Most were female. Most came from middle-class families. Most were white. For most of these students, it was their first course in education. The few males in class were either in class because they wanted a filler course on their degree plan or they had tried other majors unsuccessfully and thought teaching might be an okay profession until they were promoted to some administrative post. There were the exceptions to this male perception and that was promising. After being a teacher in the public school system for 13 years, I applaud those males who overlooked the low pay and sought the teaching profession for the sheer purpose of influencing the lives of children in a positive way.

As I surveyed the class on the first day, I realized how the perception of higher education gets the commentary it does! Comments like "Undergraduates don't learn anything in those big classes," "How can they learn anything about teaching in classes that consist of 50-plus students," "All they'll get is a bunch of theory and multiple choice tests," and "Higher education is just that; higher education! It is so high that what it teaches is beyond the reality of what *really* goes on in schools. It is too impersonal." These statements were pieces that contributed to a negative perception of teacher education institutions. There is some element of truth to this perception, but I wouldn't be able to address all negativisms this semester. For this reason, I decided to concentrate on the impersonal piece.

*Day 1, 10 A.M.:* There I was, staring at 50 pairs of eyes that were waiting for words of wisdom and knowledge, waiting to learn about the *how-tos* of teaching reading (so I thought). Students did have these concerns; however, on that first day their priorities were on grading assignments and books. It was definitely a how-to kind of moment; not exactly what I was expecting. The how-tos were soon followed by the *whats*, the *whens*, and the *whys*. I could see that if the students and I were to survive this semester, we would need to develop an open communication system that would answer their questions and provide them with the information they needed. This could mean many office hours for advisement, answering phone messages, and repeat performances on, "What's the assignment? We had an assignment?"

"I heard that you canceled the assignment" "Reading? This is a reading course? I thought you would cover secondary reading. Did you say this is a secondary reading course?," etc. I could see the beginnings of a nightmare. By midsemester, the headlines would read "Baby Boomer Graduate Student Kicks Bucket Answering Gazillion Questions From Gazillion Clueless Students!"

One particular cohort of students had worked with children in schools as volunteers, grew up in homes where a parent was a teacher, or had mentored their younger brothers and sisters. This particular group of students were ready for working in the classroom, ready to study the idiosyncrasies of reading. They seemed mature and confident in their choice of becoming professional teachers. Their questions in class were focused on the subjects of reading, teaching, and children. They had been *mentored* in their perception of the role of the teacher.

This was a bit intimidating to another group of students. This group had many questions but were afraid to ask, so they sat in silence. I could see them remaining clueless, envisioning themselves as I.D. numbers, without a face in a sea of confusion. It reminded me of my undergraduate days at San Jose State. Most of my classes were quite large, but to the credit of the professors, they were great at personalizing their courses. Unlike the horror stories of many larger universities, the professors were accessible and student-centered. Their courses were informative and made interesting with sprinklings of personal experiences and an accounting of hands-on research. I was perfectly content to be a passive listener and notetaker in those days. Those students who preferred to ask questions or give profound statements could do so; I really didn't care to become involved if I didn't have to. In the 1990s this is not the case. College students have opinions and share them. (They definitely must be products of the 1960s.) It is all so familiar.

### E-mail and A Cup of Java, Anyone?

In an effort to personalize the course, I asked the students to e-mail me their questions and concerns. In return I set up a group mail system. Information was sent in mass to all my students along with personal responses addressed to individual questions and concerns. First encounters with this system of communication focused on assignments and class particulars. It was straight information only. As time passed, students asked me to mass-mail other types of information about conferences, shows, and organizations. Some requests were political in nature and fostered group interaction along with heavy debates in class.

Our class quickly became divided between those who used their e-mail and those who did not. Those who didn't quickly realized that they were missing a whole line of communication in class. By the end of the fall semester, the entire class was on-line. Conversations became more personal in nature. I felt like Ann Landers or Oprah Winfrey.

I was beginning to sense how many students come to college without an available support system. The pressures of living with a roommate, eating strange foods, planning study time, preparing for classes, planning each day, and tracking expenses can be overwhelming to 19- and 20-year-olds. Their e-mails reflected these concerns. Our system of e-mail offered a safe way for students to vent their emotions and concerns without the pressures of making an appointment or face-to-face embarrassment. E-mails from my class gradually strayed to topics other than textbook and reading theory and arrived at all times of the day and night. I have included the humorous, the brave, and the tragic as examples of creating a mentor network over the Internet. The following are e-mail dialogues.

*The Jeepster:*

Hi Mrs. Z., this is my first e-mail, I hope you got it. If you did, great! I love this (I think). I went to a concert this week and it was so cool, the "group" sang songs that could be used in reading lessons with kids. This might be a way to motivate them to read by writing lyrics to songs. Would you mind discussing this in class?

*Mrs. Z :*

So you like Jeeps? My son drives one too. Yes, in answer to your question. Having reluctant readers and writers read the words to songs or create their own is a terrific idea.

*The Jeepster:*

Thanks Mrs. Z., but I don't own a Jeep. "The Jeeps" is the name of a musical group. I like them a lot. However, I would like to own a Jeep some day. They are awesome!

This was a good lesson for me. I found that the e-mail addresses that students choose sometimes reflected their own likes, interests, preferences, and personalities and that my interpretation wasn't always theirs. Other interesting e-mail addresses included playat3@–, wildting@–, beerhall@–, yoyo222@–, lolylag@–, alcohall@, jaywak@–, agge96@–, skitter@–, george93@–, and rambo3@–.

As our communications continued, I saw the importance of being familiar with the terms and definitions of language used. It also gave me an opportunity to show how e-mail addresses might be a way to motivate elementary age students to use their clever e-mail addresses when writing their stories to each other.

Students began sharing stories and experiences on a regular basis as they became more dependent upon the e-mail system for updates on what was due and what was new among the group. The stories disseminated to everyone through our "web" created more spontaneous responses and camaraderie during class discussions. The 125 students in all of my courses didn't seem so unmanageable as they became more spontaneous in their class discussions. The following is an example of what students wanted to share with each other over the Internet.

### Three Letters to Teddy

> Mrs. Zellner, my 11th grade English teacher gave me this letter and I thought you might enjoy it. Please share it with the class. It is called, 'Three Letters From Teddy', by Dr. Evalynn Thompson. Thanks! jaywak@ jfk.edu

The letter was a tale that every teacher would love to have told. The story was about a teacher (Dr. Thompson) who didn't notice the needs and determination of Teddy, a student in her class, Through Teddy's determination and persistence, he got her attention. He was a motherless child with poor academic performance who appreciated and admired his teacher, Miss Thompson. After his persistence, Miss Thompson took him under her wing and mentored him through his school years. She decided that she wanted to become a "great teacher" instead of a forgettable one. As the story goes, Teddy continued his correspondence with her all the way through college. He invited her to his high school graduation, his medical school graduation, and to sit where his mother would have sat at his wedding.

The story, "Three Letters From Teddy" (Thompson, 1984), was an example of a heart-string grabber. After that particular story was shared, it took me two days to answer my e-mail. The students loved the story and wanted to share their own experiences with how certain teachers affected their lives and choices. In this way, the circle of teachers as mentors was taking place. Our undergraduates were sharing who made the most impact in their lives with others and the Internet became the vehicle for sharing this information.

**Who are the Gifted?  From Tmz9243**

"My English teacher gave me this," tmj3099@–.
Creative and imaginative people are often not recognized by their contemporaries.  In fact, often they are not recognized in school by their teachers either.  History is full of illustrations.  Consider some of these: Einstein was four years old before he could speak and seven before he could read. Isaac Newton did poorly in grade school. Beethoven's music teacher once said of him, "As a composer, he is hopeless." When Thomas Edison was a boy his teachers told him he was too stupid to learn anything. F. W. Woolworth got a job in a dry goods store when he was 21, but his employers would not let him wait on a customer because he "didn't have enough sense." A newspaper editor fired Walt Disney because he had "no good ideas." Caruso's music teacher told him, "You can't sing, you have no voice at all."  The director of the Imperial Opera in Vienna told Madame Schumann-Heink that she would never be a singer and advised her to buy a sewing machine.  Leo Tolstoy flunked out of college.  Wernher von Braun flunked ninth grade algebra. Admiral Richard E. Byrd had been retired from the Navy, as "unfit for service," until he flew over both poles.  Louis Pasteur was rated as mediocre in chemistry when he attended the Royal College. Abraham Lincoln entered the Black Hawk War as a captain and came out as a private.  Louisa May Alcott was told by an editor that she could never write anything that had popular appeal.  Fred Waring was once rejected from high school chorus.  Winston Churchill failed the sixth grade. Probably these people were identified as low achievers in school or as misfits on their jobs because of problems of relevance. (Source: Milton E. Larson).

**Death Mid-Semester and Other Life Crisis Experiences**

Not all e-mail is pleasant, funny, or just informational.  Some demanded a different type of mentorship and sensitivity, a mentorship that required you to read between the lines and plan how you might ease the pain.
November had rolled around and brought with it its usual epidemic of absences from class due to flu, colds, dead car batteries, and funeral excuses for dead distant relatives, family friends, dogs, cats, and a pet snake.  After teaching university courses for nine years, I was used to

receiving a long list of reasons for *missing* class during midterm examinations, quizzes, and major papers. Students would often wait until the last minute to finish term projects and study for exams. In their panicked state they would realize that "over night" may not be enough time, so the list of requests for excused absence often grew. However, this wasn't always the case.

During this particular November, one of our more dedicated students had a sudden death in his family. He remains in my mind because it was through e-mail that students in class were made aware of his grief and could offer the support their fellow student needed at this time.

Jack (the name has been changed in respect for anonymity) was one of the few males in the class. He was also one of three members of the Texas A&M University Corps of Cadets in the class, the Corps being a tradition and trademark of the university. Texas A&M University was primarily a male dominated university with an emphasis on military discipline and preparation until 1972. In 1972 the university officially became co-ed and so the College of Education was born for all those Aggies that wanted to become teachers. The Corps tradition has remained even though it isn't the largest group on campus.

Jack was the epitome of the Corps image. He was clean cut, neatly groomed in his cadet uniform, extremely disciplined, and punctual with homework assignments. You just asked, and it was done! If there was a lull in class discussion, I couldn't help but call on Jack (I knew he had read the material). He never missed a class and was always on time. After all, it was the Corps way.

One day Jack wasn't there. Another day passed and another and then a week passed. I couldn't believe it. Had our star student dropped out? Or had he been kidnapped by the *Red Pots*? (a group of students who help cut, stack, and build a bonfire that is an annual event held before the football game with the University of Texas). I received an e-mail at the end of a week from New York, his home state. The following are direct exerpts from our conversations:

*Jack:*

> Mrs. Zellner, I will not be in class the rest of this week or during the first 2 days of next week. My father died and I have the chicken pox. Please let me know what assignments I may have missed. I will be taking my midterm exam as scheduled.

*Mrs. Z:*

> Jack, take care of yourself. When you return we'll discuss what assignments are missing. My condolences to your family.

The day of the midterm exam arrived and Jack was there. His face was covered with scabs from chicken pox. He had arrived thin and pale from New York City after his brief stay with his grieving family. The class had already e-mailed their sympathies and offers of help. I sensed their strain in trying to offer some comfort to him in class. Then the week of Thanksgiving arrived. I wanted to talk to Jack after the midterm, but he hastily slipped out of class. Thanksgiving was a particularly hard time for out-of-state students who attended the university, since everything closed down for the holidays. The campus of more than 40,000 students became a ghost town.

For Jack I imagined that Thanksgiving would be especially difficult since he wouldn't be with his family, and after all, he was still recovering from the chicken pox! I e-mailed him.

*Mrs. Z:*

> Jack, I know that this is a difficult time for you. My family would like to have you spend Thanksgiving with us. If you would like to give me a call or stop by. Sincerely, Luana

*Jack:*

> Thank you Mrs. Zellner for the invitation, but I will have to pass. I have to catch up on some missed assignments so that will keep me pretty busy. I would like an extension of two days for the last assignments if possible. Sincerely, Jack

Wednesday of the following week arrived and Jack turned in all assignments. His midterm grade dropped from a straight A average to a B- due to his midterm scores. However, he insisted on business as usual with no favors. All make-up assignments were turned in before his requested two-day extension. An excellent final exam plus some extra-credit work brought his grades back to a well deserved A in the course. The class couldn't believe how he stuck through the semester. A flurry of conversation took place over the Internet regarding his situation. What Jack didn't realize was that he was *mentoring* others. He was modeling how someone their age might handle grief and obstacles in life.

What the class noticed was that their own excuses for being late to class, or turning assignments in late, paled in comparison to Jack's.

After reviewing their e-mails and thoughts of sympathy and support for Jack, I realized that the class seemed different. I was hoping that it wasn't my imagination, but I could swear that everyone was on time. Everyone was turning in their assignments on the date due. The class seemed fuller (no empty seats). The excuses got better and more believable for those who were tardy or sick (actual signed doctors' explanations appeared, a novelty!). Anyone who has ever taught an undergraduate course at the university level knows how strange it is to find perfect attendance during the last weeks of the semester when papers and projects are due.

Another student of mine, Anna, lost her mother to cancer during final exam week that semester. I gave Jack and Anna each other's e-mail addresses and encouraged them to get together with a few other students from different undergraduate classes who had also experienced recent losses in their families. I was glad to find out that these students started their own support network. The use of e-mail helped with the initiation of the group, giving each person some anonymity until he or she felt comfortable enough to meet each other in person.

### Nineteen and Pregnant

Cynthia was a beautiful student who sat in the back of my class. She was very quiet, almost painfully shy. Small group work in class seemed to help her open up and participate more with the others in the course. After three weeks of large and small group activity, I was pleased to see everyone participating in class discussions. Preparation for class was an unspoken requirement if you didn't want to look foolish in front of your peers. Everyone, even Cynthia, was in the know. As the semester clicked along, Cynthia's group was complaining about her absences, tardiness, and lack of preparation for class. They didn't want her lack of preparation and participation to affect their grade!

I sent Cynthia an e-mail asking her to explain what might be interfering with attending class on a regular basis. I suggested that she e-mail me or visit me in my office. I got a simple e-mail back.

*Cynthia:*
I'm pregnant, not married, 19 and on scholarship. I'd like to come talk to you soon. I'll let you know when I can.

After four weeks Cynthia came to my office. She was upset that her group was so down on her, but that was the least of her worries. She had missed class because of an upset stomach every evening at 6 p.m. Our course met every Tuesday night and, unfortunately, Cynthia and Baby X weren't getting along around that time. Cynthia was three months pregnant and experiencing morning sickness, but only in the evening. She was afraid to say anything to anyone other than her mother, whom she adored. Cynthia's mother was her mentor.

Cynthia was from one of the poorest areas of Houston and the first of four children to go to college. Her parents and younger brothers and sister were counting on her to succeed. In her mind, college was her only opportunity to escape from a cycle of poverty. She had no intention of marrying the father or giving the baby up for adoption. She definitely didn't want to quit school.

After discussing the matter with her parents, Cynthia and her family decided she should finish the semester as best she could and work during the summer and fall instead of taking classes. Her parents would raise the baby once it was born in the fall of 1996, allowing Cynthia to return to school in the spring of 1997. This was definitely a difficult decision for Cynthia to make since she had hoped to not miss a semester of school.

I suggested that she explain the situation to her group so that they might be more accommodating and understanding. The next week the class was bringing her crackers and snacks. The young mothers in her group were offering suggestions on how to cope with nausea, fatigue, and other common problems expectant mothers face. Cynthia seemed less stressed, and interaction with members of the group seemed less hostile as the semester drew to a close.

Knowing how determined this young woman was in acquiring an education, I think she will make it. The support she had from her family and classmates made a difference in how she felt about herself and her future.

I keep my former students posted on upcoming reading conferences, and job and tutoring opportunities through e-mail. They seem to enjoy the notes and quotes I supply them and like the fact that their former instructor hasn't forgotten them. I am now addressed affectionately as *E-Mail MaMa,* a label I take great pride in. Many of these same students are working with Dr. Jane Hughey as Writing Buddies in local elementary schools. They continue to keep in touch with former classmates through e-mail. Many have branched into using the Internet to write letters to their assigned *Buddy* (usually a third or fourth grader). This seems to be a great way of developing and improving writing skills of children as well as the writing skills of my former students.

## MaMa, Dad, David, and Nathan

When the Internet came into general use, I swear that the world shook from the thunderous applause of parents who face gigantic phone bills from their sons and daughters every month. The cyberspace highway had given us a way to communicate with our offspring without going broke in the process. E-mail became a way of mentoring our children from a distance, especially when they took off for college and unknown territory.

While David completed an internship for Lucas Films in California, he was grateful to be able to e-mail his family on a regular basis. As a budding screenwriter, he found the Internet to be an excellent way to send scripts back and forth to his brother, father, and mama for review and edits. Mentoring and family support had an opportunity to continue without interruption.

David now lives in Austin and is busy with his fledgling film company. His brother Nathan and other screenwriters and readers are able to keep the circle of support alive over the Internet. Mentorship truly takes on different images and purposes.

## Summary

The Internet seems to keep the circle of my friends and family together. The circle of graduate students and faculty that first initiated this project keep in touch by e-mail. It is a spontaneous and easy way to share ideas and thoughts with each other. Friends located miles away don't seem so far away any more since the Internet came into being. Dr. Jane Hughey has been the link in completing a circle of mentorship for me. Her dedication and inspiration to the field of teacher education, plus her support during my pursuit of a Ph.D. have been a true model of what mentorship is all about. The support and mentorship from the circle of faculty and graduate students who first dreamed of this book has kept the circle together.

I often wonder how Grandma Jenny, and those who I considered mentors in my young life, would have used the Internet. Well, maybe the "tents" in the living room would have taken a different form!

## Acknowledgments

Special thanks to the following circle of friends, students, and family for their support and encouragement: John Stansell, Jane Hughey, Carol Mullen, Donna Wiseman, Maggie Cox, April Kemp, Diane Adoue, Cindy Boettcher, Gwen Webb-Johnson.

And thanks to all of those undergraduates who shared their stories, dreams, and wishes–Ron, David, and Nathan Zellner, my favorite mentors and cyber talkers!

# Part II

# The Role of Mentorship in the Graduate Assistantship Teaching of Preservice Students

**Cindy King Boettcher**

**Maggie D. Cox**

# Chapter 4

---

# Mentoring:
# The Magical Wand in Education

## Cindy King Boettcher

As a young child I was entranced with the story of Cinderella. I loved reading about the young girl who had been transformed from a poor, lowly, mistreated servant to the exquisite young princess at the Ball. The wave of the magical wand, the delicate glass slipper, and the loving Fairy Godmother were very enchanting and made a lasting imprint on my young impressionable mind. Throughout my life I have attended many educational "Balls," and I have played not only the role of "Cindy-ella" but other roles in the story as well. I have been the young girl who was transformed because of caring and kind mentors. At different times I have waved my magical wand to help a student achieve the "Grand Ball" of success, and then I have switched hats and become the trusted Fairy Godmother to preservice and novice teachers. This story is still one of my favorites, and since Cinderella was "sweet and gentle and good as gold" (Jeffers, 1985, p. 2), she is an important mentor in the educational community. There are over 700 known versions of this beloved folktale, and because the value of kindness transcends all cultural lines, this book reflects no boundaries when looking at the mentoring process.

Cinderella was often alone in her circle of one. Her ugly stepsisters were very threatened by her beauty and kindness and excluded her from many activities in their world. She toiled hard doing menial tasks that never seemed to satisfy her family. No one observed her talents or the kind attitude with which she executed her meaningless rote tasks. As young preservice teachers leave their college campuses and enter the grand ball of the teaching profession, do they operate in their own circle of one? Do the ugly stepsisters have any relation to the way that those in position are threatened and exclude novice teachers? Are experienced teachers intimidated by the enthusiasm and beautiful ideas that young teachers bring to the classrooms? The death of Cinderella's parents left her with no loving support system. Do we in the educational field provide that support system (mentoring) so that students are not confined to the "cinder" circle of one?

**Magical Wand Number 1**

During my student teaching experience, I returned home each night determined that I was not going to be a teacher. No one had prepared me for this horrendous ordeal. After seven semesters in college I was finally attending the Ball and interacting with children, but I hated my major! It was my worst nightmare, and I was stuck because my family told me that I had to graduate and get a job!

After more than 20 years in the teaching profession, I can reflect back on what made this student teaching experience so painful in 1972. The first frustration that I encountered was being assigned to an all-black elementary school and knowing nothing about African-American culture. My cooperating teacher was a middle-age white woman who had recently moved from New York to Texas, and felt "caught in the desegregation of southern schools." She hated her assignment, and her students clearly hated her. Here I was, a preservice teacher in the middle of a power struggle between the teacher and her students. I now question why the school district would allow a teacher new to the district to mentor a student teacher. She had not received the necessary mentoring to help her feel at home in her new environment.

The first couple of weeks of school I was required by both my cooperating teacher and university supervisor to sit and observe the dynamics of the classroom. The students were in fights, the teacher screamed, and the kids showed no respect to the teacher. I was scared to death! I had never really observed any teaching and/or learning, and, as

I reflect today, the teacher clearly did not respect or value what the students had to offer.

I can only remember the reading classes in that school. The library was almost nonexistent, and the students used old basal readers with ditto work sheets. Every day the teacher had the students read aloud, taking turns by rows, and they were given worksheets covering what was taught. There was no literature, creative writing, or inviting extensions of the lessons. The students engaged in rote drill, and their answers were either right or wrong. This environment was similar to the one that Cinderella faced daily. The school atmosphere was one of a harsh existence, and the students had no luxuries in their physical or educational environment. The pedagogy of the teacher was reminiscent of the mean stepmother who required the students to do menial tasks that often held no relevant meaning to either Cinderella or the students. There were no books that showed African-American characters, values, or beliefs, and the magic wand used to enhance creativity and thinking skills was never waved!

There was a petite young girl named Vivian who ruled the class I was observing with an iron fist, or maybe it was a magical wand! I quickly decided the second week that I needed to get this student on my side if I was going to survive this experience. I asked her if she could stay after school that Friday and help me put up a bulletin board, and in exchange I would buy her a Coke and a snack. Those were the magic words! We stayed until 5:00 P.M. while I tried my best to win her trust and affection. Vivian asked me if I would go with her to church, to which I said "Yes." On Sunday she marched me down to the front pew of the church for all the kids to see, and that became the turning point in my student teaching experience. I had found my Fairy Godmother in this little girl! She had transformed me to be accepted by her culture and peers. We had reversed roles; I became the Cinderella and she became my Fairy Godmother. Her magical wand allowed me to be accepted into the palace environment in which she lived and attended school. Since I had grown up in Canada in a middle-class home, I was not familiar with the ghetto environment in which my students lived. My Fairy Godmother, Vivian, took delight in helping me understand her culture and environment.

On Monday, I observed that Vivian had the students lined up quietly when they entered the room from the playground. As I stumbled through my first reading lesson, I noticed that she would shoot the evil-eye at misbehaving students and that they would reluctantly but quickly get back on task. At the end of the third week, I had actually established somewhat of a rapport with the class, but unfortunately not with my cooperating teacher! She seemed to resent my ability to make connections with the students in her class.

Throughout the semester, I was required to make two bulletin boards a month for my teacher. I had to do a reading interactional board and a seasonal board. I spent a lot of money and many hours each weekend creating these boards and planning how I would some day use them in my own classroom. I was appalled at the end of the semester when the teacher insisted that they be left in her room because they had, as far as she was concerned, been made for her. Like Cinderella, I felt that I had worked and toiled hard week after week, and then my teacher's classroom became stitched with beautiful bulletin boards that I had made. In some versions of Cinderella, her stepsisters tore her beautiful dress to shreds. This was how I felt as my cooperating teacher ripped my bulletin boards from me. As a 21-year-old college student trying hard to graduate, I didn't even question her request!

**Musings for Mentors**

1. Mentoring is reciprocal and students can mentor teachers, as did my young student, Vivian. She showed me the values and beliefs of her culture and waved her magical wand to permit me entry into her world,
2. We, as teacher educators, need to mentor our preservice and veteran teachers in understanding and appreciating the multicultural classrooms in which we teach,
3. There needs to be better cooperation between university supervisors and cooperating teachers in mentoring student teachers. It is essential for these three parties to know the expectations of the others,
4. To be successful in the classroom, in whatever role played, we must look for ways to transform each other in a very positive and magical way.

**Magical Wand Number 2**

I finally graduated and entered my own classroom that fall, determined to save the world and make a difference in the lives of every child I taught. Now for the first time, I was going to be the Fairy Godmother. This was a tall order for a naive teacher. Many of the veteran teachers were wonderful mentors. They made me feel a part of their team and helped me to assimilate into the culture of the school. Moving to a small rural community was a cultural shock, and so I was grateful for the wisdom and guidance of these wonderful women.

In addition to the wisdom and guidance of the Fairy Godmothers that were magically appearing in my new world, these teachers provided me with many concrete materials. My empty filing cabinet became filled with activities and ideas to implement a variety of lessons. Waving their magical wands revealed critical suggestions for effective classroom management, tips on how to handle a parent conference, and advice on organizing my lesson plans and grade book. They shared methods of teaching pertinent skills and innovative ways to check for understanding of the new material. Their guidance, in effect, transformed me from a college student to a classroom teacher!

As in any new situation, there are always some teachers who resent the "new kid on the block." They were suspicious of the new ideas from the universities and resented the enthusiasm and vigor with which the new teacher embraces each day. Fortunately for me, there were several of us "new kids" and we mentored and encouraged each other. It was fortunate that none of the six of us had graduated from the same university, so we brought a variety of ideas and backgrounds to this elementary school. We would stay late on Thursday evenings and congregate in someone's classroom to air our frustrations and encourage those that needed support. Interestingly enough, the six of us have remained close to each other and still share ideas after 20 years! The value of peers can never be overestimated in teaching.

**Musings for Mentors**

1.  There needs to be an experienced, caring teacher available to help mentor the new teacher on campus,
2.  The value of peer mentoring cannot be overestimated,

3.      It is valuable to meet one day a week after school hours with fellow teachers to voice concerns and encourage each other with helpful suggestions to resolve problems. This kind of commitment will build the collegiality of the staff.

## Magical Wand Number 3

After several years of teaching, my principal approached me about having a student teacher in the classroom. I was both excited and apprehensive and wondered why the principal felt that I should have a student teacher. Did he recognize me as having the qualities of a Fairy Godmother? Were my mentoring skills visible to him as I worked with other novice teachers on my campus? Vivid nightmares of my own experience flooded my memory, and I was determined that this young woman would have a very different experience. In this new role of cooperating teacher, I again felt frustration with the university supervisor. She never took the time to explain to me what the university's expectations were for the program, and I was never sure if I was meeting the requirements for a successful experience.

Reflecting on my own student teaching experiences, I was determined to help this student teacher leave my room prepared for her own classroom. Many student teachers have a difficult time in their transformation from being a college student to a classroom teacher. Like Cinderella they hear about the Ball, but they don't know the proper etiquette once they get there (classroom). These newly transformed guests need the guidance of a "handsome prince" (cooperating teacher) to take their hand and ensure that they have a wonderful time. It is critical that they be mentored in the protocol of pedagogy.

I assumed the dual role of the Fairy Godmother and the handsome prince (see *Figure 2: My College Tale of Mentoring Cinderella*). I valued and honored her new ideas, enthusiasm, and excitement for the teaching profession. During this time I helped her learn classroom management techniques, how to prepare lesson plans, and how to cope with the multifaceted demands of a classroom of elementary students. Over the course of the semester, I filled her personal filing cabinet with creative activities and suggestions to help make her lessons more inviting and relevant for the students. This young teacher discovered my passion for children's literature and the necessity of having multicultural literature in the classroom library. She made bulletin boards for her

*Figure 2. My College Tale of Mentoring Cinderella*

different teaching activities, which she took with her for her own future classroom! On a couple of occasions, she became my Fairy Godmother, waving her magic wand to share a new idea or piece of research that she had learned in her university classes. We often exchanged roles as we danced at the ball of classroom instruction.

We would sit and talk after school about what things worked and what things could have been done differently. In our discussions, we discovered together that student teachers come with a lot of textbook knowledge but often do not understand how to put theory into practice. She discerned that teachers must vary activities to keep the attention of the students. Another valuable lesson she became cognizant of was the importance of being consistent in classroom management and procedures. Often college-level student teachers want to be friends with their young students. They quickly learn that the students need a friend who is not on their own level, but one who will be similar to a parental figure. These reflective discussions were our most valuable teachable moments of the day. We laughed and we cried, but mostly we grew in pedagogy together.

**Musings for Mentors**

1.    Be positive, accepting, and understanding of the new preservice teacher in your classroom,
2.    Reflect back on the day along with your student teacher. Help him or her to determine what worked or didn't work. Discuss and suggest ways to help improve on pedagogy, classroom management, organizational skills, and more,
3.    Model effective teaching strategies. Don't assume that students will come prepared to read your mind. Help them to do the good job they are so willing to accomplish.

**Magical Wand Number 4**

In addition to being an elementary public school teacher for 10 years, I also started a private elementary school and was principal for a decade. The school started with two teachers and 25 students ages three and four, and in 10 years grew to include 35 teachers and 350 students from preschool through fifth grade. I wore many hats in the Cinderella roles that I played as administrator. For the first time I even had to assume the role of the ugly stepsister on a couple of occasions. Because the school grew so large in a relatively short period of time, I felt it was crucial that teachers mentor each other. I had teachers in grade levels above and below each other mentoring as we added new grade levels. In this mentoring position, the experienced teachers shared the philosophy and procedures of our school. This in turn ensured a vertical alignment of the curriculum and gave a greater continuity of content and activities of subject areas. I also had teachers form mentorships horizontally across grade levels, which kept the content taught in classes at one level very similar.

Faculty enjoyed the time that they spent reflecting and encouraging each other after school hours. It was the warm, fuzzy time of the week for these teachers. This time together built a very cohesive staff of teachers who were genuinely concerned about each other, the children, the school, and the curriculum. This shared time of team-building was valuable to the success of our school. Teachers felt that they were empowered in the decision making of our school with regard to mentoring arrangements and the design of curriculum.

On a couple of rare occasions I experienced some Cinderellas who were not ready to be transformed from a college student to a classroom teacher. I had to ask them to work a little harder on classroom management, lesson planning, professional attitudes, and mastery of their content. Unfortunately, some were not given an invitation to attend the Ball the following year. They reminded me of the coach that turned into a pumpkin at midnight. No magic seemed to sustain them for a long period of time. I just could not, in some cases, get results from waving the magical wand.

## Musings for Mentors

1. As an administrator, put a mentoring program in place in your school. It will help everyone to get involved, especially you,
2. No matter how hard you wave the magical wand, for some teachers there will be no transformation.

## Magical Wand Number 5

For the past two semesters, I have been teaching preservice teachers in the college classroom. I have been able to see first-hand how much these students need mentoring and encouragement as they prepare to student teach. I find them viewing me as their Fairy Godmother. Many have come to me with stories and frustrations concerning the system and have confided in me about their problems.

One of the frustrations that the students have shared is the way in which they must take their courses. They are arranged in a hierarchical fashion that does not allow room for flexibility in the sequence that courses are taken. The problem is that students often do not have any actual hands-on experience with children until they are in their senior year. (This reminds me of my own experience!) They only get to interact with children if they are doing a reading practicum. My students have also shared with me that they are never really taught how to do a unit or how to integrate books in different content areas. There is often little if any exposure to literature that deals with diversity of culture and gender. However, the public schools do a lot of integration, and students feel that they are not prepared for the real world. Students preparing for teaching remind me of Cinderella, who is often seen scrubbing the floor when she should be learning how to wave her wand to become a catalyst for learning. Like Cinderella, the student teacher often performs meaningless tasks unrelated to what happens in real life.

Another thing that my students feel they need guidance with is the grading practice of instructors and feedback on their work. Many of the students claim that they do not get feedback on their assignments, or if they do, it is negative and unhelpful. Many of the students tell me about being subjected to multiple choice tests, which educational research clearly asserts checks only for recall and lower level thinking skills. Essay questions that cause a student to think and synthesize information are typically not given. Does assessment in teacher education programs deal with how well Cinderella can clean, and not how well she can dance at the Ball? Do we fail to see the beautiful person underneath the rags? Is there another way to look at the performance of Cinderella? Portfolios and alternative assessment measures are often used in public school settings, but are modeled by too few professors within college settings.

As one of many graduate assistants who shares these same frustrations, I have tried to model exceptional pedagogy in this area of feedback. Assignments are returned with liberal feedback within one week of submission. I have modeled portfolios and alternative assessments so that students will know how to do these curricular activities in their own classrooms. My office is open to students to come by and share concerns or rejoice in accomplishments. These young adults are the future educators of the next two generations. We as teacher educators are charged with a great responsibility of helping them enter the profession prepared to have a successful impact. We must help them to become prepared with the necessary social graces to attend the Ball!

## Musings for Mentors

1.  Teacher educators should be available to help model exceptional pedagogy for undergraduate students,
2.  Students in the College of Education should be exposed to working with children prior to their senior year,
3.  Feedback and assessment should be relevant and given on all assignments in a timely manner.

## Magical Wand Number 6

As a doctoral student, I have often felt like the Cinderella who did not get to go to the Ball. Thankfully, I have had a couple of wonderful mentors. The chairperson of my committee has been my Fairy Godmother. She has waved her magical wand and transformed me on my journey.

When selecting members for my doctoral committee, no one gave me guidance about the process. In Sadker and Sadker's (1994) book, they reveal it is no secret among faculty members who is valued, vested, and rewarded. Through comments, attitudes, and behavior, the message is clear that female faculty members have second-class citizenship on campus; and this message filters down to the students" (p. 166). I selected as the chairperson of my committee a female academic who shared my philosophy about reading, feminist literature, and multicultural education. Three other members of my committee are also female and of diverse ethnic backgrounds. When I submitted my degree plan I was strongly advised to add a male faculty member to my committee. I was told that this change would help me to get my dissertation proposal accepted. I was appalled. How many committees have been, without scrutiny, composed of all males? So why should my committee be scrutinized for its gender-based representation, I wondered. Once again, I had received an invitation to the Doctoral Ball but without the full privileges of being a guest in the palace.

In Walt Disney's version, Cinderella's only friends were animals and birds: "All of the animals loved her. She took special care of her dog, Bruno, and made sure to feed and brush down her old horse each day. The birds sang to her often, and the mice were always there to keep her company" (Grimes, 1993, p. 4). While working on my Ph.D., some of my best friends were a couple of trusted fellow doctoral students. Like me, they were the "animals and birds" (Grimes, 1993, p. 4) of the department. These were not the flamboyant leaders who were always knocking on the department head's door. We often operated in the background but took special care in mentoring each other. We provided the necessary support system by sharing ideas, editing each other's work, helping with research questions, and encouraging each other not to give up! Like Cinderella, we had created our own inner circle of friends through the need for a support system.

There is a distinct and often political line drawn in the College of Education between quantitative and qualitative research. The qualitative research paradigm is considered female and second-class by the men who hold the power to approve a student's dissertation. On several occasions, I have attended class only to have professors tell me that my research paradigm is not "good research." One professor spent an evening telling us, during class time, how to do a good 85-page dissertation, saying anything more would not be considered valuable research.

These paradigms remind me of the value placed on the importance of Cinderella and her stepsisters. The stepmother valued her own daughters (the quantitative researchers) and not Cinderella (the qualitative researcher). Wasn't there an invitation issued to all the people of the land to come to the Ball? Won't my research design be as beautiful as someone else's? Because of the mentors on my committee, I have been able to persevere on my journey to the Dissertation Ball proposal.

**Musings for Mentors**

1.    As a doctoral student, select a committee that shares your beliefs and values, and that will help you get to the graduation ball safe and intact,

2.     Surround yourself with trusted graduate student peers who will mentor you,

3.     Select your research to please yourself. If not, your transformation will not be a happy one.

## Final Magical Wand

During my final semester of coursework, the chair of my committee accepted a position at a university out-of-state. For her, it was the dream job of her lifetime. For me, it was the lowest point of my Cindy-ella experiences. I felt like the magic had been taken out of my life. How would I ever be transformed sufficiently to attend that Graduate Ball? To add to my despair, other professors began asking who my new chair was going to be. Why did I have to get another chair, I wondered.

After a couple of weeks of feeling sorry for myself, I began to rely on the magic that my Fairy Godmother had given me. Hadn't she helped me get my pilot study going? With e-mail, FAX machines, and the trusty old telephone, couldn't I communicate my ideas and receive her suggestions with ease? My committee chair had also arranged with another person on my committee to sign papers and run the interference necessary to get my dissertation approved. I decided that it was not necessary *for me* to change.

Mentoring is a multilevel process. It is also a reciprocal process. As teacher educators we can be mentored and help to mentor others. As you go to the educational balls of pedagogy, you too will assume the different roles found in the Cinderella story and wave your magical wand to positively change a life!

# Chapter 5

---

# Walking the Tightrope: The Role of Mentoring in Developing Educators as Professionals

## Maggie D. Cox

As I reflect back on the beginning of my teaching career in the late 1960s, I remember thinking that teaching was a solitary career with one adult working with many students. I had no real idea of teaching as a profession or that collegial relationships would be important. My first job was in California, which had a different type of teacher training at the undergraduate level than I had received in Louisiana. California was a national leader in educational innovation at that time. I saw this first job as an excellent opportunity to grow professionally, although I did feel apprehensive.

I was hired three days before school started. My fourth grade class included some immigrant students from Mexico who spoke only Spanish. They had never been to school before coming to the United States and did not know how to read or write in either language. I frantically sought to learn new content in order to teach California's history to my students. The curriculum guides were very useful to me, but different from what I had been exposed to in my undergraduate studies. This district curriculum used multiple texts rather than one adoption and defined classroom projects for each unit, such as having the students build a model of a Spanish mission which was half the size of the classroom. Along with the other teachers in the building, I was quickly assigned to a district-wide curriculum committee. I was both elated at the teaching opportunities and exhausted from attempting to keep up with bulletin boards, lesson plans, student needs, and my frequent lack of knowing what to do next. I found myself walking a tightrope each day as I struggled to become the teacher I wanted to be. And there was no one holding the net!

I rode to work with Joanne, the other beginning teacher at the school, who had graduated from the state's five-year program with an entire year of student teaching. Although she was extremely helpful, I felt even more inadequate when comparing myself and my preparation with her skills as a beginning teacher. At the same time, my principal was highly critical of what I was doing and how I was doing it, yet highly complimentary of my fellow beginner. I felt frustrated and, above all, alone as a circle of one. The circle seemed to be growing tighter each day.

One Friday afternoon I was sitting at my desk attempting to adjust my lesson plans for Monday to include what the class did not get done that day. There was a knock on the door and a head appeared, saying "We're going to Dottie's house right now for our Friday meeting. Come with us." It was the first time I had been invited to go anywhere with the other teachers and, as tired and disheartened as I was, I felt the need to break out of my solitary world. As I followed the hand drawn map to Dottie's, I wondered what other teachers talked about on Friday or, for that matter, any other day. It seemed I only talked or thought about teaching 24 hours a day. And I seemed to solve one problem only to be met by new ones each day. Well, I sure wasn't going to tell them how frustrated I was with my principal, my students, and, most of all, myself, I proclaimed to myself as I got out of the car.

The next hour and a half changed my life. I didn't have to tell Dottie, Eleanor, and Kim anything. Each could recall their beginning year of teaching as well as their first year at this particular school. They also had noticed the principal's attitude toward me and were quick to share similar experiences they had had with her. I finally had the courage to ask if they thought I was going to be a competent teacher or if I needed to look for another career. I was very serious about my question, but each of them agreed that I had talent and potential. Different teachers in the "Friday Bunch" offered to plan activities with me and my class so we could team teach, assess my lesson plans for effectiveness, suggest district resources to complement my units, and, finally, respond to questions about procedures or classroom management. What a relief it was to have found, after several months of isolation, teachers willing to hold the safety net for me!

## Musings for Mentors

1. Beginning teachers need to break the isolation in the classroom and within themselves through both collegial and mentoring relationships with other teachers,
2. Collegial and mentoring relationships within the school can offer the beginning teacher a sense of belonging while also enhancing teaching and survival skills,
3. Each mentor can serve a different purpose for the same teacher–instructional strategies, procedures and policies, understanding students and their needs, resources, bulletin boards, or planning for instruction,
4. If beginning teachers are assigned a mentor by the school or advised to seek one on their own, they will usually struggle alone unless a more experienced teacher reaches out.

## Looking Back on My Story

Thus began the cycle of mentoring that I continue today. I know I would never have made teaching my career if it had not been for the Friday Bunch, who accepted me as a professional, listening when I was uncertain or frustrated, encouraging my growth as a teacher. After that year, I consciously committed myself to mentoring other teachers as a living tribute to the Friday Bunch.

## Holding the Net for Others

"Can I talk with you right now, Ms. Cox?" All five foot, one inches of me looked up at all six feet of the first year social studies teacher at our middle school. It was obvious he was upset.

"Sure, come on in and shut the office door."

As soon as the door to my library office shut, his face broke and tears streamed down his face. I found myself hugging this usually enthusiastic young teacher while he tried to calm down. After he'd blown his nose, his only word was a poignant, "Why?"

I waited. He began to tell me what had transpired. "I was sitting in the lounge on my conference period, drinking a soda, and grading my seventh graders' test papers. One of the older teachers fixed a cup of coffee and then began reading the tests over my shoulder. He started laughing and said loudly to everyone in the lounge: 'Hey, you should see what this kid thinks seventh graders can do! Where did you get your degree, kid?'"

"Ms. Cox, everybody laughed and wanted to see the test. I was mortified and didn't know what to say. I could feel my face turning red. I gathered up my papers and started towards the classroom where I teach next period. Then I realized that I couldn't work in there because another teacher uses it this period. I'm a floater, you know. I couldn't think of any other place to go but here!"

His anguish over lack of a private place, compounded by his public embarrassment from a fellow teacher, brought tears to my eyes. What could I possibly say or do to make the school seem like a friendly place to this young man? We talked instead of why he wanted to be a teacher and if he could see any evidence of making a difference with his students. He pointed to a couple of the tests and showed student work that was definitely well done and yet difficult for many seventh graders. He left at the bell, not with any understanding of his fellow teachers' motives, but with reassurance in his students' abilities. He also reaffirmed his own ability to make a difference with them.

## Musings for Mentors

1. Mentors must be able to listen nonjudgmentally and communicate the positive aspects of beginning teachers' daily activities,

2. Beginners, both male and female, need a safe place in the school to express their emotional responses to the daily challenges of becoming an experienced educator,

3. Mentors may serve as a liaison between the rest of the faculty and the beginning teacher by introducing the beginner to others with whom they can work collegially,

4.  Serving as a mentor creates an opportunity for further learning in all areas of education.

## Looking Back on My Story

For more than 20 years I have been offering services to mentor teachers who are new to the teaching profession or who are new arrivals to my school. Why? One reason for my commitment is the knowledge of the impact the mentoring by the Friday Bunch had had on me as a beginner. But there are many more reasons–the science teacher who wanted to quit every Friday her first year yet had been recently selected above other teachers in the district as department head at the newest middle school in that same district; that same male social studies teacher who became team leader and is now working on an administrative certification; the experienced teacher who said she would always put enough money for a snack in new teacher's mailboxes because it meant so much to know someone cared.

## Trying a New Tightrope

Somehow approaching 50 called for drastic changes in my lifestyle. After teaching for 27 years, I decided to become an independent educational consultant. At first the change was great. I enjoyed being a circle of one with time to think and create workshops that I could present in a variety of districts and conferences. It felt so freeing to not be tied to working an eight-hour day and part of each evening while also doing teacher inservice. After I began to lead workshops, however, I realized that I did not know enough about contracts, fees, expenses, or making contacts. I needed help. Once again I was walking the tightrope without a net, thinking that I could use books and other media to answer all my questions. But it just wasn't enough! I began to call on old friends for advice and suggestions.

As soon as I began to communicate with others, I realized just what I had been missing. Opening up my circle of one to include old friends and acquaintances, as well as developing new contacts, created a renewed interest in my consulting business. I even went to the small business department at a local junior college to get advice on marketing. The circle was becoming wider and wider as I added business concerns to educational issues on which I needed to stay up-to-date. At the same time these business contacts began to serve as my safety net.

## Musings for Mentors

1.  Each time a new responsibility is added to a professional position, that teacher will need some guidance and someone from whom to learn,
2.  A mentor can serve as a personal confidante or a professional consultant, or both,
3.  Serving as a mentor, and being mentored, can occur simultaneously or at different times in one's career.

## Looking Back on My Story

It was surprising to me to discover that mentoring in the business world is a much more accepted part of being successful than it is in education. Most business people told me that finding a mentor and creating a network were the two most essential ingredients for maintaining a successful business. Business people, even in an initial meeting, were much more open to sharing ideas with me than teachers I have known and worked with over the years. After all my years in education, I am still puzzled by the reluctance of educators to share and work together.

## Time for a Higher Tightrope?

It was May and I was still developing my consulting network by visiting educators whom I knew and with whom I had worked around the state. I made an appointment to see a college professor with whom I had done a teacher-as-researcher project several years before. As I walked around the campus, my thoughts drifted back to the days when I worked on my master's degree while teaching full-time. I had always in the back of my mind wondered if I could ever get a doctorate. Would I be called "Dr. Maggie" if I did get one?

As I waited in the department of curriculum and instruction at the university for my appointment with my friend, I wondered if getting a doctorate would enhance my ability to do more consulting around the country by giving me a wider range of expertise and experience. After

. sitting down in the professor's office, I reminded him of our work together and shared my consultation brochure, asking if he knew educators in the area whom I could contact to offer my expertise in in-service presentations. He was very quiet as he read the list of workshop presentations on my vita. Looking up at me he said that he had no idea that I had such vast experience and that it would be a definite asset to the university. He asked if I had ever considered working on a Ph.D. I explained that I had taken the Graduate Record Exam and sent my scores to the university but had not initiated the application process given my involvement in my own projects. He became very excited, wanting me to apply immediately. I was reassured by his support for the university's doctoral program. I was also complimented by his enthusiasm about my credentials and what I had to offer undergraduates as a teaching assistant.

I left that day with many questions about how I could continue my educational consulting business while studying at the graduate level. While working through the application process, I continued to talk with my friend about money needed to support my study and the possibilities of graduate teaching assistantships, benefits, and fellowships. I was busy all that summer with my contracted work with both students and teachers. I waited to hear whether I had been accepted for doctoral work and whether I would be graduate teaching in the fall semester. It was a time of stress.

Upon receiving my letter of acceptance and an offer of a graduate assistantship in mid-August, I frantically met with my friend, now temporary advisor, to decide on classes to take during the first semester. I also had to order books for the classes I would be teaching, create a syllabus and lesson plans, and attend two days of mandatory orientation for graduate assistants. Classes started two weeks after I was officially notified of my acceptance.

"What was I doing here?" I asked myself. "I don't know procedures, policies, who to talk to about relevant questions, or even when any of the offices are open!" And, compounding these pressures, I got a ticket the first day while waiting in line to get my parking sticker. Was this an omen? On the drive home after my first day of teaching and my first doctoral level class, I laughed to myself upon realizing that, as a Ph.D. student in curriculum and instruction, I was again in desperate need of mentoring. I was definitely on the tightrope, but I could see no safety net below me.

I had an office mate who was also in one of my other classes and who had almost finished her course requirements. She immediately began to introduce me to other students in the program. I quickly learned to ask her first when I had a question, but I also needed to get to know more professors in order to find those who could eventually function as my committee members. What was a committee, exactly? The Writing Group came together during my first semester to talk and later to become a group of comentors. This group, consisting of a range of teacher educators from full professors to beginning teacher educators to graduate students at various points in their completion of a Ph.D., became important to me—enough to drive 90 minutes for our meetings and then turn around and drive the same length of time home. Why? These comentors continue to serve as my net, encouraging me to walk across the tightrope toward the other side, the completion of my doctorate.

## Musings for Mentors

1.  Mentors can provide new opportunities for experienced educators as well as guide beginning teachers,
2.  Traditional formal mentoring relationships in higher education are not enough for most students because of the need to express self-doubt and struggle with educational issues without the imposition of a hierarchy,
3.  Mentors can serve an important role by bringing together students and professors who share common interests within specific areas of education.

## Looking Back on My Story

The group, which is represented in this book and its chapters, offered me a diversity in approaches to, and opinions on, educational issues, honesty without brutality, pushes, hugs, and questions to ponder. At the same time, I contributed to the group in much the same way. It was during this experience that I realized that my most worthwhile experiences in mentoring and being mentored were reciprocal. This group of developing and established teacher educators serves as my net so I can walk, with some safety, the tightrope of new learning in my doctoral program. I am able to risk with less fear knowing they are holding the net and cheering me on.

## Holding the Net Again

It was a typically hectic day in my life as a graduate teaching assistant in the college of education. My elementary reading practices class was over and I was quickly gathering my materials so the next class could get setup. My mind was already leaping ahead to my doctoral level class on instructional theory that I would begin in just 10 minutes. I felt a quiet presence near the desk and looked up to see one of my most insightful and energetic preservice teachers. I asked her if she needed to see me and she replied softly that she only needed to ask a question. I nodded, and her words began to pour out with emotion: "I am excited about teaching, so I decided to substitute whenever I can until I student teach. I have been going to the same school each time, and I love the kids, but, well, Ms. Cox, can you explain why none of the teachers will talk to me? Have I done something wrong? I try to talk to them at lunch, but even when I start a conversation with the teacher sitting right next to me I am ignored. Why are they so mean to subs?"

With a quick intake of breath and a smile of understanding, I assured her that she was a valuable addition to the staff as a substitute. I added that if the teachers truly found her objectionable, she would not be called back. As to the question of nonsupport for substitutes, I could not clarify this attitude, but I could relate that I had seen this lack of support repeatedly during my career. Then I advised: "When you become a teacher, you do not have to repeat this behavior. *You* could make subs feel welcome. And perhaps you will discover for yourself where the behavior originates."

As she walked away, I pondered my role as a mentor of preservice teachers. This responsibility was new to me even though I had mentored many beginning teachers during my career in the public schools, both at the elementary and secondary levels. How did I become a mentor at the preservice level so quickly? Here I was only in my second semester at the university myself! Even with the college of education advisory program for undergraduates, the students still needed someone to talk to who had taught in public schools and who would not find their questions trivial or unprofessional.

**Musings for Mentors**

1. Preservice teachers can benefit from being exposed to collegial activities in their university education classes,
2. Teachers in undergraduate education classes should tell students stories of mentoring as a method of professional growth,
3. When preservice teachers are working in the schools, they need opportunities to ask questions about their classroom observations and to hear constructive responses.

**Looking Back on My Story**

Mentoring is so much a part of my own professional growth process that I seek these relationships. I find that the students ask the types of questions that keep me searching in the professional literature for better answers or alternatives to those already being used. This continual questioning causes me to examine my own knowledge in pedagogy and philosophy and search for inconsistencies between the two. Mentoring has become an essential ingredient in my own inquiry in the field of education.

**Taking Turns Holding the Net**

"Hi, Maggie, is it really you?"

I turned around in the hall of the education building as I heard a familiar voice. It was Pat, one of my cohorts in the 1980s during my days as an active teacher advocate in local, state, and national teacher associations. We greeted each other with a hug and immediately began to talk about what we'd been doing professionally since we had last worked together.

Pat had completed her Ph.D. at the University of Montana and was now a newly hired professor in the department of educational curriculum and instruction. I laughed as I told her I was following in her footsteps this time as we both rushed off to teach our classes.

I continued to see Pat during the next semester as our paths occasionally crossed in the hallway. I never seemed to have the time to talk at length with her about the projects in which she was involved or about her classes. Yet, I had a sense that we were to play a part in each other's lives again.

Summer passed quickly and fall semester began. The deadline for finding a committee and filing a degree plan was beginning to hover like a black cloud over me. I had to begin interviewing professors and find those who would serve me best as members of my dissertation committee. I realized it was important to me that each member be interested in my work, represent different areas of expertise in the research process and professional literature, and be helpful without being overly directive. I wanted the research and the dissertation to represent my scholarly abilities, not simply the committee's.

Sitting in my advisor's office, I began naming those I thought might fit the qualifications. I also was concerned that each of them have respect for the others so the committee itself would support each other as well as me and my work. Suddenly Pat's name came into my mind. I was determined to make an appointment to visit with her.

Luckily, she was able to meet with me that day. First we reminisced about our work in the teacher organizations. Pat expressed how much she learned from watching and working with me. With a chuckle, I asked her if she wanted to take her turn in mentoring me. She looked at me with surprise and said she'd never thought of our relationship as one of mentoring.

I explained the definition of mentoring and the model that evolved from the Writing Group's interaction. As we talked, Pat and I realized our relationship represented a strong example of the model–we worked intensely together, drifted apart, and now had an opportunity to reconnect in a different configuration, with Pat holding the net this time and me walking the tightrope.

We then changed the subject to a discussion of my doctoral journey, my goals and choices in combining language arts and environmental education for my degree program, and my research for the dissertation itself. Pat immediately began to ask incisive questions to clarify my thinking and suggested adding an element of qualitative narrative to my quantitative research project. Her enthusiasm for inquiry was contagious! She has agreed to serve on my committee. We will, therefore, spend the next few years in an intense mentoring relationship, with each of us playing the opposite role from our first mentoring relationship.

While Pat and I have been developing a new mentoring relationship, Ann, now "Dr. Ann," has also come back into my life. Ann was a beginning teacher in San Antonio during the early 1970s when I first taught across the hall from her. I had been teaching three years at the time. We had both been transferred to Booker T. Washington Elementary, after school had started, under mandated desegregation of the teaching staff. Neither of us had previously taught in a predominantly black school although both of us philosophically believed in desegregation and equality of educational opportunity for our black students.

As a first year teacher, Ann had a great desire to make a difference for her students and a need to be supported in learning to teach a culture new to her. I could give mentoring advice on lesson planning and classroom management, but both of us were equals working together to learn what we could do that would best serve the needs of our new students who had not known many white people. After contacting the district curriculum specialist for recent teaching materials on Africa to replace our outdated world geography text, we planned lessons together, teaching the same curriculum to both of our classes. Ann and I also took our students in small groups to the public library after school to allow us a chance to get to know everyone better while broadening the students' educational experiences. Not only did we work together at school, but we also spent time outside of school as we struggled with aligning our actions with our personal beliefs in equality for all.

At the end of the school year we both left San Antonio, moving out of state. Ann attended Stanford while I moved to Minneapolis and then to Houston to teach. We had seen each other periodically throughout the last 20 years but had not been closely involved in any professional work together in many years. When I answered the telephone one afternoon last spring, I was delighted to hear from "Dr. Ann."

"Would you be interested in doing a presentation at the International Reading Conference with me in May of '97."

"Of course I would! I can't believe you called. I was just talking to my office mate at the university about working on a proposal for that conference. What do you have in mind?"

Ann described a presentation focused on reading and writing poetry in the content areas. I was teaching an undergraduate content reading class at the time, so this seemed an ideal presentation for me. I asked if she could use another presenter. I described my office mate–a doctoral student in children's literature who teaches the undergraduate literature class. Ann quickly said she would be delighted to have an additional person and requested her name and phone number.

And so the circle of mentoring grows. "Dr. Ann" will now serve as a mentor to me in presenting at a national conference. She will also play an important role as a reality check for my doctoral journey. While beginning her teaching career in higher education, "Dr. Ann" will also offer me a window into the world of becoming a tenured professor.

**Musings for Mentors**

1. Taking turns in being the mentor and the mentored is powerful for both individuals in the relationship,
2. Trust developed in one type of mentoring relationship between individuals can transfer to new mentoring relationships involving the same individuals,
3. Mentoring relationships often recur throughout the professional lives of those involved.

**Looking Back on My Story**

The trust and joy found in recreating these relationships has renewed my commitment to maintain strong ties with mentors and those whom I have mentored in my professional or personal life. It is delightful to be part of a long-lasting relationship that brings you challenges as well as affirmation that you have grown. There is also an element of sadness at the loss of those who either grow away or refuse to continue to grow along with me. Yet that is inherent in developing mentorships.

**A Final Look Back on My Entire Story**

My enthusiasm for mentoring other professionals and being mentored has increased through working with this group of educators. Our conversations and writing caused me to create a personal definition of professional mentoring and to recognize the significant role of mentoring in both my life and the life of each individual in the group. As I became knowledgeable about each group member's work as a mentor, I realized the incredible creativity displayed in each person's actual mentoring style. Although each of us share the same underlying philosophy of mentoring, the methods used and the domains in which we work with our students are unique. Empowering individuals appears to be the passion and purpose of each of our professional lives. Through sharing this passion with the others, I gained a greater sense of the power and joy of mentoring. By writing this chapter about my experiences, I hope to encourage other professionals to broaden their own education through actively creating mentoring relationships. My drawing of the tightrope walker and the person holding the net illustrates the two roles in a mentoring relationship (Figure 3). I believe that successful mentoring relationships allow professionals to alternately walk the tightrope and hold the net.

**Questions to Ponder**

What is the role of a mentor? Should student teachers, students in field-based classes, and substitute teachers be warned about the "Lounge Lizards?" What about the grade level chairperson who will not share materials with others or the principal who is never available for support or consultation? In other words, how much knowledge of professional development and schools should be made available in teacher education courses? And what role do instructors of teacher education courses play in the real world mentoring of these young people?

Do teacher educators need to be taught to be mentors? If so, what would we teach them to do? Can mentors be appointed for people or do these relationships have to evolve from a mutual respect or a meeting of the heart? Does gender make a difference in the ability to mentor and to be mentored in turn?

These are only a few of the many questions to which I seek answers in my transition from a public school teacher offering professional mentoring to fellow teachers to a teacher educator working primarily with preservice teachers. What types of mentoring and induction programs are working effectively in other colleges of education?

**Final Musings for Mentors**

Do preservice and beginning teachers need a mentor in order to become confident and competent professional educators? Is the mentor an essential part of a teacher education program? Should school districts have trained mentors available for student teachers and beginning teachers? In my experience the answer to each of these question is an enthusiastic "Yes!" Whether I am a learner or a beginning professional, once I break the circle of one that isolates me, I share stories with other

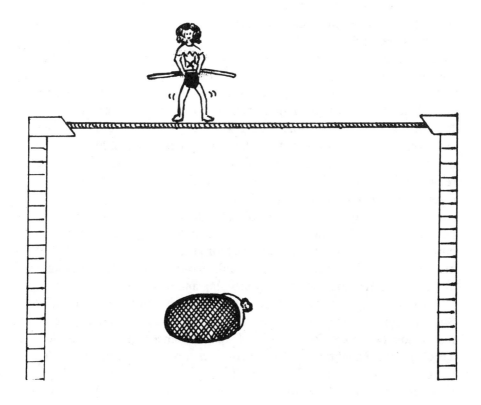

*Figure 3.  Tightrope Walker and Net Holder as Comentors*

educators and question how I might have better handled various teaching situations. Through this process I become energized and, hence, able to accept my blunders and grow in ability. I have seen those who have a mentor they can trust become more accepting of themselves and others in teaching, and remain within the profession, committed to becoming a better teacher each year. I have also seen others who remained isolated, by chance or choice, and, after a difficult first year, leave the field of education disillusioned with teaching and teachers.

What constitutes a healthy mentoring relationship? The relationship should be one in which both parties show each other respect while learning about the profession through wrestling with professional issues and concerns of day-to-day teaching. Although the mentor must be more experienced and knowledgeable in the area of direct mentoring, the relationship should allow the novice the freedom to use, adapt, or discard the mentor's advice at all times. The mentor should serve as a sounding board and also a sharer of educational wisdom, providing the novice with questions or points of view possibly different from the ones currently serving as the foundation for educational decisions. The mentor relationship should be reciprocal, one in which both the mentor and the mentored learn more about teaching and learning.

What other results can be achieved through effective mentoring? Students get teachers who will try new techniques and fight for an instructional climate in the school that enhances student learning. Teachers gain insights and courage from each other and learn the value of collegiality rather than isolation. Team planning and teaching begin to occur spontaneously. Students see teachers modeling collaboration as the students themselves are collaborating. Sometimes teachers outside the mentoring arrangement meet and work with those involved in the mentoring relationship. This is how the circle of professional development widens.

Through broadening the meaning, purpose, and process of mentoring, educators at any stage in their career can improve their professional skills while deepening their capacity for human caring. By using this model of mentorship, "teachers can leave their mark on teaching" (Shalaway, 1989, p. 265) as well as on their students.

# Part III

# School-University Partnership Programs Aimed at Mentoring Preservice Teachers

**Diane Sopko Adoue**

**Jane B. Hughey**

# Chapter 6

# Mentoring Preservice Science Teachers: The Professional Development School

## Diane Sopko Adoue

When I reflect on my journey through graduate school, it becomes a collage of memories–memories of the experiences, discoveries, failures, successes, losses, trade-offs, insecurities, and challenges. There is still more to come because for me the journey is still moving, moving forward but in a zig-zag fashion. My goal is within sight. Becoming a teacher of teachers is within reach. My mentoring of the next generation of professionals has begun. Yet discovering how to mentor and finding mentors to guide me through the maze of procedures, policies, philosophies, protocols, presentations, papers, proposals, and politics has been marked with missteps, miscommunication, and misunderstanding. The life and career of an academic is one that I chose to enter with a naive understanding of the all-encompassing nature of that commitment, but with a deep desire to add to the vision of excellence in educational opportunities for all children.

While I knew that I, as a doctoral student in education, must make numerous adjustments, rediscover the self, shift paradigms, and begin the process of teaching and learning in a new setting, the desire to remain true to myself was not diminished. The belief that the knowledge gained would contribute to my growth and to my possible impact on the teaching profession was strong. There was also the fear that this emerging person, undergoing a metamorphosis, would no longer fit neatly into familiar roles and familiar relationships. How was I to maneuver into new roles and new relationships and maintain the old, required direction from those more seasoned than myself? There was no neat map to follow. Student handbooks and graduate catalogues could not begin to state explicitly or implicitly what really lay ahead. The need for guidance from established professionals was critical. I hoped that a mentor or mentors could provide support and advice at critical junctures and help smooth the path to success. I also hoped that mentors could provide role models that exemplified what is best in education.

Sometimes my vision of the doctoral process collided with the belief system and paradigms of the established system or with professionals within that established system. The innovative practices and open-minded discourse I envisioned were not always realized. While I knew that my belief systems would be challenged, uncomfortably so, much of the time, there was still the hope that this could be accomplished in a constructive, collaborative atmosphere where mutual respect and genuine professional relationships would be cultivated. When this did not always happen it was a disappointment, a setback in the process, that took time and reflection from which to recover, to regain my self-respect and dignity. The doctoral journey is stressful under any circumstances. It can be more stressful than necessary when the search for that support system, those mentors, is met with disillusionment and disappointment. However, I have been fortunate. My setbacks, my discouraging encounters, and my unrealized expectations have been only that, setbacks. This is my unfinished story. Maybe it says something new to my readers.

## That First Year

Prior to my arrival at the university, I was fortunate to have met another graduate student who also arrived that fall to complete her requirements for residency, her course work, and ultimately her dissertation. That brief encounter during an introduction opened the door to friendship and to the mentorship she provided me. Yes, she was a graduate student too, but one who had been in the teaching profession longer, who had been a summer student in the program that I entered, and who was much more savvy about the people, the politics, and the process than most. Her willingness to share her success in teaching, to lend an ear as I expressed my uncertainties, and to collaborate with me on projects helped me move into the doctoral journey with a little more confidence than I might have felt otherwise. She and other graduate students were that first support system.

Graduate students were the glue that helped hold everything together for me. With the support of other students, who were also making sense of the graduate process, and of their new roles, I moved into the program believing that success came through hard work and a willingness to learn. It was they who shared experiences about choosing a committee: what coursework was interesting and productive, what kinds of questions you might face in your writtens and orals, how to gain monetary support to attend conferences; and when to file what.

My first appointment in teaching was one I was thrilled to be involved in, teaching elementary science lab methods two times a week and grading papers for a professor. I respected him as a professional committed to the advancement of science teaching in the elementary schools and appreciated his help and willingness to let me use some of my own ideas from the very beginning. It was a big shift to teach young adults rather than children. Although a well-defined syllabus provided most of the necessary material, that first semester was one of trial and error. The errors were correctable, the trials necessary. The second semester was met with growing confidence in my ability to teach young adults. While I was searching for my own mentors, those budding teachers began to make me feel as if I was mentoring them. Many viewed me as an expert, someone who knew what real schools and students were like and understood how to teach children, someone who was not far removed from the classroom by time and circumstances.

While I was working hard to teach successfully, read, and complete assignments, my temporary chair and I seemed to lack an avenue for clear communication. This was disturbing and not how I had pictured graduate school. My confidence was eroding. Even though I had come to learn from the experts, I still thought I understood something about the state of science education in the public schools. Experiences that first semester began to challenge my beliefs about how I would become an effective instructor of preservice science teachers. Preparing to instruct lab classes was time-consuming but rewarding. The professor I was working for was supportive and easy to talk with when I had an idea or a problem. It seemed I had lined up with a perfect mentor for becoming an elementary science educator even if he was not my advisor, but something was still missing. There was always that feeling that I could not measure up in the eyes of science educators because I had not been a secondary science teacher.

From my perspective, science needed to be integrated into the curriculum of other disciplines, or it was very likely that it would never get taught in most elementary schools. It seemed to be scheduled for the end of the day and only attended to when everything else was finished. The demands of standardized testing systems, I believed, had contributed to a narrow focus in instruction. The vision of reform in science education was severely hampered by forces beyond the classroom teacher's control. One of my goals as a science teacher educator was to open a window of possibilities for these preservice teachers. I wanted them to have a vision for exciting science instruction in their future classrooms and to see the opportunities it provided for students to construct basic and higher level thinking skills while expanding their knowledge of the world around them. Science instruction was not an island, but one part of a larger picture that focused on the growth of the whole child.

Often, my own coursework lacked the excitement of innovative teaching. Believing I had come to the university to learn better instructional strategies, to observe integration within subjects, and to see technology in action, I was somewhat disappointed. The established system was not set up for this kind of teacher education. From my perspective, reform in teacher education programs had not found its way from philosophy to practice within the university. My list of questions concerning my academic pursuit was growing more rapidly than my list of possible solutions. What could teachers of preservice teachers do to bridge the gap between university and school, I wondered? Did these young people have any idea how challenging it was to be an effective teacher? Did their observations and limited teaching opportunities prepare them for student teaching? How should I as an instructor balance a description of a modern classroom and a vision for possibilities? My students looked so young, so eager, and so naive. What was my role as an emerging teacher of teachers?

### Critical Incident: An Opportunity for Professional Growth

Perhaps it was conversation in the lunchroom/workroom, perhaps it was just a need to fill a space, but it was still important in the turn of events. The temporary department head spoke to me briefly about a graduate teaching position that needed to be filled in one of the university's professional development school (PDS) programs. Was I interested? Well, yes, I was. That summer session, I attended a class that included literature concerning PDS schools and was excited about the possibility that I might get to work in one. I was vaguely familiar with the university's involvement. In fact, most of what I knew was centered around only one school, and not the one where the position was available. This opportunity was one I wanted to investigate further. The department head suggested I visit with the university liaison for more information concerning this partnership position.

My first step was to seek out my peer mentor and share the news, and ask for her input. My second was to contact the professor and schedule a time to talk. Both convinced me that this was something I wanted to be a part of. Even though I enjoyed my current position and was delighted with my boss, my intuitive side was telling me to "go for it." Hadn't my temporary chair told me that one should have a variety of experiences while in a doctoral program? Hadn't he said that too many students find a comfortable place and stay there when they should be gaining experience in other areas to prepare for an academic career? I might risk losing a position in which I had gained competence only to find myself unhappy with the new one. I didn't even know where the school was that I would hold my classes in. In any event, the decision was made on my part. I was ready to move. I waited to hear from the professor who headed the program.

Meanwhile, my current boss warned me that I would be worked to death at the PDS. Nonetheless, I thought this kind of a program was on the cutting edge of educational reform and I wanted the experience. Another key factor was that I would be the instructor of record. This was not an easy position to gain in the elementary science methods courses. Going off-campus was the only way. It looked like I would teach the science methods and coteach the social studies methods course. That was not how it worked out.

Two weeks before the semester started I received word that the position was mine. My excitement turned to anxiety when I was informed that I would be teaching both the science methods and the mathematics methods classes. The new department head was in charge now. Graduate assistants were receiving assignments that included more work, without more pay. Whatever the reason, many of us felt overwhelmed and unappreciated. How could we manage a high standard for teaching and still meet the requirements of our coursework? I, for one, got into high gear. There was no time to waste in preparing my content and writing the syllabi. I turned to others for help. Professors and peers alike served as my mentors. The advice of those who currently taught these two courses was sought out and received. The generosity with which individuals shared their outlines, syllabi, textbooks, and advice was amazing. In particular, one professor invited me to attend his undergraduate mathematics labs to enhance my hands-on manipulative skills. I was grateful. My students needed the same standard of excellence that was offered on campus.

For me, there are always those first faltering steps. A time when I feel slightly like an impostor. Again, I was faced with trying on clothes that I was not quite comfortable wearing. Here I was, a teacher and possible mentor to 32 eager cohorts. My new boss placed total confidence in my ability to accomplish the task. I did not want to disappoint anyone. The other university staff at the PDS were supportive and friendly. It was wonderful to be in a real school, with children. This, I thought, was a place where preservice teachers, immersed in the school culture, could grow and wed philosophy and practice. Here was a community of diverse professionals working for excellence in education for children; where, as their motto stated, "Everybody Learns, Everybody Teaches." The honeymoon was soon over.

My first schedule was terrible. After school the cohort students were tired and, early in the morning, we were interrupted by announcements. These two days challenged my resources physically and creatively. I had 40 minutes to drive to the main campus, find a parking space, and walk one-half mile to the building after my morning mathematics class. My one late morning class seemed like heaven in comparison. My students and I met in the school library with chairs more suited to children in elementary school than adults whose knees didn't quite fit under the tables. Within the first two weeks, my classes had been moved or canceled four times because of the school schedule. I was studying day and night, attending mathematics labs, and felt exhausted from preparing lessons. This opportunity was indeed working me to death. The already stressful level of my life began to escalate. My science side was warning me to seek counsel. "Only the fittest survive!" I kept thinking. My own coursework was also challenging. Maybe I had attempted too much.

Fear and friendship sent me back to the counsel of my first boss and faculty mentor. His listened sympathetically. I was surprised at how calm I seemed while talking because I certainly didn't feel calm on the inside. His advice was sound: "Go talk to your boss," he said. "He is a man of character. He needs to know how you are feeling." That advice was followed, and I took an important step in career building. I needed to learn how to express my concerns without sounding like I couldn't do the job. At the same time, a professional needs to be candid about the reality of the workload. My talk with him was tempered somewhat, but I tried to express how overwhelmed I felt on some days and how undervalued I felt my contribution was when my classes were moved about. He too listened quietly. During that conversation, I realized I had a truly remarkable ally. Here was a man who wanted everyone concerned to be successful. His gentle manner and kind words boosted my confidence and helped me realize that I was only in a transition stage. He said he would do everything possible to make sure that my workload was made lighter in the spring. Meanwhile, I knew I could go to him for advice at any time. With the help of this newfound mentor, my faltering steps became more confident strides. As I watched the confidence of my own students grow in this culture, I knew that I had made a good choice and that I wanted to stay. All of the interruptions were a part of what comes with real schools. This environment suggested what is best and worst about schools. No lecture or observation could substitute for this experience.

Working with these preservice teachers was a bonding experience, wherein my own mentoring, more nurturing than anything else, was permitted and appreciated. I was breaking the circle of one as collaborative relationships, not strictly expert to novice, formed and developed. What I had to offer was not the answers to all of their questions, but a belief that they could find answers within themselves, their experiences, their reading, their talking with classmates and cooperating teachers, and within the experience of knowing children on a personal level. If they wanted, I would stay after class and help a cooperative group work through problems with an assignment. I focused on how they could facilitate the learning of students within the context of the classrooms to which they were assigned.

The preservice teachers learned to work together under difficult circumstances. Friendships developed. When one was too tired or overwhelmed, others would pick up the slack. Here they were, taking five university classes and spending the rest of the day working in classrooms. A supportive faculty surrounded them, modeled and mentored, and learned from them as well. The diverse student body opened the preservice teachers' eyes to the real world and to the circumstances of children that were quite different than those they had known as children. These children taught them daily about success and failure, love and anger, security and poverty. The preservice teachers became mentors or role models, in their own right, that were loved and admired by their young charges. The circle was always expanding as everyone extended oneself and tested his or her own abilities.

As the semester progressed, some preservice teachers began to come to me with questions concerning the students in their classrooms. They shared their successes during methods classes and in the quiet halls of an empty building at the end of a busy school day. My phone would ring in the evening with a tentative voice at the other end. Soon they realized that I really didn't mind the interruption as I listened and counseled. Each preservice teacher became a face with a name and a personality, a beginning educator with a growing sense of self-efficacy. Their individual strengths were acknowledged and their weaknesses were accepted. Each was committed to the welfare of the students in this school and to his or her own personal growth. Our individual circles, those of instructors, teachers, students, and preservice teachers, became a complex chain that provided strength to the emerging professionals and to the school within which we all worked. The multiple voices became a choir. No one was alone, even during a solo.

I watched, listened, and learned. The synergistic nature of this PDS provided multiple perspectives from which to emerge a better teacher educator. Multiple mentors encircled my personal experience. From the classroom and special education teachers, I found that inclusion worked when a professional support system was coupled with a strong commitment to focus on the needs of the individual child. From the librarian I learned that even librarians could be tolerant of possible science spills and messes as long as we promised to clean up. The administrators gained my admiration because of their commitment to building a community in which all children could learn and succeed. The collective body of teachers served to strengthen my belief that educators could change and adapt when they were committed to the welfare of the children in their school. The children in bilingual classes reminded me of the flexibility of children who must walk into and leave to adapt to a world so different from the one they had known. Even sitting at a cafeteria table with a preservice teacher and her class, watching the custodians as they repaired and cleaned, and viewing the ill children waiting on cots in the nurse's room were reminders of all the people who supported and worked with the teaching staff and for the children. The art work in the halls, the noise from the gym, the laughter on the playground, and the reprimands for poor behavior were all part and parcel of what it means to be in a school.

As a developing teacher educator, I was able to stay in touch with the reality of this complex culture and the needs of the preservice teachers. My mentoring of them was based on this reality. My circle of concern was tempered with my circle of influence. There were many mentors who served them and me. We could take from each what we needed, but we were also required to bring our own gifts.

## Conflict Arises

If my story sounds too good to be true at this point, it was. As the strain of a physically demanding semester was ending, I decided it was time to select my committee. Other graduate students had given me plenty of advice in the past. Selecting a committee, they said, was the most important step in the process. Horror stories were shared, some true, some myth, about committees who held up students' graduations. Other students seemed to bask in the light of their choices. My problem? My major support was coming from mentors outside of my area of focus. It was imperative that I find committee members within my area of specialty. If I did not get a degree plan filed before summer, I would be blocked from registration. My search began in earnest.

It seemed logical to just talk to prospective committee members, show them the coursework I had completed, and ask if they were willing to serve. Those faculty members that I was able to visit with were cooperative. Some suggested another science education class or two, but no significant additions were otherwise made to my list. It looked like the process wasn't going to be too cumbersome until I sat down in a particular professor's office and started to talk openly. I don't know exactly at what point the conversation shifted from pleasant to confrontational, but once we got on the wrong track it seemed to escalate. Nothing had prepared me for this difference of opinion to turn to anger.

The conversation changed when we began talking about the jurisdiction of the newly formed governance committee that would oversee graduate students in my area of focus. Some students had received notices to attend meetings, while others had not. We did not know if this discrepancy was intentional. Maybe it was fatigue because we were all busy getting in our grades, finishing papers or exams, and hoping for a break during the December holidays. But, I felt that I needed to state my case. I did not believe I could continue with the workload assigned to me as a graduate assistant and keep up with my own coursework to my standards. I was informed that his governance committee could not protect me at the PDS school.

An offer was made for me to teach a course on campus. Without any hesitation, I declined. I liked where I was, I explained. I did not want to adjust to a new course. Furthermore, the teaching environment of the PDS provided a more authentic situation for preservice teachers to grapple with the teaching/learning process, I explained. The body language and tone of voice changed. I knew intuitively that I had said something wrong. Perhaps the implied message that on-campus coursework was not as authentic for preservice teachers should have been avoided, but it was too late. After a rather unpleasant reprimand, I left knowing that I had angered someone with whom it might be difficult to reconcile. There was no sympathy for my perspective of the rich experiences in the PDS school. Why was I so outspoken about where I wanted to stay? Why did I feel it necessary to defend graduate students in general? What kind of mess was I now in?

Things went steadily downhill from there. As I mulled over the situation, reflecting seriously, I believe I had been unaware of an implied message. In seeking counsel from this particular person, the assumption was made that I was now under his jurisdiction. Following this disturbing encounter, a message was delivered by my adversary that the science education people had met and decided I should be back on campus. If I was going to be a science teacher educator, they wanted me to teach labs again and attend the professor's lectures. They could not be assured that a quality science methods course was being conducted off-campus because it was out of their jurisdiction. It wasn't the position I objected to as much as the treatment I likened to that of a wayward child, one that I found offensive for a person of my age and life experiences. Why wasn't I in included in the discussion about my own professional development and graduate education?

I did not want to leave the culture of the professional development school, where I interacted with professionals who provided excellent models in a setting where teacher education reform was a reality. A difficult decision was made. If my position within the context of the PDS school was unacceptable to my governance committee, I would change my area of focus. The PDS experience was too rich to leave. The mentoring relationships I had fostered there were serving to broaden my scope and understanding of teacher education. My boss was supportive. He realized what kind of stress I was under, some of the politics involved, and appreciated my contributions at the PDS. He communicated a strong belief in my ability to teach well and helped me focus on other possibilities for support. Once again, he listened, made suggestions, and modeled professional behavior. I was thankful for this encouraging mentor. Here was someone who respected the contributions of the faculty at the professional development school and respected the graduate students with whom he worked. I felt our relationship was collaborative. We considered what was best for the whole community of learners within the context of the PDS.

This uncomfortable spotlight, forming a circle of light around me, was broken by shadows other than my own. Peers, friends, and family members reminded me that conflict could not be avoided at all costs. Sometimes we emerge a stronger, better person afterward. But, I had also learned to avoid signs of weakness and felt I had been foolish for expressing my concerns and showing signs of fatigue during the semester. Yet, this was not how I wanted my own students to feel. This was not the message I wanted to send when I moved into the academic arena as a full-fledged member. Collaboration in a supportive environment fit my vision of preparing future teacher educators.

**Looking Back**

As I reflect on the conflicts that arose when I was assertive about the preferred direction of my career, I wonder why it would surprise members of the faculty that a graduate student was not following their prescription. Not surprisingly, from the very beginning, I had found the greatest support system within a small circle of other graduate students. Learning to be an academic professional was modeled for us daily by the explicit and implicit messages that we receive from faculty members. You need to publish was one explicit message, but no specific advice was forthcoming. You need to present at conferences, and an application would appear in the mailbox of one student to be shared with the others. You need to take your teaching less seriously and concentrate on research, some would say. The advice was often contradictory and confusing at times. Why would a teacher educator want to model anything less than the very best teaching practices I asked myself? Who should I ask for editing and writing advice? Which conference would be best suited for a presentation of my research? Who will provide the best advice and guidance during my dissertation research? The answers to these questions and many more are critical to maneuvering through the process successfully. There was no question that finding mentors is critical. But what does it mean to mentor? This role can be confusing as well. Is there one great mentor out there for all of us? I seriously doubt that the demands of academia permit any one person to be all things to any of us, even when good intentions are involved.

The mentoring I received from my PDS boss was obvious. He took me to luncheons, where our research project was acknowledged. He introduced me to people and shared insights about who I needed to know within the context of the PDS movement. He lent books from his personal library. He was willing to serve on my dissertation committee, but fully acknowledged that he was retiring soon and was not a strong researcher. Therefore, he insisted I talk with a professor who was noted for his research and his ability to work with graduate students in a supportive, collaborative fashion. This was an important step in my search for a committee that I fully appreciated. But throughout it all, my helpful, supportive boss never wanted to dominate me or any of the people around him. He was always ready to give credit where it was due and stand at the sidelines and cheer his students and colleagues on. There was no ego to be stroked.

The fall semester ended. With the help of my mentor, I found a well-respected professor to serve as a chair or cochair and decided to wait on making any further decisions concerning my committee. When the spring semester began I returned to the PDS school to teach. The new group of preservice teachers needed my attention, personal concerns would take a back seat. This group proved as interesting and earnest as those in my first cohort class. The semester was more relaxed. More time could be spent talking casually with teachers and administrators in the building.

Several previous students of mine who were now serving in student teaching positions sought my advice and counsel once more. I was flattered and pleased to help them in any way I could. Our relationship deepened as we exchanged ideas and possible solutions to their day-to-day problems in the classroom. I encouraged them to try instructional strategies and lessons they had developed during the previous semester. I was a nonthreatening, nonjudgmental ally. They shared their weaknesses and failures. They also shared their successes, joyfully, knowing that any congratulations and praise was authentic. I watched them blossom even further and thought about how lucky the children in their classrooms would be. They invited me to observe in their classrooms and requested letters of recommendation as they began to apply for their first teaching position. We shared time away from the workplace laughing and getting to know one another better. I knew they needed to let off steam with some griping and complaining. I sympathized with them, knowing that this was a necessary and healthy release from the pressures of being a novice, of feeling like they were working under the intense scrutiny of others.

Their friendship and willingness to share of themselves reaffirmed my own commitment to prepare teachers for public school. Our exchanges provided further insight into the developmental processes involved in becoming a capable teacher. I watched and marveled at the youthful enthusiasm. I felt I was on the receiving end, that I had been given a special lens to view their transformation from student to teacher. But they believed they were gaining something too. During one of our informal meetings, we discussed the way they addressed their cooperating teachers. I suggested that they could call me by my first name now, but without exception, they did not want to do so. "You are not just our instructor," I was informed. "You are our mentor. You are what we want to be like." They could not have given me a greater compliment. In focusing on their needs and being willing to share whatever help or wisdom I could, they felt my contribution had been significant. I, however, know that I gained much more than I ever gave. The relationship with them was reciprocal. They had entered my circle and I theirs, each gave and took what we needed.

## Musing for Mentors

Maybe in the grand scheme of becoming a teacher educator, each of us needs to select from various role models those qualities that best emulate what we want to become. Perhaps we need to glue together this collage of characteristics juxtaposed against who we are and who we are becoming. In my personal search, I tried to be a good observer and listener. Sometimes that failed me, but more often this sensitivity helped me discern who was willing to invest something of themselves in my future. It is what mentors do. They mentor without regard to what they will get in return. Their reward is an intrinsic one. They do not exert power or play power games.

The responsibility to mentor the next generation of educators must be addressed, individually and collectively. The support system for preservice teachers is expanded within the context of the professional development school. There is a collective sense of learning together, of being able to test yourself within the parameters of a safe environment. These preservice teachers are surrounded by a variety of possible mentors from which to choose. This environment serves to enhance their understanding of what it means to be a teacher. My own personal experience has strengthened my resolve to do a better job of modeling the kind of support I want from others.

Graduate students are often just as isolated as the novice teacher. The structure of institutions often produces working conditions and competitive environments that do not build collegiality. These conditions are counterproductive. Graduate students preparing to become teacher educators need the support and counsel of seasoned professionals. The circle of one, isolation, can be broken when educators acknowledge the legacy they can endow to the next generation. Our talents and contributions are enhanced when we form a collective body of supportive practitioners. I believe we need improved mentoring practices and a redefinition of mentoring itself. This is not an emotional argument as much as a logical one. Too much talent is at risk if we fail to have serious discourse concerning mentoring practices. The mentoring circle can take on a new shape, one more in keeping with the multi-dimensional, complex nature of human relationships in which the culture of the profession is learned.

# Chapter 7

---

# Creating a Circle of Many: Mentoring and the Preservice Teacher

## Jane B. Hughey

### Mentoring Defined

Our rich English language is known for its many shades of meaning and connotative flexibility. Consequently, when we use the term *mentor*, it conjures up different words and shades of meaning for each of us. What exactly do we mean when we say *mentor*? Traditionally, a mentor has been defined as a wise and knowledgeable person who undertakes a special commitment to counsel, teach, and advise a younger and less experienced person. Further, the two comprise a mentoring circle of two. The interaction between the two has usually consisted of a deep and extended relationship, or individualized learning and guidance. With the mentor's guidance, the novice grows in wisdom, knowledge, and experience. What a wonderful practice! Most of us have experienced a similar kind of mentoring in our lives, either from a family member or a teacher or perhaps a close family friend. I know I have. It is probably a universal in human nature for such a relationship to exist, but what do we know of its origins and its underlying implications?

Most dictionaries or encyclopedias tell us that Homer created *Mentor* to be Odysseus's trusted counselor and teacher. Theirs was a circle of two–one teacher, one student. Odysseus, you remember, symbolized the inquirer and adventurer in all of us; thus, it was his mission to sail mythical seas in search of answers and truths. With the aid of Mentor, his wise and trusted counselor and teacher, Odysseus succeeded in exploring the wonders, mysterious creatures, and events of the world surrounding him.

Today, explorers–and aren't we all explorers–sail the seas of outer space, the scapes of the Internet, and the mysterious facets of our intellect. Like Odysseus, we too are looking for answers and truths. Like Odysseus, we need the guidance of a mentor to increase our chances of succeeding on our exploratory voyages. In our present fast-paced lives, our need for encouragement and guidance is greater than at any other time. Our modern world is different from the simple, smaller world of Odysseus. Our lives and our activities extend from shore to shore and from galaxy to galaxy, from everyday events to the fantasies of virtual reality. We no longer live in close-knit communities where one generation provides mentors for the next. Instead, we live in a mobile society where we are often strangers in new communities. It is no surprise that we are hesitant to approach a newfound neighbor or teacher and say, "Would you help me, encourage me, mentor me?" In earlier times, only a few were fortunate enough to be selected for the teaching and guidance of an individual mentor.

Today, on the other hand, education is offered to many rather than a select few. The pace is faster, the knowledge base is greater, but the rich opportunities for long and deep reflective associations are fewer. What, then, has happened to the mentoring of a more traditional time? For some, it still exists on a personal and individual basis, wherever and whenever someone encourages and teaches another. But for others it is a scarce commodity. Because it is such a precious commodity, however, we need to recapture and redefine its essence for today's world. We need to widen the circle to include the many.

## Mentoring Redefined

Perhaps we can best redefine mentorship for our current purposes by looking again at its origin. Mentor advised Odysseus; then Athena (goddess of wisdom and the arts) took on the guise of Mentor in order to teach Odysseus's son Telemachus. Although the relationship was still a circle of two in each of these cases, a chain was established, and the ability to mentor was passed from one to another. Briefly now, let us look again at the traits of the original mentors. In a trusting relationship, the wise mentor taught and counseled someone. So how do the shades of meaning for mentorship differ today from this original concept?

Current studies delving into the value and use of mentorship in today's teacher education programs find that mentors fill a variety of roles; among these roles are guide, leader, good listener, enabler, organizer of experiences, coach, role model, supervisor, trusted colleague, developer, anthropologist, and collegial collaborator. It is easy to see that the mentoring of our time reflects the same basic traits as the traditional model, but there is one significant difference. The tightly closed circle of one-to-one mentoring has expanded to include a greater number of participants in the process. Mentorship may now take the form of teaching and counseling not only from one-to-one, but also from one-to-many, from many-to-one, or from many-to-many. Such are the brief history and textbook definitions of mentoring, but how does the process play out in practice? How has it affected, for example, my own personal experience?

## Mentoring Experienced

Most of us have experienced mentoring in our lives, even though at the time we probably didn't call it mentoring. Indeed, I had many mentors who were wise and trusted counselors all–from parents and grandparents to friends and colleagues to teachers and professors, and yes, even my children. Mentoring, it seems, has always been present in my life. From early childhood, I was always told by my parents, "You can do whatever you want to do," and then they showed me how to go about achieving the goals I had set. My questions were usually answered by a supportive, "Let's look it up." One of the bedtime stories I remember most fondly, and subsequently read to my own children, was *The Little Engine That Could*. Always in my experience was the idea that anything was possible. Reading, learning, and discussing issues and ideas were a part of our daily routine. When, on occasion, a goal was temporarily unattainable, my family lovingly encouraged me to try again. These family mentors not only furnished me with advice and encouragement, but they also modeled these traits for me day in and day out. This strong family mentoring has followed me from my youth right up to the present.

Early in my academic career, in the sixth grade as a matter of fact, my classroom teacher, Lottie Baker, entered a piece of my writing in a statewide contest and celebrated my winning. Of course, the composition was written on the topic of "My Favorite Teacher," who happened to be Mrs. Baker. Thinking back, I guess she was my favorite teacher for the attention and encouragement she gave me in general and for her celebration of my attempts at writing in particular. Because I grew up in a small and stable community, there were numerous others who played guiding roles in my growth.

Yet even as an undergraduate in a larger setting at the University of Oklahoma, I found mentors among the professors in the English department there. Dr. John Raines took a special interest in my writing abilities and continually encouraged my growth in this area throughout my studies in that department. He probably had the greatest influence on my desire to teach, too, because he made teaching seem an intellectual challenge, and at the same time he established a warm and comfortable relationship with his students. He modeled for us the importance of teaching.

Once out of the cocoon of being a protected student and embarked on my own career of teaching, I was fortunate during my first few years to find myself in a small rural consolidated school. I say fortunate because the school was small and the more experienced faculty had the time and inclination to help a young new teacher get off to a good start. Once again, a specific mentor appeared for me. He was the superintendent, and his office was just down the hall from my classroom. He would regularly stop by my sixth grade classroom to listen in, to compliment a lesson, or to give a tip or two about how to handle a specific situation. While mentoring continued for me, I now found myself on the other side of the circle. It was my turn to counsel and teach others. In this small consolidated rural school, giving back was easy to do because everyone knew everyone else and the setting was open and comfortable. Students would stay after school to talk and ask questions until the school bus

arrived. Getting to know them well was just part of the daily routine–
the chain of mentoring at work.

There was another facet to the business of mentoring that I had not yet
discovered. It was collegial comentoring. I first became aware of the
value and practice of collegial comentoring when I moved into another
community and began teaching in a well-established private school.
Collegial interaction was the order of the day. Everyone mentored
everyone else. There were evening sessions once a month for faculty at
which we would congregate for the sole purpose of talking about our
classes, the students, teaching techniques, and new educational theories.
Everyone felt secure in raising questions and making suggestions.
Because of this warm collegial interaction, it was a time of tremendous
growth for me.

In these early years, I primarily taught English/language arts at the
middle and high school levels. Probably because of the early
encouragement I had received, I always included writing in my
instruction. Novice that I was, I was not conscious of its implications at
the time, but teaching writing automatically placed me in a mentorship
role since most of my students revealed much more about themselves in
writing than they did in direct conversation. The result–my students and
I established closer relationships simply because they had shared with
me their hopes, fears, and goals through their writing. I often found
myself writing back suggestions and advice in response to their
questions or comments. More importantly, however, I learned volumes
from the students about their needs. They were, in essence, mentoring
me.

During this time, an event occurred that set the stage for the
remainder of my life. I suffered the loss of my husband to a terrible
automobile accident. My sister-in-law became the mentor who
counseled me and encouraged me to return to school in order to continue
my own growth, and in turn, to better nurture my two tiny sons. My
children's gentle and wise pediatrician, Dr. Ben Nicholson, also gave
counsel and guidance that helped me understand that I needed to be
happy and fulfilled in what I was doing in order to be able to give the
best to my little boys. He was right. My resulting decision was to return
to the university for my master's degree in order to enhance both my
teaching skills and my opportunities. Dr. Nicholson's counsel, although
brief, was one of the most important bits of mentoring I have ever
received. Its repercussions ever since make me realize now that

mentoring does not necessarily have to exist on a long-term basis to be strong and effective.

In retrospect, most of these early mentoring experiences existed primarily in a circle of two. But now, the wider circle of collegial comentoring I had experienced appeared again with even greater meaning. Along with many other women these days, I was bold enough to set out on the journey toward my doctorate when my own children completed their education. In this venture, I found tremendous encouragement and a warm welcome at Texas A&M University; however, rather than waiting around for serendipitous mentoring, at this point I sought out those who would act as wise counselors and teachers for me. Without such support, it is almost impossible to move successfully through a doctoral experience. Some of my mentors during this time were the professors directing my program of study, and some were colleagues and fellow doctoral students. Although I had experienced it before, it was from this small group of fellow students that I learned the broader and deeper value of collegial comentoring. We gravitated toward each other out of a mutual need for communication and support. We studied together, cussed and discussed issues and the demands of the program, and *always* encouraged and celebrated each other's successes–which we still do. From this experience, I found the circle of one expanding to become a circle of several, with interactive mentoring at the core.

I suppose, like many other things, we learn how to mentor from our role models. All of my nurturing experiences seemed to be, and I believe were, spontaneous and unsolicited. Most of my early mentoring was one-on-one. But the shift to a wider circle, to a circle of many, was now firmly also planted in my experience base.

Today, in the role of university professor, the circle continues to grow in order to meet the needs of the times and our department's large enrollment. In our college, and the same is true in many other institutions of higher education these days, the ratio of faculty to undergraduate students is often as high as one faculty member to 200 students or more. Because of the sheer numbers and the resulting critical limitations on our time, the one-on-one mentoring of earlier times is difficult at best, if not impossible.

**Mentoring a Circle of Many: The Jones Story**

"So what does all of this history and personal experience have to do with preservice teachers?" you may ask. The answer is "needs and solutions." First, the needs. In my university classes, there are hundreds of junior level preservice teachers clambering to absorb enough information and experience to be able to teach the crucial basic skills of reading and writing by the time they have finished their certification and are in the field–within a short year or so. The large impersonal lecture hall approach stops short of preparing these future teachers for the challenges they will face teaching young students in a reading-writing workshop classroom. From my university experiences of the past three years and from discussions with supervising teachers in the field, I am convinced that preservice teachers need the experience of seeing the connection between the theories they are learning in their lectures and the application of those theories in the working classrooms they will soon enter. They need a place to *rehearse* and an opportunity for discussion and problem-solving with regard to the results. Eureka! They need a circle of mentoring that is wide enough to put its arms around all of them. In support of this idea, Frankl (1969) maintains that if real mentoring is to occur, participants must truly encounter one another.

With classes of students numbering in the hundreds, where, oh where, in this day and time, could we find spontaneous one-on-one mentoring for each of them? Impossible. Maybe, just maybe, there was another solution. Could we, by chance or by design, create a field-based experience for them that would put them in touch with some level of modern day mentorship? Well, that was what we hoped to do when we set out to establish a school-university *writing buddy* program. In keeping with the fundamental conditions set out by Goodlad (1988, p. 80), we wanted a partnership that offered frequent opportunities for teachers, preservice teachers, and university faculty to share experiences with others in similar roles and for them to reflect on how theory and research can inform practice, and vice versa. The Jones Elementary Writing Buddy program was the outcome of our efforts to find such a school-university partnership. Without the field-based mentorship we have developed as a result of this happy combination, our preservice teachers would still be attempting to learn how to teach a reading-writing workshop from a large lecture hall experience.

We made the initial contact with Jones Elementary School with the help of Donna Wiseman–our former facilitative department head. The contact was made on the basis of what appeared to be a mutual need for both parties. From this point on, we set about to establish a school-university writing buddy collaborative. The Jones program was carefully planned with the input of its stakeholders–the Jones principal, six Jones lab teachers, Luana Zellner–an insightful doctoral student who has been a facilitator and liaison from the inception of the program–and myself as university faculty. Luana's primary role included finding the small, but necessary, amount of funding necessary to compensate the lab teachers. This may seem a small factor, but it is vital to the survival of the program. At its inception, the program was not, however, structured along the lines of a formalized mentoring program. Rather it was designed on the basis of what we considered to be an effective experience for future reading-writing workshop teachers. It was designed to promote effective learning and teaching for all of its stakeholders–both in the content area and in learning how to teach, or mentor if you like. I digress here, however, to discuss the parallels between what a number of researchers are discovering about mentoring practices and what we are doing in the Jones Writing Buddy program.

## A Slight Digression

Many teacher educators have been exploring ideas and procedures for training mentors to satisfy our current educational needs. One group, the Association for Teacher Educators (ATE), has said that the traditional definition of mentor includes a relationship that includes expectations of a level of commitment and comprehensiveness that are not currently found in many educational mentoring programs. "The aim [today] is to help individuals develop the human potential of others" (Bey & Holmes, 1992, p. v). In fact, an ATE Commission has adopted a set of 10 mentoring principles to address the role and preparation of mentor teachers. Most of those principles underlie what is happening in the Jones program. For example, at Jones Elementary School the program is complex and the activities of the preservice teachers include support, assistance, and guidance. The activities of all parties require time and communication in order to facilitate self-reliance in the novice preservice teachers. The program involves the local school in collaboration with an institution of higher education and is consistent with school district goals. The mentors are selected based upon identified criteria and are prepared and offered incentives for their work. Essentially, the Jones program uses the "team approach," which is defined by Bey (1992) as a "triadic link among the university supervisor, the cooperating teacher, and the student teacher" (p. 113). The difference, however, is that our circle is even wider than the triad, and the student teachers are preservice teachers. Bey further suggests that the mentor teachers and the university professor work closely together as a collegial team to implement the program, and indeed we do.

## Back to the Jones Story

How then were we able to set the program into motion? Back at the university, the decision was made to try to find a match for the writing buddy program, a match meaning an elementary school that was accessible to the university students and that had a need that matched our need. The match also had to be one in which the participating parties were interested in and committed to voluntary participation in the program and all that that entails. Roles of each of the participants had to be clearly established and coordinated. Elementary school curriculum and university course goals had to be identified, compatible, and coordinated. The lab content taught by the cooperating classroom teachers had to be coordinated with university lecture and syllabus. Groups of elementary students had to be matched as writing buddies with preservice university students. Elementary school and university class schedules had to be coordinated, and on, and on. There is no question about the complexity of the program's process or function.

The match was made with Jones Elementary School based on our mutual needs–their need for help with their children's writing instruction and our need for a third through fifth grade population large enough to accommodate the number of students in our classes, and more importantly, a principal and faculty who were willing to be observers, teachers, and guides to our preservice teachers.

Once our mutual needs were identified and agreed upon, we began–together–to design the field-based experiences. Support and guidance were built in at every level. The Jones program is designed to use mentors to support the professional growth of our preservice teachers and to offer them an opportunity to learn from a wider circle—a circle that includes Jones writing lab teachers, Jones classroom teachers, Jones third through fifth grade students, and each other, all in addition to the university faculty. After several planning sessions, which included both the Jones designated lab teachers and university faculty, the program was approved. Its format is illustrated in *Figure 4: Concentric Circles in the Mentoring of Many.*

**The Mentoring of Many**

Approximately 100 preservice students attend two hours of lecture each week with me, in which we discuss reading-writing theories, learning styles, classroom management, and implementation strategies for the reading-writing activities. Four lab teachers and I meet often to coordinate our teaching efforts and to discuss the program and its progress. We also meet at least once each semester to share with each other ways to improve strategies and communications and to maintain program integrity.

In addition, preservice students travel to Jones Elementary once a week for a two-hour session. One hour of this time is spent working with their writing buddies in the regular classrooms. During this hour, the classroom teachers are present to supervise and assist them, should assistance be needed. However, after an initial observation in their supervising teacher's classroom, the preservice teachers are fully responsible for the lessons and their interactions with their writing buddies. Each preservice teacher is matched with two to four children, and they work with these same children for the entire semester. The second hour at Jones is spent in a writing lab with Jones teachers. Preservice teachers are divided into two labs in which two classroom teachers team up to work with approximately 50 preservice teachers. The lab teachers have a dual role: they model by demonstrating strategies for the writing buddy lessons and they answer questions and discuss issues or situations that the preservice teachers may raise. I am also at Jones on these days, observing the preservice teachers with their writing buddies and attending the lab session. I am constantly learning just from watching and listening. With so many circles operating at once, it is essential that one person be cognizant of all that is going on in order to keep the channels of communication open.

There are other ways of facilitating communication, however. Optimally, mentors encourage their mentees to reflect upon their initial teaching experiences (Reiman, 1988), and we do this.

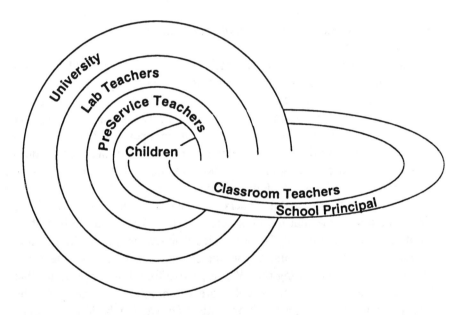

*Figure 4. Concentric Circles in the Mentoring of Many*

In this wider circle of relationships, vehicles for communication and feedback are built-in from writing journals to holding discussions in both lab and lecture classes. From the beginning of the course, the preservice teachers are asked to keep three different journals each week.

## Mentoring through Journal Writing

One type of journal is a *reflective journal* written to me in which the teachers comment on theories or approaches we are discussing in lecture and how they fit into the actual classroom practice they are experiencing. I read these journals twice each semester and respond to teachers' comments. It is a valuable learning, monitoring, and support vehicle for both of us.

The second journal is one that the preservice teachers write to their supervising classroom teachers. In this journal, they ask for advice about lessons they are preparing, ask questions of the classroom teacher about specific student's learning styles, or express their excitement or frustration with their progress. Although an occasional teacher may have had a stressful day and not be able to rise to the occasion, the Jones classroom teachers are wonderful about responding to the preservice teachers with encouragement and advice.

The third journal puts our preservice teachers on the other side of the circle since it is one that the preservice teachers keep with their writing buddies. With this journal, the preservice teachers are put in the position of being the responders and encouragers; they are, in essence, learning how to "pass the mentoring on." We have also found in our program that the mentor and the mentored roles are often interchangeable. As the preservice teachers begin working with their writing buddies at Jones Elementary, they find themselves in the role of mentors, and yet they also find themselves learning from their caring charges and, in the process, being mentored.

In their journals to me, before beginning their initial assignment at Jones Elementary, most of the preservice teachers have written openly of their apprehension, insecurity, and nervousness about their writing buddy responsibilities. Would the children like them? Would they be able to teach them? Could they come up with enough, or even adequate, lessons? What about discipline? Few of them have ever been in a classroom in the capacity of being directly responsible for children and their learning. Most of their field experiences up to this time have only involved observation. Consequently, for many, this is a first! For example, one of the preservice teachers writes:

> At first I was nervous then frustrated, but now I'm comfortable as well as thankful. Being a mentor for H & J is more to me than just helping them to become better writers. It is time when I'm there academically, socially, as well as emotionally. A mentor does more than help out with school. I've become someone who doesn't just bring more homework, but am someone they know and depend on.

Obviously, her initial nervousness and frustration melted into self-reliance and confidence as she became more comfortable with her role.

A few, gratefully not many, preservice teachers who have not received the support they have wanted or needed have written entries similar to this one:

> The classroom teacher has honestly not been much help. She has only responded to my journal once and she didn't really even answer my questions. It's definitely a worthwhile experience, but I do wish I had more guidance from the teacher at Jones.

My response to her was to keep on writing to her teacher each week. With persistence, eventually the bond would probably be established. The vast majority of entries, however, read more like these:

> My classroom teacher has been an encourager, and she is very willing to help if we need something. I feel that all three parts [lecture, lab, classroom] are working together to (1) help me teach the students and (2) help me as a future teacher grow and learn. *All of the useful ideas have given me more confidence in teaching.*

> My classroom teacher is helpful. She will talk to us as a group after the program ends at 3:15 to answer any questions or to tell us about problems or strengths in our individual groups and students. She has started to come around and see what each group has done that day. *I feel she is truly interested in helping me work our kinks in teaching my group of 'special' (as she calls them) students.*

> I think this is an excellent program. Not only do I benefit by getting to try out lessons on my students, but these children are getting essential individual attention. As a preservice teacher, this program allows me to interact with students on a teacher/student level, it forces me to interact with other preservice teachers, and most importantly, *I get feedback from actual teachers if I have a problem or a question.*

This preservice teacher feels the interactive mentoring between her writing buddies and herself:

> I really enjoy being a mentor. It is neat to see that C & M are excited when I come and think about me on other days in addition to Thursdays. I feel like I am making a difference, not only by helping to teach them writing skills, but by giving them individual attention. *It is learning for both of us, I only hope that C and M are learning as much as I am.*

Expressing a view of the mutual benefits of mentoring for both student and teacher, this entry explains:

> This class has been a great help and has provided me with much needed experience. The class and the lab for this class have actually provided me with many ideas for my future classroom. The simple act of putting us in the classroom and getting interaction with the students has given me much needed experience. The lab instructors are also a great help. They put us in the place of the student, so *we see things through the eyes of the student while learning how to be an effective teacher.* My personal view on this form of mentorship is that it is incredibly effective and will benefit both students and teachers in the end.

This preservice teacher finds value in writing journals and in working with his peers.

> The journal between our teacher and me has been very helpful. It allows me to ask questions I might not ask out loud as well as find out valuable information about our writing buddies. Finally, talking with my peers has perhaps been the most valuable experience. Since we are all in this together we understand and try to help each other as much as possible.

Overall, I have found in the four semesters that the program has been in existence that Gold's (1992) view of the mentor is crucial: The mentor, she says, needs to be an accepting individual who knows how to communicate genuine feelings of acceptance to the beginning teacher, develop listening skills that demonstrate an understanding of how the beginning teacher feels, and also have the skill to communicate that this is of great importance. Even Joubert (1899, p. 158), almost 200 years ago, showed us that "Children need models rather than critics." The reflective journal entries of these preservice teachers bear this out.

## Mentoring Benefits in the Circle of Many

We have come full circle from the mentoring of one to the mentoring of many. Perhaps we could compare the mentoring of many to a pebble thrown into a pond. The pebble creates a circle in the water, and then another, and another. Its effect grows and expands. Mentor counseled Odysseus; Athena took on the role of Mentor for Telemachus; our families and teachers assumed that role for us. Spontaneous mentoring will always exist because people of like mind and interests will always be drawn together. We will always have our Lottie Bakers and our Dr. Nicholsons.

Today we cannot afford to wait for the spontaneous right match for all of our future and beginning teachers. While our needs grow, so do the wider and wider concentric circles in mentoring. Furlong (1995) reports that "one of the most common complaints made by student teachers about their professional development has always been that ... real learning does not begin until they enter the classroom" (p. 175). Teaching, they say, is essentially a practical activity. Thus, "student teachers, at a fairly early stage in their professional preparation, need to begin the process of teaching." Why, then, should our prospective teachers wait until the end of their program for the experience of the classroom when the benefits to all are so pronounced? Why not widen the circle here and now?

A multitude of experiences from this program have demonstrated for us that everyone benefits from the collegial comentoring that occurs. The child is the focal point, and like a pebble, the child is the catalyst that sets the widening circle in motion. Beginning with the child's benefit as the foremost consideration, in a collegial atmosphere, preservice teachers learn what they need to know about working with the child from the classroom teachers and their university instructor. The preservice teacher who wrote, "The teachers help us see things through the eyes of the student while [we are] learning to be effective teachers," expresses this idea succinctly. In addition, while the classroom teachers mentor the preservice teachers, they, in turn, learn new techniques and different approaches for working with their own students from the university setting.

At the university level, we are immeasurably enriched by having a testing ground for the theories and philosophies that we teach and by having the opportunity to examine their practicality in classroom applications with actual students. Through observation and discussion, we learn to "see through the eyes of *our* students" and we also learn to be more effective teachers for them. The children benefit both cognitively and affectively by having a caring buddy who comes to give them special lessons and a large measure of undivided attention each week. Through her support of the field experience, the Principal benefits by enriching the children's experiences and the school's curriculum; in addition, her teachers are able to keep up with current theories and practices in the field. The process establishes and widens the circle of communications, counseling and teaching, all along the line. Lastly, it provides action research in the field, working with classroom teachers as researchers in their own right. When the university level is open to voices and relationships from the field, we are impelled to more meaningful action research.

Writing this chapter has opened my eyes to new insights about mentoring. Auden (1962, p. 22) quotes E. M. Forster as saying, "How do I know what I think until I see what I say?" In reflecting on the circles of mentoring in the Jones program and having had the opportunity to articulate my reflections, I see much more clearly some of the program's facets and interactions that had heretofore been somewhat vague or unclear. The process of writing this chapter is quite similar in many ways to the preservice students writing their reflective journals. It has caused me to explore at a deeper level the contributions and mentoring interactions of all of the involved parties. I have examined closely the mentoring influences of each participant on each of the others plus my own role within that circle. In so doing, I have discovered the valuable mentoring power of the writing buddy children on the preservice teachers–an influence I had not given the weight I now know it deserves. Through their multiple journals, three preservice teachers have told us what they need in the way of guidance and have shown us more effective ways of building the mentoring circles. I have seen the importance of my role clearly as the thread that ties all of the circles together. When there is a mentoring circle of many, operating within a limited time frame with brief but vital communications, it is important to have a thread that binds us all together. Examining the many facets of the program with fresh eyes has certainly stimulated my thoughts and ideas about other and new ideas for the program.

At a different personal level, fellow chapter writers have offered encouragement and also questions that helped me to re-examine at yet a deeper level some of the observations and assertions about the Jones program. Working with them has reminded me once again of the important lesson I thought I had already learned–how quickly we forget–that it is often incumbent upon us to seek out those who can and will interact with us as collegial comentors. We are all enriched by the exchange.

It is obvious that with programs like the Jones Elementary Writing Buddy program, we can widen our circle of mentoring to include the many. Such programs can become pilots that help us discover the kinds of mentoring experiences that work best or models that demonstrate the effective mentoring that preservice teachers can receive in a first classroom experience. This mentorship is not necessarily the deep or extended one-on-one mentorship. It is not necessarily a situation in which the mentor and the mentored choose one another. For some, the effects are direct; for others, the effects are indirect. It is, however, a form of mentoring that provides opportunities–in the real setting of a working classroom–for novice teachers to reflect on successes, problems, and unknowns through journals or class discussions; to learn how to ask for help and receive counseling and advice from their mentors and colleagues; to learn skills and techniques that build confidence in content teaching; and to develop an awareness of personal learning/teaching styles and classroom management.

The preservice teachers who have experienced this expanded triad of mentoring are excited about their future in the field of teaching and feel that they have gained in both in skill and confidence. They see their contributions as important. Their education, and ours, has been enriched by our participation in this wider circle of mentorship. We all leave the program ready to pass the mentorship on to yet the next circle, expanding effective education as we go.

### Acknowledgments

My students are excited that their experiences are contributing to this chapter and were most cooperative in sharing their reactions and thoughts about the program. A profound thanks to the Jones Writing Buddy preservice teachers in Reading 467 for their contributions.

A tremendous thanks also to those of you who have provided suggestions and encouragement in my writing of this chapter, and especially to Carol A. Mullen and the *Circle* for letting me enter and participate in the project at this late date.

# Part IV

# The Search for New Patterns of Mentoring within Higher Education Circles

John C. Stansell

Carol A. Mullen

William A. Kealy

Donna L. Wiseman

# Chapter 8

# Mentors and Mentoring: Reflections of a Circle with/in Circles

## John C. Stansell

On an early spring afternoon nearly 30 years ago, I sat waiting at the back of an English classroom in a south Texas high school as the last class of the day filed out. I was a student teacher in my first week of observation and anxious to find out when I might move from the role of observer to that of teacher. We'd been told that we'd probably start out working with a small group, or maybe teaching a brief lesson to one class, so when John, my cooperating teacher, walked up and asked if I was ready to get my feet wet, I quickly said that I was.

"So," he said, "do you want to take them tomorrow?"

"Sure," I answered, wondering exactly what I'd just agreed to.

"Okay," he continued, "I'll be in the workroom if you need anything. I'll stay in the room if you want me to, but I'd probably just make you self-conscious, so I'll stay out of your way and you can ask me in if there's anything you want me to see. We can talk at the end of the day, or anytime you have a free moment."

I listened to him say this in something like a state of shock. I'd just agreed to take all five of his junior English classes, starting the next day and presumably continuing until the end of my student teaching period. I suppose I could have backpedaled and asked for a more gradual entry to the teaching role, but it really didn't occur to me to do that. Despite knowing me for no more than a week, John seemed confident enough that I would survive, maybe even succeed, and I didn't want to seem reluctant. I went home and got to work.

The next day I taught all five classes, and continued to teach them all until my student teaching ended. John and I talked only infrequently, after school or in the corridor between classes, about particulars–individual students and the strengths and problems and quirks they had, and the need to provide something worthwhile to the particular students who made up a particular class. We talked some about teaching strategies–not the things that phrase usually denotes, but rather those small moves that can invite a student into a group, or bolster confidence, or offer a moment's relief during an intense discussion, or address adolescent egos run amok. I learned a good deal from hearing John speak about his experience as a teacher and what he'd made of it. But when I spoke, John listened as if he expected me to say something he might learn from. He came to the room two or three times, at my invitation, to observe my teaching. When I felt something had gone poorly he first asked what I thought might have helped and, sometimes, offered another option to think about. Mostly, as he had promised, he just stayed out of the way.

During the six weeks of student teaching in this setting, I had my moments of uncertainty and of struggle. Some plans just didn't pan out, some activities produced less-than-wonderful results, and some students were not as well served as they should have been. But there were also some successes, and I gradually realized I could trust my on-the-spot thought and action, as teachers must. I came to know that, while not always successful, I was also neither ignorant nor helpless. Would I have come to this realization if John had played the role I'd originally envisioned for him? Maybe, but I doubt it.

**Musings for Mentors**

1.  Perhaps one critical quality for mentors is the willingness to step aside and let neophytes find their own way, with the assurance that the mentor is available if needed,

2.  Wherever mentors may position themselves in relation to the beginner's circle of one, they can do much to build a beginner's

sense of belonging to the profession by treating the beginner as an contributing member of the profession.

## Looking Back on My Story

For a while, both during and after that semester, I thought of John as a good teacher of high school English students who left something to be desired as a mentor for student teachers. To me, he was just a likeable fellow who gambled on turning things over to his student teacher very early on and got away with it. Though I was glad to have taken the plunge as I did, I thought he had avoided his responsibility to show me how to function, both in my classroom and in the larger world of the school. And maybe he had. But I eventually realized that, regardless of his motives, John had done important things for me. Either by accident or by design, he had created a situation in which I could empower myself, make my own decisions, and find my own way. He did this not by breaking my circle of one but by standing attentively at its outer edge, meeting me on the boundary from time to time so that I could use his perspective and understanding to examine and triangulate my own knowledge.

## With Circles on the Frat House Pool Table: House: High School Teacher

The following September, I began teaching in a place I would remain for the next seven years, a place I still recall fondly and occasionally visit. My teaching career began there, my wife Sally and I became parents there, and we bought our first home there; yet in many ways my work as a teacher was often a solitary experience. With a couple of notable exceptions, my contact with other teachers was as a circle with other circles that shared a common space and moved in similar patterns. In Louise Rosenblatt's (1969, 1978, 1985) transactional theory of reading, interactions are described as billiard balls colliding. People that interact affect each other as billiard balls do when they collide; their speed and direction are altered, but they remain essentially unchanged. Using Rosenblatt's framework, the teachers in this town's high school were like the bright-colored balls on a pool table. We interacted, occasionally changing each other's direction somewhat as we jostled about, but we did not experience what Rosenblatt has termed "transactions"–deeper connections between people, interpenetrations through which all involved are changed.

This small southeast Texas town's high school had an enrollment of between 1,100 and 1,400 students during the years I was there. The school had many veteran teachers and few new ones. In my first year, I was the only new teacher at the high school and one of only four or five in the entire school district. My first new acquaintances, besides the principal who had interviewed me for the job, were in the English department I joined–Liz, the department chair, and Roy, a teacher who had come there about three years before. I would gradually meet all the teachers and principals, become well-acquainted with most, and form close friendships with several; yet we were more like neighbors than professional colleagues. Though we did often "talk shop," the topic was usually of faculty politics–who's currying favor with whom and for what purpose, who has the principal's ear–rather than of learning and teaching, or of linking theory and practice. It seemed that we collectively viewed ourselves as subject matter experts who felt little need either to seek or to offer much in the way of pedagogical insight. Though there were individuals who didn't share this view at all, and others who didn't share it entirely, its predominance among us, together with the prevailing gender politics, strongly shaped the dominant process and purpose of mentoring among teachers to be much like the rites of a fraternity initiation.

Occurring mostly in lunchtime conversations reminiscent of frathouse bull sessions, male mentors offered "the lowdown" on "the lay of the land" in the school and community. Mentors provided interpretations of the identity, background, and motives of influential people, and of those seen as not exerting any real influence despite their highly visible attempts to do so. Though they were given as authoritative, these interpretations did vary and sometimes clashed; yet an interpretive community had long since developed that featured many shared frameworks and perspectives. I moved fairly quickly from being the initiate member of the lunchtime circle of circles to helping initiate new members. To this day, I don't know whether mentoring even occurred among female teachers, not to mention what it might have been like. I do know, though, that there were a couple of mentors who worked outside of the frathouse.

**In Circles On the Frat House Porch: Liz and Roy**

My two colleagues in the English department, Liz and Roy, were mentors of a different kind.  Liz and I talked on occasion about our understandings of students and of learning to write and respond to literature, and how these understandings affected curriculum. A far more experienced teacher who was nearly twice my age, and was my department head to boot, Liz could easily have assumed a dominant role in these conversations, but didn't. Though we sometimes disagreed, we listened to one another and thought about what we had heard and revisited some of the same topics several times during my seven years there, and we also became friends who enjoyed sharing a funny story (we're both incurable storytellers, and we appreciated and enjoyed each other's tales and willingness to listen) or having a chat about other things.

As department head, Liz encouraged us all to think about curricular innovations that were then attracting interest in NCTE circles, and about the rationale and research support for them.  She was one of the few teachers that engaged me in thinking and talking about such things, offering me perspectives shaped by more experience than I had, while at the same time respecting and showing a genuine interest in the differing views I often expressed.  Liz was also the first female colleague I would work closely with, and the first of several female mentors.  Although I did not consciously recognize it at the time, she, too, showed me that mentoring did not have to be what I had once imagined it to be–a one-way process of being "shown the way" by one whose knowledge and authority were unquestionable.

Roy also helped show me this different side of mentoring.  He and I taught in adjacent classrooms for several years, and since we were both school bus drivers as well as teachers and lived in the same part of town, we often shared rides to and from the bus barn.  Thus, we had many more opportunities for conversation than Liz and I had.  Roy is, among other things, a devoted punster; I remember well the day that he stepped inside my classroom door near the end of the class period to ask whether I'd heard about the fisherman who retaliated against some annoying seagulls by throwing rocks at them.

"No," I said with some apprehension, "what about him?"

"He vowed," Roy answered, "to leave no tern unstoned."

As colleagues and friends, our relationship tolerated each other's brands of humor as well as fairly divergent views about teaching and schooling. Though Roy was much closer to my age than Liz, he was also far more experienced than me and could have claimed some authority for his views on those grounds. He didn't, though. Like Liz, he offered his own ideas, teaching practices, and rationales, and he listened to mine. He never hesitated to question or challenge me, but it was always clear that he expected the same treatment in return, and he got it.

Roy also never attended the frathouse sessions. I'd known and worked with him for some time before I ever noticed this, and while he was on friendly terms with all the "regulars," it seemed as if he'd made a conscious choice not to be one himself. From comparing the topics of our many conversations to those I was part of in the frat house sessions, it became apparent to me that Roy's focus was different. He was neither naive nor inarticulate about power relationships, and he clearly recognized that schooling is inherently political; yet far more often than those in the frat house, he thought and spoke about learning and teaching and curriculum, about teachers and students and the kinds and qualities of interactions that they have. Through him, and through Liz, I was able to recover and maintain a pedagogical perspective that was at risk of being lost in the frat house. Through them, I was also beginning to develop my own notion of mentoring, gaining my first hints of the transactional connections that could be involved.

## Musings for Mentors

1.  Mentors may be very effective even when they may not consciously see themselves in a mentoring role. We all set examples that others may choose to follow,
2.  Whether we choose to follow a mentor's example may depend on the extent to which the mentor values our thoughts, ideas, and perspectives and on the depth of our connection with the mentor.

## Looking Back on My Story

Liz and Roy, as well as the denizens of the frat house, may never have consciously thought of themselves as mentors despite the impact they had on me, and probably had on others. They were quite possibly just being themselves, thinking and speaking of the things they saw as important and responding to others in ways that had become second nature to them. As mentors and teachers, we often underappreciate the power of the examples we provide, the unconscious demonstrations we offer others of how things might be done, what might be seen as important, and how one might choose to behave in a particular role. Yet as Frank Smith (1981) pointed out some years ago, such demonstrations are the basis of our learning. If we are not inclined to believe that what is being demonstrated is hopelessly beyond our powers of understanding, and we attend to it, then we learn what is demonstrated. We would do well to examine what it is we demonstrate to others in our daily work, and consider whether it is something we wish for others to learn.

## From the Frat House to the Academy

As I talked with Liz, Roy, and others and reflected on my work over the years, I gradually decided that working toward a master's degree would be desirable. In my third year, several other English teachers and I volunteered to teach classes intended for students who were struggling with reading and writing. None of us had ever had a single college course directly related to this assignment, nor any other kind of preparation, so we struggled to extrapolate from what we did know and believe a set of principles and practices we hoped would be beneficial. After a while, we dared to believe that we just might be helping the students, but we also had many questions. All of us felt the need to find out whether there was any defensible basis for our emerging beliefs and practices, and this need led me to enroll in the master's program at the newly opened branch campus of a larger university in our region. The branch campus was about 50 miles away and that made commuting to the program's evening classes during the school year and taking a full summer's course load viable. In the summer of 1973 I enrolled for my first classes, thinking that I'd complete the degree in a year or two and continue teaching in the same school with the benefit of new and examined knowledge. Like so many plans, this one didn't turn out in quite the way I expected.

### Master's Mentors: Bill, Dave, and Dorothy

My first graduate instructor, Bill, was a full professor in his mid-fifties and was head of the division of education at the branch campus. He was a man of serious purpose and demeanor, greatly admired and respected by the faculty and the students, who also had a twinkle in his eye. Though we students were a bit awed by his accomplishments (which we learned of from other faculty, given Bill's modesty), and had made him into something of a legendary figure, we also really liked him. He had a way of making people feel welcome, and of listening to whatever they might have to say with the complete attention that reflects genuine respect. He made students feel valuable because he believed they were.

I doubt that any of us who began our graduate journey with Bill could've had a better beginning than he gave us. In later years, I would metaphorically describe the experience of being a public school teacher as the Chinese water torture–you don't notice those individual drops as they fall, I'd say, but one day you suddenly wonder what's become of your forehead. As I talked with classmates who were teachers in other schools in the area, I realized that we all had stories to share about the many little things that had slowly but steadily diminished our belief in our intellectual and professional selves that we had had when we left college. The frequent indications from various quarters that we teachers were thought incapable of making decisions about curriculum or anything else of substance, the many reminders of widespread belief that "those who can, do; those who can't, teach," were individually easy enough to dismiss. But collectively, they had eroded our confidence and our abilities to direct ourselves more than we realized. Bill's contrasting view of us was a welcome and much needed antidote.

Since the campus had just opened and was in the process of getting itself organized, none of us had yet been assigned official advisors. Near the end of that first summer term, as I was finishing the course with Bill, I decided quite on my own that an introductory course in educational administration might be a good idea, assuming that if I decided not to pursue a principal's certificate, the course would count as an elective. One day a couple of weeks into the second term I ran into Bill in the corridor outside his office, and he asked what I was taking. When I responded, he asked me to come into his office for a minute.

"Have a seat, John," he said, and as I sat down he added, "and tell me something. Do you want to be a principal?"

"I'm not completely sure, Bill," I lied. I was pretty sure I didn't particularly want to be one, but I was attracted by the higher salaries of principals, and this was definitely not something I cared to admit to him. "The course is interesting, though," I added lamely.

"We need to keep good teachers in teaching," he said abruptly, "so I want you to give something a try. We have a new faculty member coming aboard this fall who's really outstanding. Her work's in the area of language and reading, and I think she has a lot to offer an English teacher. Take her class this fall and see what happens."

At the moment it just struck me that Bill was being uncharacteristically blunt, but I soon realized that Bill was reminding me of my own questions about whether I was doing anything beneficial for my struggling students, and how these questions had propelled me into this program in the first place. Maybe this soon-to-arrive wonder would indeed help me find some answers. I decided to take her course.

And that decision led me to meet, study with, and learn a very great deal from Dorothy. Finishing her doctorate after a lengthy career as a public school teacher, she began her first semester at this campus teaching the course I took, an introduction to linguistics with an emphasis on language learning. That semester, she reintroduced me to B. F. Skinner and Noam Chomsky, and she pointed me toward their original work—Chomsky's (1957) *Syntactic Structures* and his (1959) famous review of Skinner's (1957) *Verbal Behavior*–rather than the textbook summaries that I had encountered as an undergraduate. As I developed a term paper exploring these works, an effort that would influence my study in this field from then until now, she pushed me ahead with questions that helped me clear up some of the muddy areas in my thinking and resolve some contradictions that were at once apparent to me and also more than I really wanted to tackle. In class and out of class, she was a charming, witty character who enjoyed a good laugh (even at her own expense) and who captivated people with the intensity of her interest in language, her commitment to learning about it, and her unwavering belief that what we know about language and language learning must be the basis of practice in classrooms. She was, and is, a living example of one of her own favorite ideas, that given half a chance, language is fascinating. Her intense interest was contagious, and in combination with the work she introduced me to, it began to draw me toward the idea of a career that would revolve around what she did—investigate something engrossing and share what you find with others. I was pulled very gently, really imperceptibly at first; soon, though, I began to get what Dorothy would call a "little nudge."

By the next semester I'd decided on reading as my area of emphasis for the master's degree, and Dave was assigned as my official advisor. I promptly made an appointment to see him, and thus began the real push toward doctoral study.

In one of our first few meetings as advisor and advisee, after we'd taken care of the degree plan and course selection business that needed to be done, he settled back in his chair and said, "Well, John, when are you going to start your doctorate?" Though I was enjoying my classes, the idea of study beyond the master's degree had never occurred to me. His question couldn't have been more startling, and I had a number of thoughts concurrently, including "surely, this is Dave's idea of a joke." Another one was what I actually said in answer to his question:

"Dave," I said, "I can't do that. I'd have to give up my teaching job, and we have two kids to raise. Besides, my family might not want to move."

"John," Dave instantly responded, looking over his glasses as if dismissing my lame excuse, "would you like to know how old my children will be when my graduate school loans are paid off?'

"Not especially," I answered. "But even if we could survive on loans and graduate assistant pay, what about my family? They may not want to pull up roots."

"Why don't you ask them?" he said.

Well, that would clinch it, I thought. Sally wouldn't be at all eager to make this move, and our kids would surely hate being separated from their friends and all four grandparents. I could ask them, hear their predictable answer, report it to Dave, and be off the hook. I wouldn't even have to face the issues of whether I could really earn a doctoral degree and whether I was prepared to leave my teaching job and own friends and extended family. Things were definitely looking up.

"I'll ask them, Dave," I said, "but I think I know the answer already."

"John," Dave answered with another over-the-glasses look, "just ask them. You might be surprised."

Not long after that meeting with Dave, I did mention Dave's question to Sally.

"What'd you tell him?" she asked.

"I said I just didn't see it happening," I answered, "with our kids to raise and our families to think of. Besides, I'm really pretty happy where I am, doing what I'm doing."

She listened and nodded without comment, as spouses do when they're catching up on each other's week. I chose not to ask how she'd feel if I decided I really wanted to do this, and our conversation moved to other topics.

I'd agreed to ask that question, but I didn't say *when*. It was the spring semester, and I was teaching my classes, driving a school bus, commuting to classes two evenings a week, and serving as Junior class sponsor during Junior-Senior Prom season. I didn't have much time to think about doctoral study, and I really didn't want to, either. The crowded schedule made an excellent excuse.

But while I was avoiding the issue with all my might, Dave and Dorothy were both thinking about how they might encourage me and talking to each other about it. Every time I saw either of them, they found a way to bring up the subject, and I began to wish they'd just give up. Dave asked me more than once if I'd talked to my family, and I pleaded lack of time. Slowly the semester drew to a close and I hoped the whole thing would soon be put aside with the unclaimed term papers and other residue of a term completed, and forgotten.

A few weeks later I registered for the first summer term to take my second course with Dorothy and a course with Dave. I checked with Dave to be sure that all was in order for August graduation, and began to look forward to starting the next school year as an actual holder of the master's degree. Early in that first term, though, Dorothy approached me with a proposition. She said she knew I was reluctant to uproot my family, and that she'd been thinking about the present and future need for more faculty at this campus because student enrollment was growing and expected to continue to grow. Then she dropped the bomb, the first of two that would fall that summer.

"So," she said, "why don't you go and get your doctorate and come back here and teach with us? We're going to need more people, and I think we can hire you if you can get the degree in two or three years. I've talked to Bill and Dave about it, and we want you. I'm going to talk to the Provost about it and see what he says."

It's a massive understatement to say I was surprised by this. I was surprised, flattered, intrigued, delighted, interested, and frightened all at the same time. About all I could actually do at the moment was ask if there was really a guarantee of a job if I got the degree, and Dorothy made it clear that they wanted me as a colleague and would do what was necessary to pave the way.

For the next couple of days, I mulled it over. The more I thought about it, the better it sounded. I could spend a few years in graduate school, then return to a place close to family and friends and work with good colleagues I already knew and liked. But I was still reluctant, and soon began to get a serious case of cold feet. I decided to do what I'd promised Dave. Ask my family, and let them tell me what I predicted they'd tell me, and then it would be decided.

So, a few days later, I came home from class and asked Sally how she'd like to live in another state for a few years. Then she dropped the second bomb.

"When do we leave?" she asked.

Rapidly losing my excuse–a family that didn't want to undergo all this–I quickly proposed that we talk to our children about it. After all, they'd have to be far from their grandparents and friends, and I couldn't picture their liking that idea. So we talked to them. And they, too, were ready to go.

Now, of course, I was trapped. Now I had to confront my own fears and insecurities, as well as career goals and priorities. It wasn't an easy thing to do, but with my family's help and a good deal of hand-holding from Dave, Dorothy, and Bill, I decided to apply to two institutions for fall semester acceptance. As I was mailing applications, I learned that our school superintendent was retiring and that our high school principal was being reassigned. This meant that whether I stayed or went, things would be different. Soon after the first acceptance letter came in late July, I finally made up my mind. I talked by phone with Carol, my soon-to-be doctoral committee chair at Indiana University, about a graduate assistantship, and she said she did not have one available to offer at the moment but would surely be able to find something for me. I said that moving there and enrolling without a job in hand seemed like a big leap, and I'll never forget her response: "If you come, John, we won't let you starve." I resigned my teaching job on August 10, and we put the house up for sale and started packing. On the day Richard Nixon resigned the Presidency, we left for Indiana.

**Musings for Mentors**

1. We sometimes think of mentors as individuals who are so nonconfrontational in their dealings with us that they would never presume to tell us what they think we should do, or offer advice that forces hard choices. But without such input, we may not otherwise know all our options, or be willing to make the necessary choices among them,
2. Mentors do not work in a vacuum but in a context that shapes, and is shaped by, their dealings with the mentored.

**Looking Back on My Story**

Dave, Dorothy, and Bill were excellent role models and mentors for me, yet they collectively made my life very difficult in the months between Dave's asking when I was going to start on my doctorate and my decision to do so. There were moments when I resented them. Who did these people think they were, I thought, to pressure me this way to do something I'd said over and over again I was reluctant about? I felt insecure, even afraid, about leaving familiar places and people, about whether I could really pull off earning a doctoral degree with that dreadful dissertation requirement at the end. I also felt guilty about leaving teaching and uprooting our family. And then, when Sally and our children seemed eager to be uprooted, I felt another source of pressure. They, too, like my faculty mentors, seemed to be relentlessly asking me to ignore all that and do what *they* wanted me to do. I eventually realized that they were asking me to face my fears and guilt, not ignore them, and to do what *I* really wanted, but had neither realized nor acknowledged. Without all of them, my family mentors as much as my faculty mentors, I would have remained in the comfort zone I'd developed for myself. Because of them, I've had the great adventure of doctoral study and a professorial career.

**Circling the Ivory Tower: The Doctoral Program**

As we drove from Texas to Indiana, with our two children in the back seat and all we could pack into the big rental trailer we were towing, a voice in my head kept insistently asking "What in the world do you think you're doing? You've got four hundred dollars to your name, no guarantee of a job either now or later, no place to live, and no idea of what this doctoral program and the people involved in it are like. Your family's going to be far from home, away from all their friends and relatives, and you'll probably all freeze to death the first winter." Being delayed two days by car trouble didn't help since we arrived in Bloomington on a Saturday, the day after late registration ended. I drove into town, past the courthouse square that looked pleasantly like the ones back home, and asked Sally to get out the directions to Carol's. She had said to come by as soon as we got to town so she could know we were there and get us oriented, and before long we were at her front door. As I knocked, the voice in my head spoke again; but when she answered, it was quickly silenced for good.

She welcomed us, insisted that we stay with her overnight, and said that she'd help us find an apartment tomorrow as she handed us newspaper ads to look through. Over coffee, she reminded me that classes began Monday, told me she had an assistantship just about arranged, and said I'd have to be at the office Monday morning to register for classes and meet the professor I'd be working for, so we'd need to find an apartment and get moved in quickly. The next morning, she drove us all over town on a semi-frantic apartment search. Late that afternoon, we found one in a brand new complex, which was surprisingly affordable since it was on the outskirts of town. She drove us back to her place so we could get our car and tow the trailer to our new home, and we thanked her for all her help, not imagining that she'd insist on returning with us to help unload. At dusk, after helping us lug all our furniture and belongings inside, she told me to be sure to be at her office at 8:00 the next morning as she drove away. As Sally and our children began arranging things in the apartment that Monday morning, I drove to campus with a very different outlook.

### Moving in Student Circles: Rus, Roger, Nancy, and Diane

That first week, I met several fellow doctoral students, and was surprised at being told by a couple of them that there was a noncredit seminar series that we were all required to attend. They said it was organized by doctoral students so they could present papers and dissertation proposals to each other for discussion and feedback prior to the conference or formal proposal hearing itself. Faculty were invited to attend, and were asked on occasion to present their work as well. I could see the value in these things, but the idea of a required seminar not involving course credit made me a tad suspicious: Was this a kind of doctoral program snipe hunt I was being sent on? I asked Carol if it was really required or just encouraged, and her answer left little room for doubt (unless she was part of the scam, too, which seemed really unlikely), so I decided to go. Nancy, a doctoral student I'd met a day or two before, was presenting a draft of her dissertation proposal. It seemed interesting enough. She planned to study first graders learning to read in their classrooms. So, I figured I'd go and listen and learn something about what a proposal looked like and what kinds of responses people give to them.

The seminar room was packed with every student I had met and several more that I had not. Everyone listed very intently to Nancy's summary of her proposal, and it seemed that virtually everyone asked tough, harshly worded questions. The scene reminded me of movies where suspects are being grilled by hard-boiled cops, and as I sat there taking it all in, a couple of questions did occur to me. But, I thought, what do I know? I'm the new kid on the block, and the others' questions seemed to have covered the territory pretty thoroughly. I doubted that my questions would have really added much, so I kept quiet. But as soon as the seminar ended, I found out that this was not a place for spectators.

As I walked over toward Nancy to say hello as she gathered up her presentation materials, she looked up and saw me coming. Her expression was not a happy one.

"Well, *you* were a lot of help!" she said.

"What'd I do?" I asked, wondering what on earth she could be upset with me about.

"Look, John," she said, in a voice used to explain something that should be obvious to a turnip, "I have to defend this proposal to my committee in a couple of weeks. I *need* this feedback to make the proposal strong."

"Uh well gosh, it seemed strong enough to me," I answered weakly, "and my questions probably weren't all that good anyway. I mean, heck, I just got here. I'm just trying to learn what this stuff is all about," I answered, scrambling for some kind of excuse that might keep her from deciding that I was a total loss. She looked me in the eye and said, calmly:

"It's about asking questions, John. And it's time you started doing that." Then she turned and walked quickly out of the room.

There was a lesson in this, I decided. Thinking about the students and faculty I'd met in the last few days and how they behaved toward each other and toward me, it began to dawn on me that here, everyone–even the new guy–was presumed to have some knowledge that would generate questions, to ask those questions, and to challenge any assertion that seemed suspect.

Everyone seemed to relish what looked at first like verbal muggings, where the attacker and the intended victim both came off as self-assured to the point of arrogance. There were clearly defined camps whose membership was determined by shared theoretical frameworks, and a perpetual state of war existed between them. But there was plenty of combat within camps as well as between them. "Do you *believe* that crap?" was probably the single most frequently asked question in response to conclusions drawn by any student or any faculty member from any body of evidence. Yet Nancy had obviously wanted this treatment from me as well as the others, and they all seemed to depend on it for something that went well beyond ego-nourishment. And, rather than being grumpy with each other in such an apparently hostile climate, they seemed quite friendly.

At the Friday afternoon happy hour sessions at a local pub (which we were also expected to attend), people from opposing camps that had spent much of the week at each other's throats greeted each other amicably and enjoyed an hour or two of good-natured talk. This camaraderie was also evident around campus, in classes and study sessions, as well as quick chats at the coffeepot and at frequent potluck suppers that attracted large numbers. Friendships, it seemed, were as strong across camps as within them.

What we had here, I came to suspect, was not a collection of arrogant prima donnas. Instead, this was a group that used every device they could, including hostile-sounding questions, to prompt thought and reflection about things that mattered greatly to them–ideas and theories and research findings within the field they had chosen to study as a life's work. They needed to be questioned, as well as to question, in order to examine thoroughly the things they had observed, read, or heard. And this examination was not just done to win arguments. Though looks of satisfaction were worn by those who gained the upper hand in arguments, the real purpose of them was to probe, to explore, and to bring one's theoretical, empirical, and pedagogical ducks into line. And friendships flourished because each of them valued what everyone was doing, that is, studying their chosen field and pushing its boundaries as they pushed themselves and their thinking. What we had here, I decided, was a community of scholars, and a strong community to boot, where the differences among theoretical camps were more an asset than a threat.

## Musings for Mentors

1. The process of mentoring described above may look more like a process of mutual disempowerment. But in a community united by a shared field of interest, purpose, and respect for members' competence and commitment to that purpose, both its intent and its outcome may be empowering,
2. Perhaps we overlook potential mentors whose perspectives differ greatly from our own, not realizing what they may offer, precisely because of the differences that allow them to offer so much.

## Looking Back on My Story

As I joined this community, I realized that Nancy, Diane, and I were part of one of these camps and that Roger and Rus were part of another. All five of us argued with each other, both across theoretical lines and within them, and all of us also helped each other in more ways than can be described here. The morning after Nancy's celebration of her successful dissertation defense, she helped me collect my dissertation data; she and her husband Ed showed Sally and me that marriage and family life could flourish concurrently with the rigors of graduate school, and we helped them move from their apartment to a house. Diane and I helped each other through an experience that was, in different ways, new to each of us: team-teaching a class of high schoolers one summer with an integrated language arts curriculum in which learning centers were the central activity. Rus and Roger and I helped each other through our last statistics course, and they both helped acquaint me with courses, professors, and the process of looking for jobs. We all had other close friends among the doctoral students who were there together, but it is these four people that became the brothers and sisters that I, an only child, had never had. We became this close not in spite of our collective differences, but because of them. Within this community we realized that even though we'd learned much through working with people who shared our theoretical framework, those who represented different frameworks also pushed our thinking, leading us to new investigations and insights. We realized that in the absence of those differences we would not have those insights, and in the absence of those people, we would not have confronted those differences. We learned that even our theoretical foes were our allies and friends.

## Carol, Bill, and Jerry: In Faculty Circles

It was Carol's work that attracted me to Indiana, and I'd planned before I even arrived to ask her to chair my doctoral committee, so as soon as I got my feet on the ground we began to work on my degree plan and talk about things to read and dissertation topics. In my second year I would work for her as a teaching assistant and as her administrative assistant for a funded project. I got to know her quickly and well, and the same was true of Bill, with whom I had my first doctoral course in reading that first semester.

A native of North Carolina, Bill's familiar Southern mannerisms were welcome to me. But in class, he seemed always on the attack. I was just beginning to get comfortable with the "Do you *believe* that crap?" questions other students would fling at each other and at me, and to understand what they were really all about, but I was unnerved by a professor's use of this genre. This seemed to be a horse of a somewhat different color, and I left class that day thinking it would be a long semester. Rus, though, explained to me that Bill expected from us the same as he gave, and that he was doing the same thing we did with each other—trying to push his own thinking as well as ours by goading us into asking him questions as strong as his own. With that in mind I was fairly quickly able to hold my own in class, to appreciate Bill's vast knowledge of reading research, to hear him praise students' ideas and analyses as well as challenge them, and to discover that he shared several interests of mine.

But Jerry was a different story, at least at first. His office was at the opposite end of the suite from Carol's and nearly that far from the cubby where my desk was, so we didn't cross paths that often. All I knew of him during my first semester was what I'd heard, and the word was that his theoretical orientation and mine were rather different. He and another colleague were heavily involved in an undergraduate program, and he spent a good deal of time at a site away from the school of education building, so he had relatively little contact with the grad students. I had met him through Roger initially, and Roger seemed to enjoy their frequent haggling over interpretations of articles in the latest issue of the research journal we all read from cover to cover each month. I eventually weighed in with him once or twice, asking for his assessment of some article so I could pounce on what I predicted he'd say. Through my own experience with him, as well as what I'd seen and heard of his dealings with others, it was obvious that he was a very bright, articulate fellow who relished an argument and whose occasional harsh remarks were balanced by his often self-deprecating sense of humor and his willingness to compliment a point well made or an idea compellingly advanced. An interesting guy, I thought, but probably not for my committee. Our interests at the time were pretty different, and I'd heard about the problems that committee members from different camps could cause.

So, my committee included Carol as chair and Bill as one of the members. But a year later, Bill would leave to take a faculty position in his home state, and I was faced with finding a replacement. I went in to talk to Carol about that, and I was really surprised when she suggested Jerry as a member. I asked what she thought about his theoretical stance, and she acknowledged the differences. She went on to say that they'd been talking a good deal about theoretical matters lately, and it was apparent that she thought well of him and thought he'd be a good member of my committee.

One reason she thought so highly of him was that he was in the midst of rethinking his own theoretical framework, a tortuous undertaking that Carol had herself experienced some years earlier. Though none of us knew it at the time, Jerry's intense struggle with his own beliefs and with evidence and arguments that challenged them would first result in his embracing a framework Carol and I worked from, and it would eventually result in research they collaborated on that would bring them international renown as it explored and expanded their shared theory. All we could see at the moment, though, was Jerry entertaining questions of the most wrenching sort. I figured that if he could value challenges of that magnitude enough to let himself be vulnerable to them, I might well have much to gain from having him on my committee.

So, a few days later I met with Jerry and explained the dissertation idea I had and asked if he'd be willing to serve as a member. He agreed, and became the relentlessly questioning critic and supportive, helpful colleague he has been for many years. After my dissertation defense, he spent a couple of hours with me, first describing the strengths he saw in the study and then going through many changes and additions he thought would strengthen the final document. I sat there thinking that if I did all he suggested it'd take several more months of work, a prospect I wasn't too thrilled about. When he finished with his last suggestion, I waited for him to ask me to show him the results when I was finished. But instead, he suggested I consider his changes, talk to Carol about them, and then make all of them, some of them, or none of them. My surprise at this last option must have been pretty obvious, because he quickly explained why it was included. No study is ever really finished, he reminded me; you just reach a point of having given it all you can give it, and you're the only one who can say where that point is.

I include this story because it illustrates so well Jerry's essentially empowering stance as a mentor, even though his responses to my work (and everyone else's) were sometimes pretty acerbic. Carol's mentorship was, and is, just as empowering, and though her criticisms were usually framed in milder ways than Jerry's sometimes were, they too could be a bit like an elbow in the ribs.

One day not long after I had completed my degree, I was back in Bloomington trying to put together a grant proposal, and Carol and Jerry asked me to speak to their doctoral seminar class about my dissertation. As I spoke, I was suddenly aware of saying something that wasn't coming out right. Jerry and Carolyn, sitting in the back of the room, immediately turned to each other and said something as I frantically backtracked to try to correct myself. After class, I asked what they'd said to each other as I made my gaffe. "Who trained him?" was the answer from both of them. Then the three of us walked out of the building, laughing.

We laughed because we'd all been there before in our dealings with each other. Each of us had heard the other say something that either seemed to contradict earlier remarks, to go beyond available evidence, or to ignore some of it. Each of us had leaped from ambush upon any such opportunity, and each of us had seen products of our thinking ambushed in such circumstances. But we'd also each heard the other speak highly of our work, and our mutual respect and regard for each other was both strong and visible. We were mentors who relentlessly challenged each other, but the object of challenge was always ideas and evidence, not the competence or worth of the individual and his or her contributions.

**Musings for Mentors**

Teachers at any level of schooling are powerful figures, whose expertise affords them a position of high status and whose words and actions can therefore disempower students. Yet when conditions are created for students to be powerful in their own right and to claim their own expertise, a climate of mutual mentoring can arise where everyone is both teacher and learner.

**Looking Back on My Story**

By the time I left Indiana's School of Education, I was well aware of its reputation as "Barracuda U." But while many outsiders thought of it as a place where people lived to intimidate and demean others, I knew it as a place where I never felt either intimidated or demeaned. It was always evident to me that underneath all the bluster and surface sarcasm was the clear conviction that students and faculty were very competent people, and that what was visible to the outsider was simply the device of choice used to sharpen and deepen everyone's thinking. The professors I've spoken of here, and others not mentioned, helped me and many other students not only to learn more about language and literacy but to have confidence in ourselves and our work. And my fellow students and I helped the faculty we worked with in the same kinds of ways.

**Final Musings for Mentors**

I've learned much about mentors and mentoring in the 20 years since I left Indiana, a good deal of it during the year I spent working with Dave, Bill, and Dorothy again back at the branch campus where I'd been a master's student. But the experiences that are recounted above are the ones that really shaped the notion of the mentoring relationship that still guides my thinking about working with colleagues and students.

At its best, the mentor-mentored relationship is mutualistic (Patterson & Stansell, 1984). Although one person may initially approach the other in search of something valued–advice, support, or help with a problem–it is when each is aware of having something of value to offer, and when each is also aware of needing the other's contributions, that the relationship becomes most helpful and empowering to both.

This kind of relationship is also transactional, rather than interactional (Rosenblatt, 1969, 1978, 1985). The individual circles of one become linked, part of a new and larger circle, rather than just caroming off each other, affected but essentially unchanged. Framing the mentoring relationship in transactional terms also echoes a phenomenon of mutualism. When organisms such as an alga and a fungus grow together for mutual support, they form a new organism, a lichen, which differs from both original organisms. And since mentoring relationships are often established across lines of power and status–between teachers and students, between senior and junior colleagues, between those in any sector of life who exercise power and those upon whom power is exercised–it is when those relationships become mutualistic and transactional that the lines delineating our places in the hierarchy, as well as the hierarchy itself, can be called into question.

But these relationships are not easy to establish. At minimum, they require of those who would be mentors a genuine conviction that those who may seek them out also have valuable things to offer, insights and understandings that the prospective mentor needs. They require as well the mentor's inclination to challenge not just the abstract notion of hierarchy but one's own privileged place in a particular hierarchy. And there is much in the experience of those who may be sought as mentors that tends to suggest their place in the hierarchy as the rightful, well-deserved one. I remember Kay, my first doctoral advisee, bringing these points home to me in a way I could not ignore. At the time, I'd recently been promoted to associate professor and tenured, and was far more full of myself than I realized. After listening to me pontificate one day about how she and I were colleagues, she looked across the table and said, "You know, you talk a better game of that than you play." Surprised, I asked what I'd done that led her to think that, and she told me. After hearing a list of particulars that undeniably reflected a consistent pattern, I realized I had some soul searching to do. More than ten years later, I doubt that I or anyone else ever completely outgrows that need to examine ourselves and bring our actions into line with what we claim to believe.

These relationships also call for qualities among those who seek the help of a mentor. They must at least be capable of seeing value in their abilities and insights, and of viewing both the hierarchy itself and their niche within it as something other than natural and inevitable. Yet experience disempowers some people so completely that it's hard to imagine a set of circumstances that would convince them of their competence and worth.

There's an old story about a pretty thoroughly downtrodden fellow who left the room at the conclusion of his final defense, whereupon the committee quickly agreed not only to award the degree but also that his dissertation was a fine piece of work. But when the committee chair went into the hall to find and congratulate him, he was nowhere to be found. After a frantic search, the chair found the student cleaning out his desk, and, in exasperation, asked what on earth he was doing. The student answered that since he'd just flunked his defense, he thought he'd better move out. "Oh, no, you're wrong!" said the chair. "You didn't flunk. In fact, we all think you did a fine study and we want to congratulate you on it!" The student look at his Chair in disbelief, and said, "And to think I respected *your* judgment!"

Over the years, I've known some students like him. Some are undergraduates, some are working toward the master's degree, and some are doctoral candidates nearing completion of their work. I've also known a couple of faculty colleagues like him. They will not be easily invited into a mutualistic, transactive mentoring relationship.

Knowing that such people exist, and that establishing a mutualistic, transactional relationship is always challenging, it can be tempting to settle for mentoring relationships that demand less of all concerned, even though they also offer less. There are, to be sure, some benefits that result from other kinds of mentoring relationships. My relationship with John as his student teacher is but one example of how an essentially empowering situation can result despite the absence of deeper, transformative connections. Yet in their absence the kind of growth I and others experienced at Indiana would not have happened. Nor would the growth among members of the group whose writings comprise this book have ever happened. Our individual circles of one would not have joined together in a larger circle across lines of gender, rank, and experience, wherein all parties needed and were enriched by the stories and questions of all others. Our experience together, as well as those earlier ones of mine, highlight for me the key features of those mentoring relationships that are pedagogies of possibility (Simon, 1987). And they point, not just to what *might* be, but to what we now know *can* be.

# Chapter 9

## Post-Sharkdom: An Alternative Form of Mentoring for Teacher Educators

### Carol A. Mullen

Doctoral students need to be socialized to see themselves as mentoring figures and to be assisted in their growth in this professional direction. Too few thesis supervisors guide their dissertation candidates beyond the work of an acceptable research study. More than a dissertation needs to be completed if graduate student-researchers are to become faculty members. In a paper (Kealy & Mullen, 1996) that studied characteristics common to highly productive and mutually rewarding supervisor-thesis student relationships, we investigated the following:

1. joint participation of activities,
2. activities related to real-world goals,
3. value of participating in a unique or defined culture, and
4. construction of mentor image for those who are mentored.

In this chapter I explore the value I place on the construction of a mentor image or identity. I ask, "What is the interest of academia or teacher educators in helping to mentor student educator-researchers?" Mentors who assist their dissertation candidates to understand themselves as beginning mentors are potentially making a significant contribution to the profession. Teacher educator-researchers or supervisors who write about their own journey and practice of research display the potential for functioning as genuine collaborators. Those who promote quality relationship and mutual development by sharing their research stories take responsibility for engaging in a common quest of knowledge with their thesis students. A portfolio of writing can be generated by supervisor and thesis student as a form of not only coauthorship but also comentorship. With my former dissertation mentor, the metaphor of being "roped together" was used to both theorize and demonstrate current examples of such practice. The developmental phases of our comentorship provided the context for this discovery (Diamond & Mullen, 1997).

## Forming Comentoring Relationships in a Sharkdom World

My comentor/former thesis supervisor and I reflected on each other's research experiences through writing and by producing interconnected conversational narratives. We had begun our professional development journey together not as cowriters or even as supervisor and student, but as a knowing participant in each other's personal and professional lives. We gained trust by providing mutually shared glimpses into one another's real struggles to build meaningful relationships both inside and outside the university context. We often analyzed human interaction, research development, and promising directions within graduate school and higher education. Through this process of learning about one another, we carried on as research associates, sharing bits and pieces of our own literary writings on education. We took each other's constructive feedback very seriously. And we grew to appreciate one another's world-view and to contribute insights on issues of power and knowledge that afforded opportunities to better understand oppressive circumstances and conditions in the academy and in prisons. We both celebrated a liberatory praxis and spirit that turned us to discover new connections within cross-cultural contexts using, as reflective tools, educational story, self-narrative, literature, and metaphor.

Through conversation, cowriting, and playing off generative metaphors (as of imprisoned selves and of butterflies emerging), we fed each other's desire to understand and practice innovative forms of qualitative research. Through the aesthetic process of helping to share new combinations in each other's reflective accounts, we developed an educational approach to the concept of duography. We defined *duography* (for original source, see Gergen & Gergen, 1993) as a collaborative form of self-narrative in which two individuals reflect on how each other has contributed new understanding to a selection of events and ideas taken from their lives. Unlike an autobiography or a biography, a duography features writing and response in order to produce a dialogue and, eventually, a narrative form of relationship. Duography is well suited to comentoring forms of intellectual and friendship formation and, to what I am depicting inductively in this chapter, a post-sharkdom world. As my former supervisor and I prepared our own duography we engaged in textual conversation with other collaborating comentors, such as Mary Catherine Bateson and Gregory Bateson (Bateson & Bateson, 1987), Barone and Eisner (1995), and Connelly and Clandinin (1988, 1990).

During and subsequent to the development of my dissertation, my comentor and I wrote a series of self-analytic stories or personal narratives. These "fieldnotes" gained meaning in the extensive, sustained inquiries we came to view as our duographic practices. Themes of the importance of asserting self and voice and of struggling with authoritative discourses, often imposed on self-authoring, became revealed in our shared writing. We looked at subjugated and dominant forms of knowledge and at metaphorical and literal forms of confinement within academe and prisons. By exploring a less traditional style of inquiry, we sought to "break out" of the claustrophobia of accepted research practice.

Without my knowing it at the time, I was giving birth to the new interconnected metaphors of sharkdom and post-sharkdom. I desired to uncover the best that could come not from hierarchical relations imposed from the outside (sharkdom), but reimagined from the inside (post-sharkdom). Duographic writing is an example of a positive academic experience within a sharkdom world. Duography itself has the potential to provide creative opportunities for emerging and established teacher educator-researchers to respond with empowering energies to seemingly inflexible contexts, and to recreate these for the benefit of others. In this sense, the concept and practice of duography launch a vitality of creative patterns and alternatives needed within a sharkdom world.

Our comentorship gradually became a form and example of post-sharkdom in a place of community, intellectual growth, and wellness. We engaged in a self-study form of collaborative practice that included others as textual voices and contributing authors. We invited colleagues to cocreate and to aesthetically embrace situations sometimes fraught with interpersonal problems, institutional pressures, and a power differential that can affect the productivity, artistry, and emotional well-being of the individual (Diamond, Mullen, & Beattie, 1996; Phillips & Pugh, 1994; Salmon, 1992). However, in our work we found it easier and less threatening to consider interpersonal tensions and dynamics between and among coauthors in texts other than our own. Might this dynamic be parallel to couples who locate their own problems within the relationships of others? Nonetheless, the opportunity to have produced a number of manuscripts with my former supervisor in a context that was mutually engaging and rewarding was at the very least unusual in the academy. Professors and graduate students who would stop by our door as we worked together asked questions that revealed their surprise and, in a few cases, hidden desire for intellectual closeness in an otherwise sharkdom world.

## Developing a Robust Mentor Image or Identity

The mentor image or identity could be treated as a critical dimension of the thesis supervisor–student relationship. The effort is to help socialize emerging teacher educators to perform their own voices in a variety of institutional contexts. On a practical level, the development of a mentor identity will also assist those pursuing faculty positions to perform multiple departmental, college-wide, and institutional responsibilities. However, this dimension of practice is currently understated at best, and virtually nonexistent within traditional graduate school contexts and relationships.

In a study of teacher training, mentors extend the least amount of effort necessary in educational settings and, at best, function as caregivers or guides (Edwards, 1995). The same paradox may be at work in contexts of higher education. Within the school system mentors are responsible for fashioning the future of the teaching profession, yet benefit from maintaining the status quo and resisting change (Edwards). In other words, there may be some advantage to mentors in *not* helping to invest a mentor image for developing students. Within this scenario, teacher educators reserve their energies for other agendas and consequently monitor their individual effectiveness. In this context a picture of academia as sharkdom emerges: Academia may be a place that perpetuates isolation, competition, and abandonment at the expense of transformation for the development of the profession. What happens to the individual and the expression of selfhood in this scenario?

In the attempt to metaphorically represent some of my life experiences within academia, I use layered images of sharks and associated symbols (see *Figure 5, Diver's Dream of a Post-Sharkdom Mentoring Community*). This photomontage conveys a world wherein first-hand underwater discoveries can be made about one's relationship to sharks, that is mentors, in the academic world. Read from left to right, a transformation occurs in the images. Major changes are indeed echoing throughout my personal and professional life. In the original artwork, the sharks on the left-hand side are black-and-white. They are associated with an unavoidable stare (see eyes in triplicate) that penetrates nets or walls. While permitting their own freedom, they restrict that of the diver/student. Also in the original but on the right-hand side of the collage, the sharks are in color. Just as in the artwork, the sharks have also become less stark and miniature in my own life. But then this change in perception may be expected given that I am "growing up" within these sharkdom/academic waters.

Sharks continue to represent my image of the academy as an underwater landscape steeped in problematic activity that has a grip on persons as institutionally conditioned, or at least inwardly fearful, beings. Even this association with academia as sharkdom is not static, however. Like my new university and cultural experiences, which in part integrate my earlier academic life, the images associated with sharks are sometimes even clearly inviting. How might this be? After I enter a window (leaving one academic home for another), an opportunity for new life emerges from within the depths of my collage/life-experience. I become swept away in the creative work of being an academic who has become empowered to make choices while fostering a diverse network of support. While discovering new places, persons, and contexts, I am synthesizing my past experiences in an effort to provide insight into the complexity of mentoring interactions between students and their mentors. The struggles, concerns, and frustrations associated with power and control in doctoral programs responsible for preparing teacher educators require multiple perspectives. These can become known through the liberation of personal mentoring stories. The circle of one isolates the mentored from the larger process of becoming socialized as a teacher educator-researcher.

*Figure 5. Diver's Dream of a Post-Sharkdom Mentoring Community*

The shift I seek is from *sharkdom* and its dimensions of competition, exploitation, and abandonment, to *post-sharkdom*. The latter is an alternative form of mentoring for educators and students alike. Within the world of post-sharkdom, the individualism, power, and status that shape traditional academic relationships are confronted. Communities of comentors, intent on breaking the circle of one through reeducation, might share leadership and tasks as well as dreams, fears, and truths. Self-study collaborative projects can be taken on by those who value joint human effort and the revitalization of life in academe. Such projects are ideally forged among selves without a human cost, despite institutional rules and games of sharkdom. Post-sharkdom also births a world of players who are mindful of the socialization involved in becoming shark-like within graduate school contexts.

This book project grew out of a collaborative self-study project. It has been, for me, an opportunity in part to test my own metaphoric understandings of the stresses and healing that can occur in joint work among professors and graduate students within the context of some fairly pervasive shark-like realities. As one of my graduate students confided in a taped interview, the experience of being marginalized, for example, can continue despite webbings of support for one's work and vision:

> Sometimes marginalization is a conscious choice but *I know* what I would have to do to be accepted by the majority culture at this university both in terms of graduate students and faculty members. I've chosen not to do it because it goes against everything that I believe about education and my philosophy of education. But I know exactly what to do. I know what research paradigm to choose, what methods to follow, everything. [italics reflect speaker's emphasis]

Having completed my doctorate in curriculum and teacher development in 1994 within two years, I was clear about wanting to become a professor of education. Indeed, I was driven to be where I am now as a junior faculty member within a well-established research institution. Although I had several mentors during my seven years of teaching within the technical community college setting in Canada, I nonetheless mostly benefited through my own powers of observation. I also gained from my capacity to evaluate my own professional needs and directions and to spend less time on agendas that would only benefit others. I increasingly thought of myself as a blossoming academic and published author interested in innovative perspectives on issues of teaching and research. These two tracks of teaching and studying emerged concurrently for me, and I completed my doctorate at 32 years of age–jobless while providing research services to teacher educators, hungry for a university teaching position, and ready to mentor others.

While earning my doctorate I was fully immersed in a publishing journey that placed me *at-risk* as I sought for opportunities to reflect on the internal workings of academe. In the words of a Hispanic preservice teacher who participated in my study on cultural forms of self-identity, "What makes you at-risk is your living situation, learning abilities, your teaching, and what you've been taught or not taught, not whether you are a minority" (Mullen, 1997a). During our life-history interview, this student teacher did not focus on race, ethnicity, or gender as critical aspects of her cultural identity. Rather, she elaborated on and gave attention to values, life-circumstances, and philosophies of teaching and learning. Developing educators who think critically about issues and sources of being at-risk, for example, are probably engaged in ethical forms of practice and professional development. Within the academy we need to share such robust images of mentor identity for the purpose of promoting personal voice within the context of strong mentoring relationships and frameworks.

## A Critical Incident of Being At-Risk during the Doctoral Process

During my doctoral studies in graduate school, I was essentially at-risk, despite my need to find my own way. I was also at-risk despite sometimes rewarding comentoring experiences with professors and graduate students as well as correctional professionals and prisoners. While sharing comentoring research projects with others, I functioned autonomously, mentoring myself to stay alert, focused, and productive. Not consulting with anyone, I undertook preliminary research for my dissertation in my fieldsite, a correctional setting responsible for educating prisoners. I later turned my research in corrections into a book that explores issues of education and innovative curriculum programming in jails (Mullen, 1997b). The twist is that I also address issues of "correctionalism" evident in paradigms of knowledge advanced in our field as protocols of qualitative research.

Being at-risk is being reconceptualized here, then, to embrace those who mentor themselves through their doctoral programs, research sites, and dissertations but it also needs to conversely embrace those who are so closely roped to their mentors that they are virtually unable to think or act for themselves. This scenario represents an extreme portrait of my own. It is one that I have witnessed in full operation in select pockets of a number of universities. It is also a scenario that brought together the members of our self-study group. We wanted to celebrate our comentoring webbings within and outside the group and to share these on a deeper and more sustained level. We also formed as a kind of refusal. Despite the novel forms of research and teaching that compelled us individually and that shaped our deeper relationships in a few graduate seminars, we worried about being stifled. We refused to feel suppressed by institutional voices and agendas to the point of being afraid to think or act for ourselves even though some members were rightfully fearful of consequences. And we expressed concern over what kind of impact the institution might have on our own graduate and undergraduate teaching, authorial voices, and personal relationships.

During my own doctoral studies, what I wanted and consistently demonstrated to others within the university setting and what was available in the way of support were often in conflict. It was as though my intellectual capacity was being assessed in terms strictly related to my development of the dissertation *and* my advancement of mentors' research efforts and agendas. I became committed through this process to the value of offering writing and publishing opportunities to my own graduate students. In a sense, I write alongside their course papers and dissertations, and they write alongside my own works, and somewhere in-between we produce conversational texts that reveal shared issues and concerns. Indeed, this book on mentorship is the product of just such a gesture in this direction. Currently I mentor at a distance connecting three university environments.

No one communicated how I might become a professor of education or even how they themselves had become teacher educator-researchers. I felt compelled to hear these stories, but they remain virtually untold to this day. Every now and then a cryptic hint was dropped during my doctoral study, like the time when I was discussing Catherine Bateson's (1990) book, *Composing a Life*, with a professor other than my thesis supervisor. This professor commented that Bateson had been born into a personal family lineage of higher education. This context, in turn, provided her with an opportunity for developing a tacit understanding of university systems and connected life-systems. I, on the other hand, had not had this opportunity nor had I learned the critical stories of how universities function internally. If this comparison had not been made I probably would have understood the initial comment in empowering terms. I probably would have felt good about my *being there* despite my lack of academic family heritage. But was this the message–that I had very little chance of succeeding and seeing in a world in which the growth of novices depends exclusively, or even heavily, on generativity, or on providing guidance to the next generation?

Recently I read Mead's (1972) autobiographical book, *Blackberry Winter: My Early Years*. I am struck by the conspicuous role of lineage in her narration with respect to how greatly influenced Margaret Mead, Catherine Bateson's famous mother and well-known anthropologist, had been in her contact with scholarly parents and associates while growing up within an academic family environment. Consistently attributing her talent, sophistication, and vision to her family roots, she writes to the effect that she

> heard constant talk about university politics and financing, about the stratagems and ruses adopted by ambitious men, and about those who made their reputations by quoting, or almost quoting, without acknowledgment from the work of others. In some ways my upbringing was well ahead of my time–perhaps as much as two generations ahead. Mother's advanced ideas, the way in which all children in our home were treated as persons, the kinds of books I read and the way all I read was placed in historical perspective, and above all, the continuous running commentary by my family on schools, on education, on the way teachers were treated by the community, and the relationship between good schools and much-needed higher taxes. (pp. 35, 85)

As the mentoring circle of my graduate years gradually becomes larger and less thick with the passage of time and other circles come closer in contact, I am convinced that forms of discrimination can be so subtle as to be almost undetectable. The central role of the mentor is to nurture and even promote special gifts in all promising student researchers despite their family lineage, class, and ethnicity. This all-embracing mentoring activity must endure regardless of the perceived odds of the professional success of the mentored. Looking to teachers and authors as models and to my own writing as a place to recreate my past and create my own future, I became a "maker of [my own] way," or to the "way" that I have made and that has remade me as well (Freire, 1996, p. 97). Many persons of humble origin have successfully made their way through and beyond graduate school, only to inadvertently educate along the way. Such passageways through underwater landscapes are steeped in dominant ideologies of those who are deserving and undeserving to obtain a higher degree–and then to use it to mentor others.

## Questions to Ponder on Becoming a Teacher Educator-Mentor

Doctoral students are generally not taught how to become teacher educator-researchers or mentors in a chosen academic field. Nor do they typically engage in conversations about how to develop their own mentor identity or how to promote that of others. Despite the emphasis on autobiographical and biographical writing in courses and circles of academic narrative discourse, this strand or thread of life history is under-acknowledged. Why is the process of teacher educator development not a subject of concern within the literature and in our daily lives? Why is it that "no distinct line of research can be traced with respect to mentoring in academic settings" (Sands, Parson, & Duane, 1991)? Is the process of teacher educator development so obvious in its shaping influence that it is not worthy of attention? What would happen if strong mentoring networks were created to promote a robust sense of mentor identity for graduate students and beginning professors? Or, might it be that doctoral students are expected to somehow learn the academic culture, its values, and practices by trial and fire or through Bateson-like texts, or even whispering corridor talk?

A final possibility points to how graduate students, forced to discover new ways of working and functioning as teacher educators without guidance, are actually generating new approaches to their field. Could it be that institutions of higher education are tacitly doing their job? Are students left to discover how to push boundaries in rethinking established protocols and methods of research as well as their philosophical justifications and underpinnings? If so, then I need to revise my metaphor of sharkdom so that there is more "post-sharkdom," or healing and renewal, within it.

Yet another possibility exists that makes me think that some teacher educators resist passing along their experiences to those pursuing graduate study. Persons who are territorial will be protective of their intellectual line of research that claims space within journals and presses of education as well as specialized departmental units. Like a parent who competes with his or her own children, mentors may withhold key insights and important information from their dissertation candidates.

The more able the doctoral student is to seek support from those who know more, and to initiate and sustain symbiotic relationships with powerful others, the more likely will be his or her success. Indeed, graduate students' knowledge, expertise, and talents may be overlooked in favor of one's loyalties, affiliations, and hard work. Graduate students who can fend for themselves and accept abandonment as part of the experience of swimming alone while being the shark probably have a better chance of surviving in academe (Mullen & Dalton, 1996).

Although literature on the socialization process of professors of education and the graduate school context itself is slowly becoming available (e.g., Bateson, 1990; Caplan, 1994; Clandinin, Davies, Hogan, & Kennard, 1993; May, 1994; Mead, 1972), it is still scarce. Such person-situated inquiries would have been considered irrelevant to the work of teacher education and research not long ago. Today they are probably considered threatening. I received the following as forms of support, albeit infrequently, and at my own initiation: the sharing of suitable job openings, personal storytelling, cooperation in the writing of letters of reference, and participation in coauthored writings. In conversations with faculty members whose Ph.D. graduates obtain tenure-track college positions, there is emphasis on active sponsorship: the facilitation of job search, research and employment contacts, emotional and intellectual support, and strategic writing for publication. To what extent these tenure-track Ph.D.s were assisted in finding suitable positions–or learned instead on their own during the abandonment phase of their higher degrees–is a story that shifts emphasis depending on speaker and context. The key seems to involve the sustainability of the mentor-mentored relationship not as a static set of relations but as a comentoring arrangement. This narrative relationship needs to be responsive to the closeness and distance of life, its situations, demands, and changes within individuals. Personal needs and rhythms, as well as professional goals and ideological directions, also change and affect what is required of such a critical relationship (see Figure 1, in Preface, for a visual image of lifelong mentoring).

The building of crucial mentoring relationships can enable collaborative support systems to function within a world of post-sharkdom. Efforts to be collaborative in academe require that educators engage in the development of their own ethical self. Researchers in a post-sharkdom academy will need to bring forward their own educational histories, critical thinking powers, and dreams of influence in a larger community of scholars.

Andrew, a white American faculty member who is simultaneously a military leader, has sustained for a decade a comentoring relationship with his major professor. When I asked him about the quality of vision that sustains their writing relationship, he referred to shared goals, a common set of values, and an interconnected academic heritage. When I inquired about the origins of their relationship and what might be generalized from their beginnings, he emphasized the importance of oral tradition and knowing one's own story of academic heritage. During our taped conversations from 1995–1996, Andrew shared a traditional world-view of the academy that has worked for him over the years. His snapshot below represents a view of storytelling in its inextricable relationship to academic heritage. In turn, academic heritage is linked to those efforts at creating a research organization of academic communities that can have an impact on society through history:

> Although research organizations in university departments can serve a mentoring function, they have the potential to do much more. The larger view is that such organizations themselves can serve as parts of a larger organizational framework that allow groups of scholars to bridge gaps of distance and time. Such an organization of research organizations has the capacity to be aligned along a common set of values and shared heritage. Where this often starts is with legend and narrative. In the fashion of an oral tradition, for example, a professor may tell a story of an academic lineage that began with the founder of a particular school of thought. This person would have disciples and they in turn would have disciples, and so on, leading up to the person telling the story. It doesn't take too much to deduce that if the newcomer, in turn, becomes a part of this person's lineage, the student will become connected to an academic heritage.

### Looking Back on My Story of Becoming

The process of becoming a teacher educator is unlike the process of becoming a school teacher, or any other type of professional for that matter. Although it can be argued that both forms of teacher development take place within a mostly traditional, competitive, and individualistic context, no systematic or dependable mentoring network exists for teacher educator-researchers. If one is fortunate, the thesis supervisor will perform an authentic mentoring function, caring about the holistic well-being of the dissertation candidate.

Given inadequate support for their professional goals and dreams, graduate students may be functioning within a larger picture that escapes attention. For those mentors who themselves had unhappy or even traumatic dissertation experiences and who developed unhelpful pedagogic styles (Miezitis, 1994), a greater force is at work in the socialization of the graduate student. Yet, doctoral students do learn to survive not only as teacher educators but also as caring persons. Given pressures and constraints such as these, how do doctoral students become caring professors of education? Without direct, consistent, and favorable leadership within the graduate school context, doctoral students often struggle on their own—or learn to chum with trusted others.

## Studying Mentors and Mentoring Prospects to Guide Development

The term post-sharkdom may beg further narrative clarification, as does its predecessor, sharkdom. While writing my dissertation, I often inquired about the series of steps that one can adapt in preparing to enter the professoriate. I also studied those everyday practices and ongoing writings of my colleagues and mentors in order to learn how our personal voices and insights could blend and function in coauthored writings. I wanted to understand the responsibilities and commitments of professors, especially in a world of reform. Universities, or at least some university researchers, were beginning to work within the context of multicultural/liberatory practices in education. My own role is geared toward helping to expose and modify the gap between institutional voices and voices of diversity.

As I shared with mentors my stories of survival within academe and in my personal life, I learned some of their habits of work and methods of research. I also became a passionate researcher and was surprised to learn the extent to which my professorial colleagues were themselves participating in a choreography of becoming shark-like. The saving grace was that this process was painful for some, especially for those who preferred self-isolation over political immersion. Nonetheless, except for junior faculty, most of the others were politically astute in the sense that they knew how to appear relaxed, pleasant, and open within their respective educational communities, while actually being in a state of "ever-alert scrutiny" (Rosen, 1986). Sharks, too, sleep with their eyes open and can appear limp in divers' hands or even "on board" ships just before springing to life (Lawrence, 1985).

Despite my hard-won insights, blocked in part by my own junior faculty status, the process of learning to dance with sharks is implicit, if not mysterious and even secretive. Like sharks, "professors are territorial, fighting to maintain paradigmatic boundaries, circles of graduate students/teachers, and specialized departmental units" (Mullen & Dalton, 1996, p. 59). Socialization processes can restrict and even incarcerate the writing and vision of professors and graduate students taught to replicate *what is*. *What is* is defined, for example, as seemingly innocuous "intellectual structures of disciplines and methods of pedagogy" (Grumet, 1988, p. 100).

Throughout these chapters on educators' lives and writings, we each attempt to redefine mentorship and to situate its meta-socialization processes in our own writings and lives. As indicated earlier, sharkdom is about the process of becoming shark-like and politically astute within academia. Post-sharkdom invites a reconceptualization of mentorship that is constantly vigilant of institutional and interpersonal dynamics. Post-sharkdom is also a world wherein ugly transformations may be seen to unfold as people force new ways of being not close to their own minds and hearts. On a brighter side, post-sharkdom also values constructive efforts to learn and share in community with trusted friends. Our work as colearners on this book project has contributed to breaking the circle of one that isolates each of us to varying degrees, and at different times. In my role as a visiting professor from Canada, this breaking of the circle of one has been a profound experience for me. Although I am engaged in daily situations of comentoring graduate and undergraduate students, I am only beginning the journey of proving my worth as a valuable faculty member.

As I prepared during my doctoral studies for the long and difficult journey of becoming a professor of education, I searched for mentoring prospects that would guide my development. I sometimes displayed (and still do) the qualities of "mechanical efficiency" and "single-mindedness" (Copps, 1976, p. 19) of sharks in the sense that I am driven to produce according to timelines and with predictable precision. I, nonetheless, still needed nurturance, which included mutual forms of emotional and intellectual support and respect for personal voice, work habits, and interpersonal styles. I was told by my mentors that I worked hard at trying to create relationships of nurturance. Even before I began my doctoral program, I had published a paper based on my master's thesis. It took into account how I was being mentored through close collegial connections that had been formed within a unit to study narrative inquiry approaches to teachers' biographies and students' voices and images (Mullen, 1994).

As I undertook the work of my doctoral program, I attempted to create a writing and publishing network with at least five comentoring colleagues. To varying degrees, these micro-networks have been successful in that manuscripts written and revised have either been published or are in review. I often wonder what remains of the human heart after such intensive explorations that can and do place stress on working relationships. Nonetheless, I had been socialized to believe that publication in refereed journals was the ultimate credential that would help me to secure a university teaching position and then tenure. Realizing that being a prolific writer and committed fieldsite researcher was not enough, I looked eagerly for strategies that would lead to the publication of my writing. I produced the initial drafts of a series of coauthored papers, quickly picked up on and extended invitations to share in writing ventures, and, typically with female academics, negotiated every word side-by-side for days and months. I shared (auto)biographical research inquiries into the multicultural literacy contexts of jails with an educator who was doing the same but in inner-city schools (Feuerverger & Mullen, 1995). With male and female academics, I also studied graduate school contexts that have the capacity both to nurture (Kealy & Mullen, 1996) and exploit (Mullen & Dalton, 1996) the professional and personal growth of educators and students.

I have struggled with academics to find innovative ways to represent our collaborative relationships and the qualities of partnership. Lives inevitably become entangled in the act of sharing critical incidents that sometimes engage the "underbelly of the shark." Taking risks also encourages fuller and richer discovery of another's cultural identity, authorship, and worth. This form of coauthorship has proven most beneficial to my own intellectual development because it is laden with emotional sharing and professional support. However, the drawback for me has sometimes been a kind of tension that develops when I take more responsibility for regulating and researching a writing project and schedule, pushing a manuscript to completion.

Papers prepared for publication typically require much more attention to detail than manuscripts prepared for conference presentation. This additional effort requires a careful demonstration of the concepts under study, greater awareness of the implications of the research, sensitivity to the particular philosophies of educational journals, attention to the most appropriate place(s) for one's writing, knowledge of relevant bodies of study and one's own situatedness, and technical knowledge and editorial skill. Dissertation writers need to learn these dimensions of publication, but if their efforts and writings comprise the majority of the work, then they should be given first authorship. Otherwise they will be socialized to believe that power and status are the ultimate shaping forces in determining authorship and voice within academic publication. The final stages of writing can prove critical and even transformative as new horizons of thought spontaneously emerge. Well-developed ideas configure differently and more powerfully as one's writing life reveals undercurrents of new insight. This is a special time for coauthors to influence one another and to recreate paradigms of knowledge.

## Building Crucial Mentoring Relationships to Facilitate Success

In order to break the circle of one that potentially engulfs and stifles dissertation candidates, mentors will need to assist them in building crucial mentoring relationships to facilitate success. Mentors can begin simply by using written and oral exercises to expose a student's goals, needs, perspectives, and issues. Mentors can also benefit by recognizing the strengths of graduate students in anticipation of dynamic and caring interchanges. In this way, spheres of mutual influence can be built over time and comentorship eventually established. For example, doctoral students who are especially keen are typically well read and have working knowledge of multiple bodies of literature. For this reason, such students may have developed a sensibility that underscores unique educational perspectives and approaches to problems of research design and method.

I have discovered that, without exception, graduate students become empowered when encouraged to combine their passion for knowledge with personal voice and authorship. Not without struggle, frustration, and even pain, my students write regularly in a spirit of discovery as a form of self-study and shared educational practice. As comentor, I guide student-researchers and colleagues within micro-sociocultural contexts wherein their own life-experiences can be metaphorically interpreted and built into the design of a project and vision. In this way, when imaginations and passions are engaged (or enraged), efforts will often follow, having an impact, for example, on one's circle of graduate students, who often have students and/or children of their own. Such an impact has the potential to subsequently make a difference in paradigms of correctionalism that promote a view of personal voice and experience as anecdotal, irrelevant, or even silly.

The mentoring philosophy I have absorbed as a graduate student promotes a narrative view of the individual as a maker of meaning in schooling contexts. This philosophy of self underscores the value of sharing and constructing meaning in educational communities. To simply generate meaning, however, is not enough. A philosophy of self in community needs to account for whose meaning is being encouraged, endorsed, and validated. The process of generating meaning needs to be examined as well as perceptions of the process. Any discrepancies between espoused and actual processes will need to be discussed, which may benefit reflections on communal forms of discourse and negotiation of meaning. Finally, the representation of particular voices and not others will need to be considered in relation to the writers' moral views and sociocultural orientations.

What I am building to here is the hard-won insight that doctoral students represent an at-risk population. Completion rates are approximately 50% as it is (Hunt, 1994), and fewer (even the national statistics on how many are vague) obtain employment in their areas of specialization. How many mentors understand the real issues involved in their students struggling with, or even dropping out of, higher education programs? To what extent might the circle of one–of isolation, competition, and abandonment–be a culprit in this picture? Female graduate students and professors are generally very skillful at developing collegial connections but struggle to "build the crucial mentoring relationships that facilitate professional success" (Keyton & Kalbfleisch, 1993, p. 1). However, when we do attempt to build networks, our actions may be perceived by those who choose not to join as threatening the status quo. We female academics do not have a long history of having grown up within academe and of having developed solid networking capabilities. Beginning teacher educator-researchers may feel isolated even while attempting effective and sensitive forms of mentorship within a "chilly climate" associated, in part, with harassment and a general lack of caring (Saunders, 1995). An alternative is to engage in post-sharkdom formations of community, with the intent to improve a broader set of relations. Here the three-strand braid within our mentoring model (see Figure 1) is fully operationalized as multiple mentoring figures interact, acknowledging and sharing each other's personal and cultural stories and participating in each other's daily work through a unified project. But even these groupings may inadvertently promote experiences of alienation from the majority culture and, hence, unanticipated transitions to new communities and places.

Resourceful and determined, my young "Hispanic" (a self-referential term) preservice teacher-participants search for mentoring opportunities that are aligned with their community building efforts. Maria, for example, has found ways to mentor herself within community and in light of a virtual absence of sponsorship available at her university:

> Through the National Hispanic Institute [NHI] I've been taught that if you want something to happen, and if it's not there, you have to make it happen and you have to create it yourself. It's a hard and long process, but eventually it will come about with the help of others, with your contacts, through networking by meeting people, through getting your education [by] going to graduate school, and going back to your community. Then the children who are growing will have that there for them, and it won't be as hard as it was for you. (interview in Mullen 1997a)

Isabella experienced a critical moment of seeing herself through the eyes of two students while substituting in an elementary school. This brief exchange inspired her to want to build school community as a Hispanic role model while contributing to her own professional dreams:

> I'll tell you this story. I went into substituting at [name of school]. I listen to the kids when they're not talking to me a lot just to hear what's going on in their life. What really struck me one time was I had these two Hispanic girls walking around and they said something about me. They looked at me and said, 'You're our teacher?' I said, 'Yes, I'm going to sub today.' I told them to look at the board. As they walked off they said, 'We never had a Hispanic teacher before.' That just hit me. I mean, they might never have thought that I can be a teacher because they've never seen an Hispanic before. That really hit me right there too to think that these kids don't know how far they can go if they never see it or they're never told anything. Like my Mom I just have this thing. Be the best you can be wherever you are. If the school system is my program, then I want to keep progressing as teacher, vice-principal, principal, and then superintendent. Just keep going and make the best of it. I guess that goes back to my Mom and how she brought me up but when I heard those two little girls, I just knew, 'Wow, I've arrived and I'm here.' (interview data, Texas A&M University, 8 February 1996, cassette recording)

Universities will need to better understand the mentoring situations and aspirations of undergraduate and graduate students and teachers in order to strengthen programs of study. In the context of my former graduate school as student, some of the teacher educators had more knowledge than myself about the process of publication and which journals were most appropriate for our manuscript submissions. Why this knowledge was made scarce, I do not know. Nonetheless, like Maria, my student-participant, I too "want[ed] to make something happen" and so I "create[d] it myself" only to learn that it is a "hard and long process" that does, ironically, "eventually come about with the help of others" through making contacts, networking, and giving back. I developed a passion for researching the journals, sharing information, and making decisions that paved my coauthorships and wider connections and communications. I learned to manage upwards.

Graduate students chum through the need to develop not only their course papers and dissertations but also their writings for publication. The more ambitious students (other qualifying descriptions also come to mind) often contribute the data, information, and even insights in order to experience being sponsored by an established academic. Their own research sites may even provide the context for advancing coauthored studies as well as generating new or reconstructed knowledge in the field. It is as though the implicit learning for understanding the dynamics of publishing within the graduate school context is knowing how to "chum" with the best.

Chumming is also a force within post-sharkdom for graduate students and professors who question systemic inequities and exploitative forms of research and practice. Within our own circle of writers, some of us took turns during the self-study phase of meeting to initiate leadership and tasks related to ways of connecting and defining our focus. Such initiation takes time perhaps because it is key to sharing power and to tackling/dissolving/transforming hierarchical academic structures. As I see it, we are struggling to build an authentic community within academia while countering our own shark training.

We made a commitment in our group to elicit personally lived stories of mentorship from one another, and to provide support during this process. I attempted to monitor my own tendency, through this context, to jump to abstraction in order to protect the identity of others and to ensure my survival within academia. I worry about repercussions of offering a picture of what is involved in surviving within higher education or in learning to dance with sharks. I was told to worry several years ago by a self-isolated tenured professor whose opinion I very much value but whose dispassionate engagement in research and community sent a conflicting message. Might I be vulnerable whenever I write personally about conditions that place developing academics and their perspectives, or conditions of work, at-risk?

## Breaking the Circle of One through Inviting Voices of Reform

The concept of being "at-risk" can be broadened to include unchallenged academic perspectives that potentially marginalize groups of people. In my research with Hispanic preservice teachers (Mullen, 1997a), I engaged their special meanings of mentorship in a larger effort to hear their voices and stories about participation in a traditional academic culture. My Hispanic participants function as developing mentoring figures within cultural and minority-based organizations; within their extended families; and on behalf of junior-level college students for whom there is no (or very little) formal mentorship available for them. With knowledge of their mentoring influences and experiences gained through life history interviews and self-identity portfolios, I hear my own voice about issues of being at-risk differently.

My participants are at-risk because they represent a minority culture for which there exists a 50% high school drop-out rate and almost no lineage or record of academic success within European-American (white) school environments. Currently, a disproportionately large number of Hispanic students also fail undergraduate and graduate programs of education (Dilworth, 1992). Hence, a pressing statewide and national concern is to "change the high proportions of failure among students from diverse racial, ethnic, and socioeconomic backgrounds" (Winfield & Manning, 1992). I, nonetheless, withhold the label of "at-risk" for the sake of argument but mostly for perspective-building. Norma, one of my preservice teacher-participants, strongly feels that labels are judgmental and that they undermine the success and leadership of individuals.

'At-risk' is a very strong term. 'At-risk' is a big label. This is coming from the educational point of view. As far as I'm concerned, if I have a student in class and I tell him he is at-risk that child is not going to learn anymore because he's thinking, 'I'm at-risk.' It's the same thing as if you tell him, 'You're emotionally disturbed.' It's really hard because there are those kids that I would consider

at-risk. Those kids that don't have anything to eat at night or they don't know
when they are going to get to eat. You need to show them that there is something
else. As a child, for instance, I came from a single parent home, but I was never
in a school where it was a regular thing to get shot or to find guns. At-risk cannot •
be so broad. It can't be like all minorities are at-risk because that's not true. We
don't know every circumstance. Kids are at-risk of quitting [school] if they don't
want to learn about pronouns or anything because they haven't eaten, or slept, or
they don't know if they are going to be there the next day. (interview data, Texas
A&M University, 13 February 1996, cassette recording)

Hispanic preservice teachers are struggling to develop positive images
of themselves against such single-minded cultural representations. The
very term "at-risk" can literally put at-risk persons who struggle to make
a difference for themselves and for others.

As a further point of criticism, the very term "at-risk" can literally
place at a disadvantage those Hispanic preservice students who have
inherited a national mindset. My 11 participants each illustrated their
involvement in extracurricular activities on a mentoring scale that
enables them to guide themselves and others. They want to achieve
beyond their scholastic goals in an effort to make a difference for the
teaching profession. The point is that a network of prevailing beliefs
substantiated by statistics potentially reinforces the very conditions that
place such persons at-risk. New understandings of minority identities or
of the changing needs and situations of future minority teachers is
therefore needed.

A new, transformative language represents students and teacher
educator-researchers as cultural resources whose lived experiences,
commitments, and dreams offer insights into more advanced forms of
mentorship. As exclaimed in conversation by an African-American male
executive in a corporate context, we as a society are prevented from
mentoring successfully unless we consider the whole human system and
being. Words like minority, he added, beg the question, "In what
context?," preventing us from communicating across cultures. A
transformative language celebrates holistic life-systems and underscores
how my focus is "not on management but on what it means to educate
people capable of a vision, people who can rewrite the narrative of
educational administration and the story of leadership by developing a
public philosophy capable of animating a democratic society" (Giroux,
1993, p. 12). The commitment to develop a robust mentor identity in
students, teachers, and researchers can help shape this new story of
leadership. The effort, then, is to ensure that "no student [including at

the graduate level] should leave any classroom [understood literally and metaphorically] unchanged without the empowerment to rewrite his or her own life [and the lives of other imprisoned selves] in even a subtly different way" (Steinberg, 1995, p. 66).

Just as I see the potential to set some conditions for reform within graduate schools through personal storytelling and in breaking the circle of one, I am aware that my own description of doctoral students and preservice teachers as "at-risk" requires careful consideration and new stories or old stories rewritten. Nonetheless, by breaking the circle of one, the very conditions that typically isolate individuals can be openly questioned.

**New Stories of Mentorship within Life Systems**

Persons in authority can enable the teaching profession within schools and universities by encouraging students to develop an image of themselves as mentors. To this end, my studies of the doctoral process and Hispanic college students suggest that a strong mentoring network within colleges would benefit the adaptation of the mentored to university and school systems. Rather than leaving the critical socialization process of how one becomes a teacher educator implicit, universities can support the construction of strong mentoring networks. Thesis supervisors and course instructors can include mentor images and identity in their work on autobiographical and curricular theory and personal practical knowledge construction. Doctoral students who teach their thesis supervisors are seeking broader alternatives to traditional supervisory practices within graduate school contexts. Hispanic preservice teachers who participate in mentoring structures and relationships are setting high standards for themselves. They are searching for a foothold in an academic world that views them as at-risk of failure. Yet, my Hispanic participants perform mentoring functions in excess of academic loads.

Doctoral students can also be assisted in achieving their community-oriented goals and dreams of leadership through a strong mentoring framework. If the socialization process of doctoral study had been made explicit to me, I would have better understood the traditional, competitive, and individualistic context that underscored my education. I would have understood the role of power in determining, for example, the order of first, second, and third authorship on manuscripts submitted for publication. I could have then better prepared for and negotiated the discrepancy that is sometimes the case in the work actually carried out by all participating parties. I would have also better understood the need for a collaborative, action-oriented research environment that addresses such imbalances through positive and supportive mentoring relationships.

"Post-sharkdom" is an original term intended to capture the importance of emergent teacher educators learning to dance or survive with sharks. The concept of "sharkdom" was developed in conjunction with my colleague, Jane Dalton. It was revisited and elaborated here in the context of mentorship. While a recasting of graduate school as sharkdom might encourage wider efforts to reform graduate school internally, the work of authentic collaboration and community-building requires careful nurturance. Teaching and research that focus on metaphoric ways of engaging in discovery writing, creative expression, and interpersonal connection can promote emancipatory forms of life in a post-sharkdom world.

The name for those stories that promote the centrality of Native-American women's role in nature, and within life systems and their own tribes, is *yellow women's stories* (Allen, 1986). Yellow women's stories concern cultural self-identity issues; they are located within parables and rituals of self-empowerment. Why yellow? Because the women in the Keres tribe paint their faces during rituals so that they can enact stories about being recognized as women at the gate into the afterlife. They want to be recognized as such given the high value placed on women and their contributions within matriarchal societies. To wear the color of who we want to be and where we are going spiritually is a creative approach to a sharkdom world and to forming new connections within it. Perhaps we can all strive to be like those Native-American women who are associated with being able to create and transform, abilities that do not always involve smooth transitions in people's lives or the wider society.

Yellow women's stories celebrate how being different or how difference itself can contribute balancing elements to society (Allen, 1986). Paula Gunn Allen's "Thought Women" is the maker of creation and the hand that makes, guides, and counsels, and also welcomes home. Like Thought Woman, my Hispanic teacher-participants consistently projected images of themselves as other than at-risk. Go-getters who are committed to professional development, community activism, and mentorship of the young, each of these students refused to accept the label of "at-risk." They discussed how those in power do not know how to enter into their inner circles yet represent them as academically "at-risk" or "not at-risk," as though these two categories inherently make good sense. Terms such as "at-risk," "prejudice," "minority," and "broken home" are promoted on the outside of their inner circles. The implication is that one needs to find a way in.

One of my Hispanic graduate students, who is a mother in her fifties, referred to an image of circles as representing her cultural experience. While I conducted the series of interviews with the preservice teachers, I used this image as a template for feedback. Each one endorsed her personal relevance of this image in terms of cultural adjustment, including values, closeness, comfort, and language. Juanita, who was most articulate about this process, included these elements, some of which are evident from our exchange below. After I described the inner and outer circle, Juanita considered the role of her persona in the world and the effort of trying to keep it consistent.

*Carol:* In my class last term I had an Hispanic student in it who has the idea of an inside circle and an outside circle. As I understand it, the inside circle has one set of values and it is a place where she feels very comfortable and true to herself and her domestic family. Then there exists the outside circle which includes [this university] and which involves cultural adjustment even though she has been here for a number of years. She experiences, on the outside circle, a different language, way of being, and set of cultural standards for herself and expectations by others. It is as though she becomes, to a degree, a different person, maybe less herself, but at the same time a different self is growing through that experience.

I also got the impression from her portfolio and our conversations that there were circles within circles. Within the family, core members represent the very tightest circle yet they embrace relatives beyond their own immediate selves. Indeed, there are many, sometimes seemingly countless, people who belong to that core family. The small, tight family circle is in actuality a very large circle consisting of shadow coils not immediately visible to an outsider. These shadow coils represent the overlapping communities and influences through storytelling, family trips, and mentoring opportunities. Does the idea of the circle work for you? Or, is there a different metaphor that comes to mind when you think of who you are and your daily academic life, needs, and concerns?

*Juanita:* I think a circle is a very good metaphor. My family is an inner circle because that's closest to me and will always be closest to me. And the outer circle including [this university] and my friends and the everyday things that I have to go through are circling around that. I do have to change a little bit. But I try not to because I believe that people will look at you and see you the way that they want to see you. Whatever kind of persona that I give off is how you are going to see me. So I try and keep that consistent and I try and be as open and as thoughtful as I can be with any person. If there is a person who has a certain idea of how I am going to be before even talking to me or even meeting me and getting to know me, I think that person, unless they're willing to change their opinion, I think they are always going to have that in their head and I see that as being very close-minded. There is nothing I can do about it. I can't change their mind unless they decide to do it for themselves and see me as the person I am. So I don't really see the point in changing the way I am or changing how I act around certain people. There is a time and place for everything, but I don't think that I would ever change my personality for anything because I've always been taught to be proud of who I am and what I am, and what I think.

Inside, I am very comfortable with my family. My family comes first in my life. I am different in my consistency with them. I think that I am a lot gentler. I forgive a lot easier with my family because they will always be my family. They will always be there for me. But with the outside circle, I've had to learn. Because I used to be that way. I used to be very forgiving. But I got walked on a lot of times. I got taken advantage of a lot of times. I had to become a stronger person with my confidence and I couldn't let anybody walk over me. That's not to say that I'm not forgiving in the outer circle. It's just that I don't put up with anybody's crap. I have to be careful because of the way I've been taught. I've been taught to care about other people before myself. (interview data, Texas A&M University, 16 January 1996, cassette recording)

As I now picture this image of circles: The outside of the circle is white and it is made of steel with faces looking straight ahead; the inside, or family home environment, is made of terra-cotta faces turned toward one another. *Figure 6, Wilda's Collage: Home is Where the Heritage Is*, features a self-identity collage created by yet another of my Hispanic preservice teacher-participants. The meta point is that professors can mentor students through cultural forms of self-expression. Wilda's artwork, writing, and interview emphasize that more positive influences need to be generated within the Hispanic community. Leadership from teachers is required to meet this goal. Using her reflections, Wilda placed "family" at the visual "center of [her] life" and self-identity collage. Around this center, family is associated with images of tradition, heritage, home, success, pride, and self-esteem.

I imagine the inside circle consisting of multiple, interlocking clay pots representing extended families and proactive mentorships. These interlocking clay pots bring to life those shadow coils contained within

*Figure 6. Wilda's Collage: Home is Where the Heritage Is*

the larger circle of *Figure 1, Mentoring as Life: A Circular Model of Education* (see preface). Like the shadow coils which live in dynamic tension with the outer circle, the clay pots convey the richness of the dense layers of mentoring stories that are often a part of educators' and students' lives. The clay pots of Juanita's story, for example, reveal her complex interaction with inner and outer worlds and a different self or persona that is growing through her experiences.

## Alternative Forms of Mentoring in a Post-Sharkdom World

My attempt in this chapter has been to consider forms of mentorship within a traditional academic culture (sharkdom) and an evolving culture of empowerment (post-sharkdom). I have also included voices of diversity that have helped me to think about metaphors of relationship and context. The very existence of sharks is harsh, and the metaphor of sharkdom connotes an experience of professional development steeped in negativity. Images of bait, feeding frenzy, chumming, training, cage, shark embryos, feed, in-womb cannibalism, and feeding inhibitor are particularly well suited to explicating issues of abandonment, competition, and productivity. I have researched the life of sharks in order to map the process of being birthed/socialized as embryonic sharks/emerging teacher educators. I have made an effort to find other ways to think about a post-sharkdom world that embrace reform efforts in the study of mentorship. To this end, I co-opted the concept of yellow women's stories from the Keres tribal tradition, briefly entertaining it as a philosophy of mentorship.

In a larger picture, the world of post-sharkdom illustrates how a life-systems approach to mentorship could create healing and lasting relationships between people and within cross-cultural communities. The *Tao Te Ching*, the ancient Chinese book of inner peace, has been interpreted by Dreher (1990) as a philosophy committed to harmony through cooperation with life cycles and the development of personal power. By claiming personal power and internal authority, individuals can learn to make a difference for the better in their own lives and for the common good. In the context of sharkdom and post-sharkdom forms of mentorship, the *Tao* attempt is to transform relationships of conflict into "a new synthesis, a new cycle of peace" (Dreher, 1990, p. 236).

Norma, a Hispanic preservice teacher-participant, can be imagined in her efforts as guided by the philosophies of Taoism and yellow women's stories. She desires to stimulate creativity and to free individuals from stereotypes that promote inbalances in power and authority. Norma understands that, for example, unreflective and judgmental systems of meaning entangled in such words as minority, prejudice, at-risk, and broken home categorize individuals, limiting potential and even worth: "There has to be real empathy in defining these words instead of having a teacher chalk in a definition on a board or students write it down in their notebooks. We have to get at the feelings behind the words."

Norma's views on stereotypical notions of being at-risk locate deficiencies not within students but within the perceptions of those in authority and in their uses of power. If it is the case that "we have to get at the feelings behind the words," and I think it is, then mentors can use this strategy to enter into students' inner circles and life-circumstances. We can encourage a robust mentor image in our students by taking Norma's advice, which involves risking exposure and aiming to make a difference. By doing so, we help to care for those deeper and wider life-systems that are called into play within those mentoring relationships that resemble cycles of growth over time.

Faculty members who mentor one another could tell us a great deal about the socialization process and its relationship to life-systems within academe. The work of faculty mentoring faculty (Sands, Parson, & Duane, 1991) is implicit and under-acknowledged as a worthwhile topic of research. In my new university contexts I have not yet sought out the guidance or energies of any particular mentor. I prefer to learn from the range of human qualities, scholastic writing, philosophical orientations, and programmatic efforts that others reveal in fragments to me in their work, research, and interactions.

Margaret Mead (Mary Catherine's mother) and Gregory Bateson have been captured at work in a village in a famous photograph wherein they face each other from behind separate typewriters while attending to their fieldnotes (Clifford, 1990). This photograph (on the cover of *Fieldnotes*, 1990) reminds me of comentorships and coauthorships that demand closeness in the act of creating text. What might be an image for those of us who also work with multiple writers across distances and even countries? The sense of field and narrative relationship is no longer tightly defined or circumscribed. My own "snapshot" features a community of educator-writers using multiple tools of reflection to engage in a mutual purpose of inquiry. This chapter celebrates self in community, realized differently as a post-sharkdom world wherein the making and remaking of life-systems are intended to support human voice, endeavor, cultural identity, and artistry.

I am committed to a view and process of mentoring as an extended family that welcomes newly abandoned sharks and those without academic heritage or rank. Mentoring in a post-sharkdom world does not celebrate the notion that a fierce, combative struggle is needed to resolve interpersonal tensions or to improve relationships. In a post-sharkdom world, hope is manifested in practice as the mentor/mentored pair or community of comentoring selves "unveil[s] opportunities for hope, no matter what the obtacles may be. ... Hence the need for a kind of education in hope [and the realization of] hope as an ontological need" (Freire, 1996, p. 9) to be expressed in live and imagined situations. Some faculty and graduate students reveal to me their willingness to risk exposure in order to better understand the mentoring process for themselves and to improve the experience for others. Represented by the stories of educator-writers in this book, hope is made visible in repeated cycles of closeness and distance within the long, learning journey of mentorship in our lives. I am inspired by the prospects.

## Acknowledgments

I wish to thank those students, researchers, and professors who have contributed to my metaphoric examinations of higher education. Their voices have certainly made the difference in helping me to communicate my ideas. By sharing their inspiring stories of academic mentorship, all of the contributors to this book have participated in breaking my circle of one. The Hispanic students who have contributed to this process have been anonymously referred to throughout this chapter.

The cultural study of Hispanic preservice teacher identity was carried out with the support of a Sid Richardson Foundation/Southwestern Bell Telephone foundations grant.

# Chapter 10

# Full Circle: Insights on Mentoring from My Mentor's Heroes

## William A. Kealy

> Bill: You are so right about my own style of leadership in academe. I try to practice the traits that serve successful military leaders so well. I long ago decided that leadership is a matter of personal example and dedication. Graduate students work hard, but I work harder. Ray (February 17, 1995)

Back in graduate school my major professor remarked many times that there are two primary activities in which successful academics should engage themselves: increasing the knowledge base of their discipline and preparing new members for their discipline. Accordingly, research and publishing are activities that typically surround the former task, whereas teaching and mentoring are associated with the latter. More recently, a further distinction between teaching and mentoring has come to mind: the outcome of teaching is student acquisition of a pool of knowledge while, in the case of mentorship, that pool is deepened through the experience of seeing it through the eyes of one's mentor.

As I ponder the influence of my former doctoral advisor on my graduate studies, it seems that part of the mentoring experience entails a willingness to not just know but to *understand* a discipline from the philosophical and personal perspective of one's mentor. In the case of higher education, this enculturation results in a different understanding of a subject than what one would have gained from classroom instruction. Possibly this is because professors, in their role as mentors, have less obligation to represent their discipline objectively than when in their role as classroom lecturers.

In addition to being aware of the bias of one's mentor toward the discipline, one may sometimes also gain an insight into what experiences and inspirations shaped this philosophical stance. This might happen, for example, through the shared stories of the mentor's own life as a mentored graduate student. On even rarer instances, one may have a glimpse of the core beliefs of one's mentor on what qualities contribute to successful mentorship. What were the sources of inspiration that led my major professor to be a great mentor? Eventually I discovered the answers to this question, but not until long after I was enculturated, graduated, and situated in a university job with students of my own.

### Retrospectives: My Tour of Duty in *II Corps*

About one year after beginning my doctoral studies I became one of several *cadets* who participated in a research group that had a hierarchical structure similar to military organizations. The *commanding officer* was the professor who would eventually become my dissertation advisor and mentor. Newcomers to the research group were considered *junior officers* and assisted the more experienced graduate students in carrying out research studies. Like many rank structures, seniority was accompanied by privileges such as access to subject pools, xeroxing, and assistance in obtaining copies of journal articles from the library. On the other hand, with seniority also came the responsibility to instruct the more junior members in all facets of experimental research.

In addition to a military-like rank structure, our research organization borrowed some of the other cultural features of the armed forces. For example, we sometimes (kiddingly) addressed each other by rank; each study was initiated by an operational order sent to the division commander in charge of carrying it out, and we had a suitable name for our group—simply *II Corps*. Despite its gleanings from military culture, *II Corps* never inherited any of the trappings associated with the negative (and sometimes stereotypical) images of a military organization. There was no hazing, browbeating, or harassment of juniors by seniors. Upper ranks were held by an equal number of men and women and, most of all, *II Corps* was characterized by a spirit of cooperation, collegiality, and mutual respect. The experience was demanding, exhilarating, and sometimes even fun.

Equity was a hallmark of *II Corps*. Membership in *II Corps* was open to anyone who wanted to participate and promotion in the organization was based on research productivity, not popularity or pull. Because it was essentially a meritocracy, motivation was high in *II Corps*; it was not uncommon for each of us to be involved in several studies simultaneously. Consequently, virtually all members of *II Corps* had one or more articles in juried publications or presentations at national conferences by the time of our "discharge" at graduation, which greatly enhanced our employability.

From time to time while in *II Corps*, we would hear tales of another earlier, grander, and more successful organization initiated by our mentor during the 1970s that was known as The Laboratory for the Study of Human Intellectual Processes (or L-SHIP). More simply called *The Ship*, it was a research organization patterned entirely on naval organization and culture. At its height, *The Ship* had almost 100 members, operated almost 24 hours a day, and generated over 75 research studies. Though unfunded and largely unknown in its day by even those in the university where it operated, *The Ship* became legendary as most of its crew graduated, took university teaching jobs, and became mentors for a new generation of researchers.

Even as a graduate student I wondered about the rationale for using a military-style framework for establishing and guiding a research organization. Since I was, at the time, a lieutenant commander in the Naval Reserve, I could appreciate the value of using a military organizational structure as the template for organizing other types of establishments–it was an efficient way of achieving an objective, delegating authority, and maintaining accountability. On the other hand, I thought, there are other organizational structures, such as corporate and business ones, that may offer the same advantages. So the question, "Why adopt a *military* structure?" remained in my mind unanswered long after graduation.

**Critical Incidents: My Mentor Reveals His Heroes**

Late in December 1994, more than five years after my first faculty appointment, I began to regularly correspond via electronic mail with my former mentor. I use the word *former* most cautiously for, as I now realize, seven years after graduation I am still learning from Ray. Beyond our shared academic interests, we had a mutual interest in the U.S. Navy. I was still in the Naval Reserve (having just been promoted to commander) while Ray had done extensive consulting work for the Navy in the past. He also had a father who served in the Pacific with the Navy during World War II. Ironically, my mentor had never served in the armed forces.

Shortly after our renewed correspondence, Ray did something that became a catalyst for our subsequent e-mail discussions–he mailed me a copy of *The Price of Admiralty* (Keegan, 1990). The book, which outlines modern naval warfare in four battles (Trafalgar, Jutland, Midway, and the Battle of the Atlantic), was a revelation to me since I had read little on naval history. In turn, I sent him a copy of *Midway* (Fuchida & Okumiya, 1955), which presents a view of the Battle of Midway from the perspective of two Japanese participants. From then on, we wrote to each other, sometimes daily, on our thoughts and observations of what we were reading. Soon, however, our discussions turned from tactics, weapons, and vessels to the leaders themselves–the great names in the annals of naval history:

> Bill: Yes, military history is a fascinating study. I started out interested in battles and over the years switched to people. Weapons, tactics, etc. change, but the human dimension stays the same and there have to be some constants that cut across eras and wars–this is probably what Keegan is trying to do in his books, like the one I sent. Ray (January 14, 1995)

Small anecdotes about famous navy admirals began to appear in Ray's messages to me. Through these stories, Ray began to reveal his personal view about the qualities that make someone a great leader. Consider, for example, this tale involving Commander-in-Chief, U.S. Pacific Fleet during World War II:

> Bill: True story. A Radioman Third got drunk and bet his buddies that he could get in to say 'Hi' to Fleet Admiral Nimitz in 1945. So he gets to the first Marine sentry and gets hauled before the Provost. Somehow Chester [Nimitz] hears of his problem, calls him in, gives him coffee to sober him up, and has his

photographer takes pictures of them together which he then autographed. The guy won his bet, and Nimitz won the affection of the sailors. Imagine taking time to do that while running the largest battle fleet ever seen. My idea of "leadership." Ray (January 10, 1996)

In later messages Ray cited the humanity that characterized the leadership of Nimitz, Spruance, and Halsey. For example, Ray pointed out that when Nimitz relieved Kimmel (who was in charge during the attack on Pearl Harbor) and was asked when he would replace the naval staff at Pearl, he replied, "Never, as long as they do their job." As a result, many career officers did not have to, as Ray noted, "follow their admiral into an early retirement."

As I read these anecdotes I was struck by how specific traits of many of these leaders had been reflected in Ray's mentorship. For instance, the previously mentioned willingness of Nimitz to give people a second chance directly parallels Ray's philosophy of working with students:

I have always refused to take test scores and GPAs into account when entering a mentor relationship with a student. My own rise from high school dropout with a 40-hour a week job and a wife and two kids to Regents Professor has been marked by people willing to take a chance, no questions asked, sort of "show me what you can do." I adopted this same approach to graduate students automatically. I have been accused of taking only "losers," but this is not true as it has turned out. I think of such people as "lost souls" who only need structure to start going up the hill. Ray (August 2, 1995)

Upon finishing *The Price of Admiralty,* Ray immediately sent me *Master of Sea Power: A Biography of Fleet Admiral Ernest J. King* (Buell, 1980). With it was a note saying that once I was finished with the book he would send, one-by-one, biographies of Nimitz, Spruance, and Halsey. He had, in effect, hooked me into being his student again!

As Commander-in-Chief U.S. Fleet during WW II, King had a reputation for being so tough that, according to Roosevelt, he "shaved with a blowtorch." It was in the e-mail exchanges about this book between Ray and I that I began to see Nimitz' concern for people as only one end of a continuum:

Bill: It's always been interesting to me how common the attributes are between those who command men on ships and on the ground. The job's different, but the basic attributes of the people are the same. There are basically two kinds of effective ones: those who are goal oriented, tend to see people as tools to accomplish a job, and are often described as "mean," and those who do the job equally well, but love, and are loved in return, by those above and below them. Not a lot of difference in outcome, actually, but certainly in the history they leave behind. King and Nimitz are a good example of this dichotomy. Ray (February 14, 1995)

I call this character dimension, suggested by Ray, *orientation*, with *goals* at one end and *people* at the other. In higher education this dichotomy is often represented by which of the two academic callings discussed earlier, development of publications or people, that a professor may favor. Based on many of Ray's e-mail comments, it was clear to me that Nimitz was more of a role model for him than King. Accordingly, Ray devoted much of his career to the mentorship of future academics.

This human dimension of leadership (and mentorship) can be expressed in many ways that vary in visibility. Some leaders, for instance, value good fellowship and camaraderie more than other leaders who are just as equally effective. The same could be said for mentors in higher education: some mentors choose to socialize with their students, others do not:

Bill: Because of my personality, I was never able to get both the intense training and the personal regard in there together. I learned that I could either train competent academics or I could be good friends. I settled for the academics. This is leadership in the style of Spruance, and the opposite of Nimitz. It all really boils down to your personality in the long haul. Ray (February 17, 1995)

Here I stumbled upon a seeming contradiction: that one could be people-oriented (like Nimitz and Spruance) yet not have the "personal regard" that marked Spruance's style of leadership. However, as I pondered my doctoral experience, I recalled that Ray was always available and congenial to graduate students without becoming their "buddy." Rather, he was able to maintain a balance between friendship and fellowship that earned the trust and respect of his students.

Another trait besides humanity that was shared by Nimitz and Spruance was a disdain for the pomposity, self-importance, and theatrics that sometime distinguish major military figures:

Bill: As to Chester [Nimitz], here is one of my command models that I try to emulate. Unlike the flashy types such as MacArthur and Patton, he makes running a war over a third of the earth's surface look like just a regular day's work for a senior officer. No posing for the movies, cursing and running about, or memorable quotes, just winning the war as fast as possible. I like him. Ray (March 23, 1995)

This dimension of leadership, I call *persona*, is on a continuum with *public* and *private* as polar opposites. At one extreme I would posit MacArthur, Patton, and Halsey while at the other end I would place leaders such as Nimitz and Spruance (whose biography is aptly titled *The Quiet Warrior*).

While I was first tempted to label the poles of this dimension *introvert* and *extrovert*, this is clearly not the case since, as mentioned earlier, Nimitz was an extrovert (unlike Spruance) who preferred going about his business without much fanfare (like Spruance). Further, where would my mentor fit in this scheme–a gregarious, if not charismatic, personality who, at the same time, put the scholastic spotlight on his students? For example, when Ray collaborated with a student on a research project he always gave the student first authorship on the conference paper reporting their work.

To try to better understand my mentor's mentoring philosophy, I tried to graphically depict his behavior relative to that of his role models. Though an obvious oversimplification (that is bound to be conceptually imperfect), Figure 7 shows six famous leaders as circles situated along *orientation* and *persona* character dimensions. Following this plan, Nimitz and Spruance are people-oriented whereas King and MacArthur are goal-oriented. Along the *persona* dimension, I have shown Spruance and King to be private personalities while Halsey and MacArthur are portrayed as the public figures they were. I have located Horatio Nelson, possibly the greatest admiral that ever lived, in the center, ideally balancing demands of mission and crew within a life that had a rich mix of personal and public sides.

Using a dashed circle to represent my mentor, I tried placing Ray amid this sea of circles. This proved to be as difficult as hitting a moving target. By his own admission, Ray was probably closest in temperament to Spruance, yet he clearly shared some of Nimitz' traits as well. Further complicating the picture, Buell (1994) describes Spruance as an introvert who was "quiet, deep thinking, always in control" (p. 44). While I can vouch for my mentor's propensity for thought and control amid the "fog" of academia, I would not characterize Ray as an introvert. I think most of my classmates from graduate school would agree that Ray was

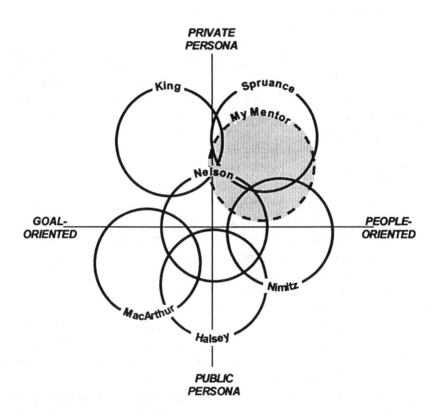

*Figure 7. Comparison of My Former Mentor with Past Leaders
Across Two Character Dimensions*

an engaging lecturer who easily held an audience's attention and seemed to enjoy doing so. Finally, one might conclude from Ray's stated preference for developing academics over friendships, that he was an aloof and impersonal mentor. However, I recall my mentor typically kept his office door open and always seemed available to talk to his students if they dropped by.

## Musings for Mentors–Is Mentorship Leadership?

After the "second mentorship" I had with Ray over the six months of intense correspondence (involving over 60 messages and almost 20,000 words between us), I was left with many questions, several of which I am still asking myself. Most prominent among them is the question, "Is leadership an important trait of successful mentors?" If this is indeed the case, I then ask, "What is the nature of leadership in mentorship?" Here I reflect on the first question, while in the next section, "Questions to Ponder," I discuss some essential leadership qualities for mentors.

Although there are many definitions for leadership, one proposed by gender scholar Barbara Bate (cited in Dunne, 1996) is particularly useful in the context of mentorship: leadership is "becoming powerful to accomplish your own goals and spreading the power you possess so that other people become able to accomplish their goals as well" (p. 73). In the sense that leadership is, first and foremost, about empowering others, leadership and mentorship are one and the same. The value for mentors in adopting this stance is that it underscores the need to be professionally competent (i.e., powerful) and to *share* this competency with students so that they can make meaningful contributions to their discipline. All too many would-be mentors fail to give their protégés a leg-up in the profession because of indifference, because they are not front runners in the field themselves, or for other reasons.

A second argument for looking at mentorship as leadership has to do with the labor intensive nature of much research in academe. In military establishments as well as the corporate sector, middle management does the detail work for senior decision makers. In the world of academe, by contrast, there is no middle management. The mentor (as the senior decision maker) of graduate students must manage all the many detailed phases and components of their research projects. Consequently, either a very small number of students will be mentored well or many will be mentored in name only.

An important key to productive mentoring is *delegation* of parts of the research task to middle management. What middle management? Mentors need to create opportunities for establishing their own middle management, consisting of upper-division students who can teach the craft of research to novices. Building such a cadre of student-researchers does not need to be a large undertaking like *II Corps*. The most difficult aspect of forming and leading such a research team may lie in learning to delegate, which, in some cases, means being open to and willing for students to make mistakes.

The concept of delegating aspects of mentoring to others is also related to the trend toward greater decentralization at all levels of classroom instruction. Teachers in K-12 settings, for instance, are diminishing their role as the "sage on the stage" and adopting new roles as information brokers who employ, in addition to traditional exposition, peer tutoring and cooperative learning strategies to impart knowledge. When teachers do this they are, in a sense, providing students with opportunities to both mentor and lead classmates in the learning process. As a result, students learn from many sources, which provides an instructional base that is potentially more culturally diverse. For students in higher education, multiple and diverse mentoring resources provide a "mentoring mosaic" (Head, Reiman, & Thies-Sprinthall, 1992) in which different persons serve different mentoring functions such as career guide, cheering section, academic tutor, parental figure, and so forth.

Another justification for considering mentors as leaders is that students need direction in learning research skills. Many times in the name of intellectual freedom, mentors are reluctant to provide students with positive guidance, and instead let them drift on their own to "discover" their own research topic. As most K-12 teachers know, when students have little prior knowledge on a topic, they need to be led in the instructional process. For this reason, I like to tell my students *what* to research, letting them concentrate on *how* to do it. This approach (the very one my mentor used with me) provides great dividends later on when students are approaching their dissertation. By then they have learned the mechanics of research and can focus on a relevant research question. However, it is impossible to lead students in the research enterprise if one does not see oneself as a leader.

**Questions to Ponder: What Leadership Qualities Benefit Mentorship?**

Analysis of mentoring environments to identify the traits of successful mentors has been a long-standing feature of the literature on mentorship. Typically, models of mentorship, as a minimum, have some version of parent-child and peer-pal components. A review of several mentorship models reveals that mentors may fill a variety of roles including, but not limited to, friend, career guide, information source, intellectual guide, nurturer, caregiver, teacher, sponsor, one who encourages, counselor (problem solver), and role model (Kealy & Mullen, 1996).

There is surprisingly little mention, if any, in the mentorship literature on the importance of leadership and vice versa. For instance, a popular book on leadership titled *Leadership Secrets of Attila the Hun* (Roberts, 1985) contains no discussion at all about mentorship. Occasionally, however, one does find references to mentoring in books and articles on leadership as one of the important tasks of being a leader. Another work by Roberts (1988) on leadership with more applicability to mentoring is *The Enculturation of Battlefield Leaders for the Twenty-first Century*. Based on the list it presents of skills needed by future leaders, I have developed an inventory of qualities that I propose mentors should both foster in their students and embody in their own mentoring:

1.  *Interpersonal skills*: The need for teamwork and team-building in a culturally diverse world. Given the complexity of current research questions and the methodologies for addressing them, the days of the Lone Ranger researcher are fading fast. Today, the key word in research is *collaboration* and graduates of higher education are expected to work as effective partners in interdisciplinary research teams,

2.  *Versatility*: The capability of using alternative methodologies and knowledge bases. Along with the ability to work with researchers from other disciplines, future professionals in academe need to have the skill of viewing problems from multiple perspectives. The inherent strengths of both the orthodox and the unconventional approaches to research need to be brought to bear on today's problems. The practice of valiantly defending one's research "paradigm" is now an anachronism,

3. *Resourcefulness*: Mentors should ensure that their students can use all the university resources available for achieving scholarly goals. Technological mastery, including computer literacy, for analyzing, publishing, and presenting research is no longer an optional but an indispensable skill in academe. The most effective way for mentors to promote the technological competency of their students is to lead by example,

4. *Integrity*: Before they graduate and begin an academic career, students should be applying high professional moral standards and intellectual honesty in both their research and in their dealings with others. First, however, mentors need to communicate to their students what these standards are and to model them in their everyday professional practice. Integrity is perhaps the most worthwhile quality in this list to pass along to student mentees,

5. *Knowledge*: An essential part of successful mentoring is knowing one's discipline, which requires keeping abreast of current research in the field. Similarly, mentors should urge their students to make a habit of avidly reading professional journals and books to acquire new ideas. Following the advice of Krathwohl (1994), if mentors encourage students to be *active* readers, mindfully and critically processing what they read, development of their natural curiosity and inquisitiveness will follow along with an abundance of research ideas,

6. *Humility*: This is not to be confused with timidity or meekness–it is, instead, the quality that holds arrogance in check. Humility, the subject of an award-winning essay titled, "The Neglected Dimension of Leadership" (Anderson, 1966), is a source of strength. Without it, a leader loses perspective through an inflated sense of self-importance, becomes complacent, and ultimately fails. In academia, intellectual humility promotes a continual thirst for knowledge and an acceptance of other cultures and ideas.

The concept of humility may be extended even further to include the "willingness to sacrifice personal comforts and perquisites of rank when necessary to fulfill the stewardship responsibilities inherent to positions of command and leadership" (Roberts, 1988, p. 17). Ray shared with me an anecdote that I believe exemplifies the quality of personal sacrifice as demonstrated by a model leader:

Bill: Talk about tough enough, there's Vandergrift who commanded the Marines on Guadalcanal. This is the same General who took his entire HQ Staff, all the support personnel, and the walking wounded, and marched them up to the line at three in the morning, put himself under the command of the Lt. Col. [lieutenant colonel] on the Ridge. They stayed there for the rest of the night knocking back three enemy attacks in their sector, and losing about a third of their people. In the morning he left the Ridge as a stretcher bearer, after he distributed his boots, jacket, and canteen to enlisted men around him. He was back in command by noon. My kind of leadership. Ray (January 31, 1995)

**Full Circle:  Looking Back on My Story**

I began this chapter with recollections of graduate school and my formal mentorship experience that ended over eight years ago. I then moved to my recollections of just two years past. Now, as I complete my story, I am amused to discover that some things have remained unchanged throughout the years. I am still in the Naval Reserve (currently a captain); the subject of mentorship continues to hold my interest; and Ray and I have remained in touch. Ray still has a passion for studying the lives of famous military leaders and is presently working on a book comparing the lives of two British generals, William ("Uncle Bill") Slim and Bernard Montgomery. In the meantime, I have yet to finish reading (and return) Ray's copy of the book on the life of Chester Nimitz (Potter, 1976).

As I reexamine Figure 7, I can see that some revisions could be made to further improve the diagram. In particular, I think another axis might be added bisecting the 90-degree angle formed by the existing vertical and horizontal axes. At one end of this new diagonal axis, located in the upper right-hand quadrant of the diagram, I would print the word *humility*, while the other end of the line (in the lower left-hand quadrant) would be labeled *arrogance*. Does my reader agree that this addition is an improvement in representing the leaders it depicts? Perhaps this humility-arrogance axis should be drawn (if it could) in a third dimension intersecting the center of the diagram at right angles to the page. In this newly configured diagram, Spruance would be portrayed as the unpretentious leader he was, a reluctant recipient of well-deserved publicity and glory.

My mentor did not have much to say about humility per se, but his thoughts about the role of humility in leadership can be inferred from his admiration of Nimitz and Spruance. Ray's reflection on his own mentoring behavior, outlined in an e-mail message he recently sent me, communicates a firm position that humility is an essential characteristic of both successful leaders and mentors:

> I take virtually everyone who comes to me. In rare cases this has not worked, but it's rare indeed. It has never been my aim to train great scientists–although that has happened in several cases. However, for those who have become famous, I was more of a guide, filling a certain role rather than doing much teaching. It is from the others that I have gained my satisfactions. The other day I sat in a proposal meeting and watched my student outline a set of studies, comment on the analyses and probable outcomes, and point out clearly where such result would fit into the larger theoretical perspective. I remembered the first time we met and her weeping because she had a "math block" and was afraid of statistics courses–an ex-elementary school teacher with absolutely no idea of what research is, nor any concept that she could do it. That was four years ago. See what I mean about rewards?

As I conclude my chapter I ask myself, "Where does my mentor fit in the proposed revision to my diagram?" Considering the qualities of leadership that Ray admires–humanity, humility, and the ability to get the job done without drawing attention to oneself–it becomes clear to me that where he is represented amid the diagram's circles is appropriate. The placement of Ray alongside Spruance, his favorite hero, makes good sense. I'm sure that Ray (Raymond Spruance, that is) would agree.

## Acknowledgment

I wish to thank Dr. Carol A. Mullen, my wife, partner, and friend, for inspiring and encouraging me in completing this chapter.

# Chapter 11

---

# Patterns of Mentoring: Weaving Teacher Educators' Career Stories

## Donna L. Wiseman

*Balance*

What does that mean?
    To a teenage girl
        It was confidence in her ability to be devoted to a marriage and a career
        Even though
        Nameless faces screamed, implied, whispered, assumed
        It wasn't possible to do both well
    To a young woman
        It was a tenuous two-faced struggle
        As a smiling teacher maintained daily composure
        While nightly her belief in unconditional love was
        Tested, undermined, challenged, and choked
    To a graduate student
        It was immersion, excitement, and inquiry
        Into not only a profession
        But into new relationships, commitments, and identity
    For years now
        It has meant trying to find a way
        To fulfill the various roles I love
        Teacher, researcher, mother, lover, friend
    But now

*Balance*

Is the wrong question, focus, goal, metaphor ...
   My life
      Is not about weighing individual parts to achieve equity
      What I have learned is to redefine my quest
      Not towards balance
      But to weaving, integrating, appreciating
      My new awareness is that I am no longer trying to balance
   Instead I

*Embrace*

Joyce Many, 1996

This chapter describes the story of a circle of female graduate students and faculty (one member was male) with whom I met from 1995 to 1996. We studied our own stories of teacher education, and reflected upon what we had learned. This writing group met to provide the support each needed during our individual phases of personal and professional development. We discovered that our conversational weavings created a circle of collegial friends stronger and wiser than a circle of one. By breaking through the isolation that each of us faced at the university, the weave became stronger. Our individual threads wove together a conversation that provided critical perspectives on higher education and supportive dialogue about the process of growing professionally.

At first we did not know why we should gather, we just knew that we needed to. Some individuals were beginning on their doctorates and in the process of accepting that they were no longer classroom teachers, but instead professionals embarking on a career in teacher education. Other members of the group were completing formal coursework and learning the research and theoretical aspects related to personal study and to an academic career. Mid-career and beginning professors joined the group at different times. We were held together by discussions and personal stories. We found that we shared common experiences, but with very different perspectives. We could not tell a story, share a frustration, describe our joy, or analyze a theory without the rest of us understanding and contributing in one way or another. The group conducted a self-study of selves and began to understand the importance of mentoring and support systems in personal and professional development.

The first conversations resembled a great ball of tangled yarn. Eventually common teaching and learning experiences began to emerge from our talk. We shared knowledge about doctoral student experiences and helped each other understand the process of becoming reeducated. Recognizing frustrations and sympathizing with familiar struggles were common occurrences among the group. The sometimes humorous situations that arose from serious matters provided us opportunities to laugh together and helped us navigate our way with confidence and faith in our own perceptions.

Sharing teaching strategies and learning outcomes that were successful in public school and university classrooms contributed to developmental and professional expertise. Articles, books, and personal writings that described and supported our conversations were the opening focus of our sessions. The voices of Catherine Bateson, Nel Noddings, and Jean Clandinin provided us with support for our collaborative research venture and the conversational narratives we began sharing. The events of our lives were connected to current theories of research and conflicting views of practice. Occasionally we would stop to try and identify the focus of our meetings, but our personal narratives would unravel our attempts to become more directed.

As one of us would share important life experiences and learnings, the group responded with related feelings and experiences. Stories led to other stories and events, and conversations were continued and reconstructed as experiences were linked to research and theory. The discussions allowed us to gain a perspective on our own lives (Bateson, 1990) as well as those emerging elements common to our experiences and interwoven throughout our writings. As we talked and listened to each other, we began to uncover insights and knowledge about our profession. The collaborative process of reflecting on our past and present experiences, and making connections to the experiences of others, helped us build a personal practical knowledge (Clandinin, 1992).

## The Nature of Our Stories

We soon realized that personal stories do not offer a singular, simple explanation of teaching and learning, but instead expand a diversity of perspectives. Our stories were influenced by the many roles we played as we engaged in teaching and learning activities. Our perspectives as parents, lovers, caretakers, explorers, teachers, researchers, and learners became "theme threads" that formed the fiber of our conversations.

Sometimes the threads were neat and orderly. Sometimes we knew how to connect the stories. At other times the examples were more difficult to understand and operated as loose ends–difficult to capture and knit together.

The stories we told were shaped by the knowledge base offered from several perspectives of theory and researcher. The theoretical threads held our tapestry together. What emerged from combining the written and published theories and narrative stories of our group was an understanding of the importance of our own experiences. Our experiences in becoming teachers and teacher educators became the basis of our personal, practical knowledge that allowed us to talk about the processes of teaching, doctoral studies, and professional teacher education as knowledgeable and knowing persons.

We accepted that the process that began with telling our own stories is one which Hunt (1987) describes as "research as increased self-knowledge," where past experiences have been brought forward to deal with the present. Hunt's concept of professional knowledge as residing in the "heads, hearts, and actions of classroom teachers" allowed us to conceptualize mentoring and support systems that valued our own experiences and influenced our theories and beliefs about teaching and learning.

Our conversations continued to return to the importance of nurturing ourselves and others during the process of becoming a teacher, a researcher, a teacher educator, or a professor. Nurturing and caring are seldom discussed in most doctoral programs, and yet Noddings' (1984) work argues that face-to-face caring is necessary for our own ethical and professional development. Noddings described the nurturing and caring relationships most commonly found among family and friends, but we began to wonder what the impact of a similar support system would be on teacher development and learning.

Our stories taught us other lessons not as pleasant. We were trying to understand and become a part of a system that encouraged isolationism, competition, and individualism. There were times that our experiences demonstrated Kerr's (1993) belief that policies and institutions have the "power to render nurture virtually impossible" (p. 10). Our stories would mirror the frustration and hurt that institutions and their processes and policies can inflict. Issues of power in our institution abound, embodied in the policies and procedures that provided for the roller coaster ride described in Pitters' (1994) account of the doctoral program.

Many stories shared by our colleagues caused us to remember, reconstruct, rebuild, and share stories from our own lives. The professors heard stories and experiences from the doctoral students that reminded them of meaningful past experiences and provided connections to their present experiences. The doctoral students heard stories from professors that explained the nature of the doctoral program, provided insight into the professorial journey, and described multiple roles of a teacher educator. The salient experiences we shared had to do with our own formal teaching and learning situations and the times we needed support or offered support to others.

Stories originated from experiences during the doctoral program, struggles present during the professorial tenure process, and the frustrations of making professional transitions in higher education. Other stories came from our young students in public school settings, future teachers in the university setting, and descriptions of our own learning processes. Narratives, stories, and personal histories have been used to develop a history and research base in public school teaching (Carter & Doyle, 1996) but there are few stories related to the process of becoming a teacher educator within the university setting. We believe the stories present a review of life experiences related to the process of becoming teacher educators can ultimately provide relevant insights into our profession.

Our conversational tapestry was woven from personal and professional stories of critical events and incidents, initial teaching experiences, professional development activities, doctoral experiences, and university teaching and research. Some portions of the tapestry were thickly and tightly woven together; in other areas we would drop the stitches and fail to pick up the loose ends, leaving them dangling. Parts of the design were threadbare, not filled in completely, leaving work unfinished. When we reviewed the nature of our work, one strong thread would appear as if woven throughout the entire tapestry of conversations. This was the case in our metaphor of the circle of one and our attempt to break through our isolation. Professional, personal, and pedagogical nurturing and support seemed to be at the heart of our conversations and were the thread that held us together.

## The Nature of Support Systems in Educational Settings

Our reflections were framed in terms of self-study–attempting to understand the doctoral program, the development of preservice teachers, and the negotiation of the teacher education professor's tenure process and professional development. Everyone in the group was involved in a continuous learning process. Those in the doctoral program began to realize that they were making the transition from being a public school teacher to becoming a teacher educator. Each of us began to realize the importance of support throughout our careers. The meetings, conversations, and interactions of our group became the setting for our learning about support systems in educational settings.

The group meetings facilitated group members in at least two ways. The group was a support system and mentored many of us through a time of frustration and transition with bureaucratic processes and changes. Many of the requirements of the doctoral program were made easier when fears and concerns were shared and processes were demystified with information. Secondly, we began to identify instances of beneficial support systems and what happened to us when the support systems were not available. Soon the concept of mentoring began to guide our thoughts. The sharing of personal experiences had provided examples of the mentoring process during many stages of our lives. The group reflection led us to an understanding of how much we depended on support systems and how often we provide the support without clear recognition or awareness.

Our conversations revealed that support can mean many things to different people. There are times that strong support comes from an individual. Doctoral students can tell stories of very strong mentorships that guide them through the doctoral program. Sometimes support comes from peers or group interactions. Many of the students in our group were brought together because of a support system formed in a class that they were all taking at the same time. The doctoral students related stories revealing that even as they were personally seeking support during their studies, they were simultaneously serving as mentors to some of the undergraduate preservice teachers who were in their classes.

Our stories revealed a need for support systems and nurturing at many points of career development. We all recognized that mentoring and support systems are needed when we begin a career in teaching, undertake a doctoral program, and move through the professorial ranks.

Experienced professors find a need for support especially when they are making changes in their lives. Nowhere is this need more evident than during the doctoral process of becoming a teacher educator. The doctoral program is a time of economic, familial, emotional, and intellectual stress. Doctoral candidates often hang on to their identification as public school teachers while envisioning the role of a teacher educator. The stress may be accentuated when changes in administrative and leadership structures in the institution contribute additional challenges and concerns. The stress can be further compounded by personal and family struggles, and transitions. By identifying those elements in our context that provided reasons for support, we were able to articulate dimensions of mentoring in our own lives.

## Personal Reflections about Our Group

One of the writing activities that we assigned to ourselves during our meetings was to express why we felt the group was important to us and what we offered to the group. I described my own teaching as an important part of my learning. When through classroom assignments I introduce topics, present a new perspective, or resolve a troublesome dilemma, I see opportunities to grow based on interactions with others. Our writing group served a similar purpose of going beyond providing a support system while developing into a learning community.

The group contributed to my own learning. Our stories, readings, and experiences gave me a great deal of grist to think about. My mother explained to me that we become a part of everyone we meet. The interactions of the group provided me with an important layer in my learning. I am not sure of the total impact of the year-long conversation on my professional development (much like my teaching), but I know that I have been subtly influenced, as can already be detected in my teaching, writing, and thinking. I may be teaching when something that someone has said in this group is used as an example, or writing when a theorist discussed in the group becomes interwoven with my ideas.

Carol Mullen, one of our group members, encouraged us to think in metaphors and pictures. One picture was particularly clear to me as I thought of the group. I don't know why I kept thinking of watching my mother braid her long hair. My mother would take her wild mass of waist-length hair and starting at her front hairline would weave her hair into beautiful French braids that contained her hair in a neat controlled manner.  As a child I was always fascinated with her long hair.  My mother was a professional women, a social worker in the 1960s and 1970s.  I remember how sad I was when she cut her hair, believing it would be more professional to have a traditional haircut.  I shared this picture with the group and the image served as an analogy to the group in two ways.  I saw the group as braiding a wildly diverse mass of tangled ideas into a neatly contained presentation of ideas.  The braid or weave seems to be appropriate to our continued efforts to make sense out of our varied and diverse experiences.  On the other hand, the idea of being able to "keep our braids" and still be professional teacher educators was the sense of our discussions.

**Collegial Responses**

A recent article in *U.S. News & World Report* (Saltzman, 1996) revealed the difficulty of establishing mentoring relationships in the business world.  The article narrated the experiences of one group of women who attempted to meet regularly and offer support to each other.  Their meetings were viewed suspiciously by some of the men.  They were afraid that the women were meeting to gather data for a discrimination suit.

One would believe that the university setting would not engender that manner of response.  Unfortunately, that was not the case in our context.  Some of our colleagues questioned the appropriateness of our meeting.  It would be instructive to know why our colleagues were somewhat uncomfortable with our meetings.  Was it discomfort with and unfamiliarity of the feminist perspective that was threaded through our conversations?  Could it have been that some faculty might have felt that their students might be recruited away from their guidance?  Or was it the term "self-study," or the personal narrative focus that made scholarly people question our right to meet?

Self-study can be seen as a threat to colleagues when it is viewed as a critique of actions, policies, and leadership in educational settings (Carter & Doyle, 1996).  While this finding has been demonstrated to be generally true in the schools where classroom and teacher research is occurring, it might also explain the resistance to the group in the university setting.  The uncovering of politics and power issues provides a situation in which well-meaning individuals attempt to silence voices.  The study of the context of the present can be viewed as a "counter culture" (Goodson, 1994). The enthusiasm for our own experiences and discoveries was not always shared by our colleagues, but the response of our colleagues certainly offered important textures and colors to our tapestry.

While some responses were negative, there were subtle and fine threads of support woven throughout our tapestry. Generally the support was offered by those who were members of the group, but occasionally the support came from outside the group, both within the college and from outside the university. Acceptance of the group within the institutional leadership was mixed. When the group and its purpose were discussed outside the group, the college leadership made it clear that it was important for this group to continue to meet. An unexpected support system was offered by a colleague at another university who also found that one's intellectual home and one's academic home could be in two different places.

**What Evolved From Our Narratives**

This collection of narratives evolved from conversations that began extemporaneously. Through sharing, reflecting on, and writing, our stories provided us with a connected, continuous narrative (Clandinin, 1992) that represented the richness of our collaborative voices. This narrative of our reflections provides interpretations of our college experiences embedded with our own histories and cultures, both past and current. The central quest of redefining mentorship ultimately focused our discussions. Our experiences at the university produced a "collaboratively woven tapestry" (Raymond, Butt, & Townsend, 1992), focusing on the role of support systems in teaching and learning.

We started out with a tangled mass of ideas, experiences, stories, and differing perspectives. Making sense of the graduate and undergraduate school contexts and the university provided an opportunity to discuss, share, and work together. Our stories illustrate the impact of support, nurturing, and personal contributions to our professional development. What follows this introductory chapter is the presentation of our stories told in our own unique voices. We became committed to telling the stories and their meaning in our own way, even though the reader may sense that the tapestry is not as tightly woven as it might have been had we established one particular manner of speaking. Some of our voices include scholarly perspectives; others of us display a voice that represents a strong sense of art, music, or literature; some represent a storytelling stance; and still others reflect a strong narrative voice. Our presentations are enriched with anecdotes, metaphors, research, and personal narratives that contribute to a rich, colorful, multi-perspective tapestry. Through these narratives we wish to share the importance of mentoring, caring, and nurturing and to offer strategies that support, connect, and mentor others who are in the process of becoming teachers and teacher educators.

## Musings for Mentors

In the preceding chapters, each of us describes what we have learned from telling our stories, reflecting upon specific events relating to mentorship within universities and schools, and investigating possibilities for change. These musings can provide guidelines for others who wish to understand more about the mentoring and supporting process. The reconstruction of our group learnings can prove instructive to the reader who also seeks to break the circle of one.

The conversational weave of our group broke through our isolation in the following ways: Groups can serve a mentoring function. Mentoring does not have to be restricted to a one-on-one process. Groups of caring, nurturing individuals can come together to encourage the individual personal and professional growth of all those participating in the process. The power of the mentoring process did not just happen without us being aware of the mentoring processes. The goal of the group was to mentor and support.

Group mentorship reflects traditional mentor relationships. Mentorship is established when there is information, experiences, and skills to be shared. The same events occur in a group, but in different ways. Expertise is shared through the group processes. Instead of one experienced faculty member being "the mentor," the entire group forms a mentoring atmosphere, with each member of the group shouldering the responsibility for support at different times and all members of the group learning from each other. The role of mentor is transferred easily from person to person and contributions are accepted as equal. This does not mean that our group did not recognize and value traditional mentorship interactions.

Group members must develop trust. Trust becomes a very important part of the process as group members tell their real stories and frustrations. This trust is developed by accepting all ideas as valuable and honoring the space and time of each group member. The foundation of the trust is nurturing and caring for each other. Trust is also knowing that what is said will not be repeated without the proper context.

Group membership must be considered. Those who are invited to the group are usually bound together by a philosophy, concern, or unified purpose. Open invitations to join during the first stages are appropriate, but eventually commitment to the meetings reduces the group to its core. At that point the group may develop strong bonds of trust that are maintained by continuous meetings, each session picking up from the last meeting. Informal groups which meet regularly without a legitimate reason may become suspect in an institutional setting. The suspicion can be dealt with by informing administrators and leaders about the goals and objectives of the processes.

Personal stories and narratives can be a strong part of the support system. Personal events in group members' own lives can serve as the knowledge base for understanding support systems and mentoring processes. The group must honor the stories and realize that each story and critical incident is valuable and acceptable. The themes recognized in personal stories become the basis of understanding events. The time spent in sharing our real lives became a very important part of the process described in this book.

## Acknowledgment

Dr. Joyce Many, a collegial friend, kindly contributed the poem (unpublished, produced in a doctoral seminar) that opens this chapter. Joyce is a member of the language and literacy faculty in the Department of Middle and Secondary Education and Instructional Technology at Georgia State University. She teaches undergraduate and graduate courses focusing on literacy instruction and graduate courses on methods of inquiry. Her primary research interests have focused on response to literature, literacy processes, and preservice teacher education.

# Afterword

---

# The Circle of One
# Has Been Broken

## Carol A. Mullen

Our chapter writers have contributed to breaking the circle of one. Through this project we experienced a degree of liberation from institutional forms of isolation, competition, and abandonment. We engaged in personal stories of mentorship, sharing a range of rewarding (and less rewarding) academic relationships. We are now affirmed in our knowledge of multiple ways to foster healthy mentoring situations. The "culture circle" is both a place and space wherein professional education takes place and new meaning is cocreated among teachers, students, and other colleagues (Freire, 1996). Each person's story is understood historically, culturally, and socio-politically, but also personally and interpersonally. Within the culture circle, members are committed to becoming makers of their own life and of remaking hierarchical schooling systems and intellectual traditions. We initially gathered to conceptualize how to break the circle of one. It had been emerging as a force within our various teaching and learning situations, and we were concerned. At the time we only knew of this need to gather more formally. We had yet to discover the meaning of the circle metaphor for its paradoxical relationship to isolation *and* community, depending on how it is experienced at a particular time. We wanted to celebrate forces that engage such making and new vitality and welcome even those that resisted and conflicted with our own.

The circle of one can damage self-esteem, creative potential, and inner development. But it can also be broken, forced open, and transformed. Breaking the circle of one invites new definitions of mentoring and plays with possibility, storyline, language, and metaphor. The traditional circle, when broken, is a challenge to tight forms of social control. A new consciousness can be shaped through new circles (persons, places, or contexts) brought together to create shared research agendas. For us, it was also the possibility of living more deeply in an interconnected space of acceptance and appreciation. Our impact was not reserved for us alone; it was also felt in outside circles in tension with our own, albeit differently. Bateson (1984) expands further the significance of overlapping "concentric worlds" as

> multiple small spheres of personal experience [that] both echo and enable events shared more widely, expressions of moment in a world in which we now recognize that no microcosm is completely separate, no tide pool, no forest, no family, no nation. Indeed, the knowledge drawn from the life of some single organism or community or from the intimate experience of an individual may prove to be relevant to decisions that affect the health of a city or the peace of the world. (p. 6)

How have we, the writers of this self-study writing project, approached the topic of mentorship in our chapters? How does our array of uses and possibilities point to broader uses and possibilities in the educational arena? And, what evidence is there that our writing may be creating new beginnings in the life of the academy?

We used mentorship to explore relations within various educational programs, relationships, and situations–some traditional, others innovative. Generally, educators speak about mentorship and colleagiality as if they were self-evident relationships, when in fact they come in a variety of forms and have disparate consequences. This we came to recognize as a group and, as writers, have attempted to demonstrate through our stories. We learned a basic principle of mentorship–that it is a process throughout life that brings mentors and neophytes close together at times, and further away at other times.

This book could help professors and teachers to be more effective (and reflective) in their relationships with students, beginning teachers, and others. Our mentoring model of education can help mentoring pairs and groups to negotiate their relationships in structured, reflective spaces. Conversations about mutual expectations can lend depth to education as an inquiry into the process of mentoring itself. Meta-questions can then be formulated concerning the lived mentoring process both in the here-and-how and over time. Desirable models or metaphors of mentorship can be discussed and reviewed for their consistency with action. Gains and losses from short- and long-term involvement can be reviewed one-on-one, in groups, or in mentoring programs within universities, schools, and alternative educational sites.

We, the writers, all share the metaphor of the circle, but differently or with a twist. It has been conveyed through this collection of images: African-American cultural center, unbroken circle, E-mail MaMa and the Internet, magical wand, walking the tightrope/holding the net, zig-zag journey, circle of one and circle of many, circle with/in circles, post-sharkdom (and sharkdom), full circle, and tapestry or pattern of mentoring. These individual interpretations of our circular model of education are also shared expressions of the value of mentoring. Our personal metaphors were experienced organically. They grew between and among us over time, providing us with a sensory approach to understanding our often tacit issues and concerns of mentoring:

> It is as though the ability to comprehend experience through metaphor were a sense, like seeing or touching or hearing, with metaphors providing the only ways to perceive and experience much of the world. Metaphor is as much a part of our functioning as our sense of touch, and as precious. (Lakoff & Johnson, 1980, p. 239)

Some of our metaphors even came to serve as templates for redefining mentoring as a shared process of collaborative inquiry.

Like our circular model of education (Figure 1), we ourselves are a circle of dense layers and convolutions, braids and coils. We experienced an intensity of contact in our mentoring relationships with each other. At times we insisted on distance, but never for prolonged periods. Through the writing of our chapters we also ignited contact with others, often significant mentors and/or the mentored, who helped us to grow intellectually and emotionally while creating a working model of mentorship in education. And, like our model, we also represent a wider circle that moves further away at times. We are only beginning to take a long view of mentoring as a process affecting the life of a self-study writing group. For some of us, this means continuing the contact through supervisory practices, professional conferences, and new writing projects. For others, the intensity of the project is still too near, or even dear.

The long view of collegial support became a reality for us through a recent experience of distance mentoring. I, the senior editor, did not anticipate moving to Tallahassee, Florida, from College Station, Texas, toward the end of our project. What became essential during these final months was availability as well as regular contact and prompt follow-through. In order to handle drafts, revised manuscripts, and new chapters, as well as queries about the project, my contact with the others became heightened. We relied on electronic mail, the mail system, and the telephone. Technology had allowed us certain capabilities, but it had also introduced problems and frustrations. The logistics and technical challenges of working with multiple formats of text and graphics were particularly time consuming. Such a daily rhythm of work in contemporary academic circles is one of the factors that has led to a "saturated self" in Gergen's (1991) postmodern analysis of technology and its impact on identity. Technological saturation is only one example of the kind of challenge facing comentoring groups committed to breaking the circle of one in an effort to overcome mentorless situations.

My intense experience of long-distance mentoring as senior editor made me even more attentive to the organic development of this book. The relationship between writers and their writing and the actual structure of the book became apparent to me. In other words, it proved insufficient to simply inform writers about new developments concerning the process and production of the book–they also had to continue to be empowered to shape it until the very end. For example, the writers continued to share new subtleties and nuances of our circular model that I attempted to assimilate into larger patterns of meaning. Our experience of long distance mentoring is an example of the larger circle of our model (Figure 1). The smaller, textured circle also comes into view here given ongoing forms of contact that draw us together. The closeness we feel even at a distance was foreshadowed in the preface:

cycling in and out of each other's lives
cycling back, checking in
sharing the real stuff of life
a relationship that looks different
depending on where you stand.

With this account of mentorship, we hope that other professionals will feel encouraged to undertake their own response to the significant question: "How can we, as educators, create a circle of communication among professional educators, researchers, and other publics invested in education?" (American Educational Research Association 1997 Annual Meeting, 1996, p. 51). As societal beings seek to not only sustain but also to actively create and recreate their own mentoring relationships, the circle widens. How to begin? Perhaps we are called forth by conversations that have already begun to emerge within our own mentoring circles:

> One opens the circle a crack, opens it all the way, lets someone in, calls someone, or else goes out oneself, launches forth. One launches forth, hazards an improvisation. But to improvise is to join with the World, to meld with it. (Deleuze & Guattari, cited in Gergen, 1991, p. 218)

# References

American Educational Research Association. (1996). AERA 1997 Annual Meeting. *Educational Researcher, 25*(8), 51–54.

Aisenberg, N., & Harrington, M. (1988). *Women of academe: Outsiders in the sacred grove.* Amherst, MA: University of Massachusetts Press.

Allen, P. G. (1986). *The sacred hoop: Recovering the feminine in American Indian traditions.* Boston: Beacon Press.

Anderson, J. H. (1996). The neglected dimension of leadership. *Naval Institute Proceedings, 122*(6), 68–72.

Auden, W. H. (1962). *The dyer's hand and other essays.* New York: Randon House.

Banks, J. A. (1996). *Multicultural education: Transformative knowledge & action.* New York: Teachers College Press.

Barone, T. E., & Eisner, E. W. (in press). Arts-based educational research. In R. Jaeger (Ed.), *Complementary methods of educational research.* Washington, DC: AERA.

Bateson, G., & Bateson, M. C. (1987). *Angels fear: Towards an epistemology of the sacred.* New York: Macmillan.

Bateson, M. C. (1984). *With a daughter's eye: A memoir of Margaret Mead and Gregory Bateson.* New York: HarperCollins Publishers.

_____. (1990). *Composing a life.* New York: Penguin Books.

Bey, T. M. (1992). Foreword. In T. M. Bey & C. T. Holmes (Eds.), *Mentoring: Contemporary principles and issues* (pp. v–vi). Reston, VA: Association of Teacher Educators.

_____. (1992). Mentoring in teacher education: Diversifying support for teachers (pp. 111–120). In T. M. Bey & C. T. Holmes (Eds.), *Mentoring: Contemporary principles and issues*. Reston, VA: Association of Teacher Educators.

Bey, T. M., & Holmes, C. T. (Eds.). (1992). *Mentoring: Contemporary principles and issues*. Reston, VA: Association of Teacher Educators.

Boykin, A. W. (1983). The academic performance of Afro-American children. In J. Spence (Ed.), *Achievement and achievement motives* (pp. 324–371). San Francisco, CA: W. H. Freeman.

_____. (1994). The sociocultural context of schooling for African American children: A proactive deep structural analysis. In E. Hollins (Ed.), *Formulating a knowledge base for teaching culturally diverse learners* (pp. 233–245). Philadelphia: ACSD.

Buell, T. B. (1980). *Master of sea power: A biography of Fleet Admiral Ernest J. King.* Boston: Little, Brown.

_____. (1994). Oral histories help tell the tale. *Naval Institute Proceedings, 120*(7), 44–48.

Caplan, P. J. (1994). *Lifting a ton of feathers: A woman's guide to surviving in the academic world.* Toronto: University of Toronto Press.

Carter, K., & Doyle, W. (1996). Personal narrative and life history in learning to teach. In J. Sikula (Ed.), *Handbook of research on teacher education* (pp. 120–142). New York: Macmillan.

Chomsky, N. (1957). *Syntactic structures.* The Hague: Mouton.

_____. (1959). *A review of verbal behavior by B. F. Skinner. Language, 35,* 26–58.

Clandinin, D. J. (1992). Narrative and story in teacher education. In T. Russell & H. Munby (Eds.), *Teachers and teaching: From classroom to reflection* (pp. 124–137). London: Falmer Press.

Clandinin, D. J., Davies, A., Hogan, P., & Kennard, B. (1993). *Learning to teach: Teaching to learn.* New York: Teachers College Press.

Clifford, J. (1990). Notes on (field)notes. In R. Sanjek (Ed.), *Fieldnotes: The making of anthropology* (pp. 47–70). London: Cornell University Press.

Connelly, F. M., & Clandinin, D. J. (1988). Narrative meaning: Focus on teacher education. *Elements, 19*(2), 15–18.

_____. (1990). Stories of experience and narrative inquiry. *Educational Researcher, 19*(5), 2–14.

Cooper, J. E. (1991). Telling our own stories: The reading and writing of journals or diaries. In C. Witherell & N. Noddings (Eds.), *Stories lives tell: Narrative and dialogue in education* (pp. 96–112). New York: Teachers College Press.

Copps, D. (1976). *Savage survivor: 300 million years of the shark.* Milwaukee, WI: Westwind Press.

Darling-Hammond, L. (1996). The quiet revolution: Rethinking teacher development. *Educational Leadership, 53*(6), 4–10.

Deleuze, G., & Guattari, F. (1991). *A thousand plateaus.* In K. J. Gergen (Ed.), *The saturated self: Dilemmas of identity in contemporary life* (pp. 218-220). New York: BasicBooks.

Delpit, L. D. (1988). The silenced dialogue: Power and pedagogy in educating other people's children. *Harvard Educational Review, 58,* 280–298.

Diamond, C. T. P., & Mullen, C. A. (1997). *'Roped together': A duography of co-mentorship.* Manuscript submitted for publication.

Diamond, C. T. P., Mullen, C. A., & Beattie, M. (1996). Arts-based educational research: Making music. In M. Kompf, W. R. Bond, D. Dworet, & R. T. Boak (Eds.), *Changing research and practice: Teachers' professionalism, identities, and knowledge* (pp. 175-185). London: Falmer Press.

Dilworth, M. E. (Ed.). (1992). *Diversity in teacher education: New expectations.* San Francisco, CA: Jossey-Bass.

Dreher, D. (1990). *The Tao of inner peace.* New York: HarperCollins.

Du Bois, W. E. B. (1903/1996). *The souls of black folk.* New York: Penguin.

Dunne, M. S. (1996). The challenges and pitfalls of peacetime leadership. *Naval Institute Proceedings, 122*(6), 72–74.

Edwards, A. (1995, August). *Possibilities for the development of mentor identity.* Paper presented at the International Study Association of Teacher Thinking, St. Catherine's, Ontario.

Elliot, B., & Calderhead, J. (1995). Mentoring for teacher development: Possibilities and caveats. In T. Kerry & A. S. Mayes (Eds.), *Issues in mentoring* (pp. 35–55). New York: Routledge.

Feuerverger, G., & Mullen, C. A. (1995). Portraits of marginalized lives: Stories of literacy and collaboration in school and prison. *Interchange, 26*(3), 221–240.

Frankl, V. E. (1969). *The will to meaning: Foundations and applications of logotherapy.* New York: New American Library.

Freire, P. (1994). *Pedagogy of hope.* New York: Continuum.

Fuchida, M., & Okumiya, M. (1955). *Midway: The battle that doomed Japan, the Japanese navy's story.* Annapolis, MD: Naval Institute Press.

Furlong, J. (1995). *Mentoring student teachers: The growth of professional knowledge.* New York: Routledge.

Gergen, K. L. (1991). *The saturated self: Dilemmas of identity in contemporary life.* New York: BasicBooks.

Gergen, K. L., & Gergen, M. (1993). Notes about contributors. In R. Josselson & A. Lieblich (Eds.), *The narrative study of lives* (pp. 225–226). London: Sage Publications.

Giroux, H. A. (1993). *Living dangerously: Multiculturalism and the politics of difference.* New York: Peter Lang.

Gold, Y. (1992). Psychological support for mentors and beginning teachers: A critical dimension. In T. M. Bey & C. T. Holmes (Eds.), *Mentoring: Contemporary principles and issues* (pp. 25–34). Reston, VA: Association of Teacher Educators.

Goodlad, J. (1988). School-university partnerships for educational renewal: Rationale and concepts. In K. Sirotinik and J. Goodlad (Eds.), *School-university partnerships in action: Concepts, cases, and concerns.* New York: Teacher's College Press.

Goodson, I. (1994). Studying the teacher's life and work. *Teaching and Teacher Education, 10*(1), 29–37.

Greene, M. (1995). Educational visions: What are schools for and what should we be doing in the name of education? In J. L. Kincheloe & S. R. Steinberg (Eds.), *Thirteen questions: Reframing education's conversation* (2nd ed., pp. 305–313). New York: Peter Lang.

Grimes, N. (1993). *Walt Disney's Cinderella.* Racine, WI: Western Publishing.

Grumet, M. R. (1988). *Bitter milk: Women and teaching.* Amherst, MA: University of Massachusetts Press.

_____. (1995). The curriculum: What are the basics and are we teaching them? In J. L. Kincheloe & S. R. Steinberg (Eds.), *Thirteen questions: Reframing education's conversation* (2nd ed., pp. 15–21). New York: Peter Lang.

Head, F. A., Reiman, A. J., & Thies-Sprinthall, L. (1992). The reality of mentoring: Complexity in its process and function. In T. M. Bey & C. T. Holmes (Eds.), *Mentoring: Contemporary principles and issues* (pp. 5–34). Reston, VA: Association of Teacher Educators.

Hunt, D. E. (1987). *Beginning with ourselves: In practice, theory, and human affairs.* Toronto: OISE Press.

_____. (1994). Have you travelled this path before? In A. L. Cole & D. E. Hunt (Eds.), *The doctoral dissertation journey: Reflections from travellers and guides* (pp. 91–97). Toronto: OISE Press.

Jeffers, S. (1985). *Cinderella.* New York: Dial Books.

Joubert, J. (1899). *Joubert: A selection from his thoughts.* New York: Dodd, Mead and Company.

Kealy, W. A., & Mullen, C. A. (1996). *Re-thinking mentoring relationships* (Microfiche No. ED 394420). Presentation at the annual meeting of the American Educational Research Association, New York. (ERIC Clearinghouse on Higher Education)

Keegan, J. (1990). *The price of admiralty: The evolution of naval warfare.* New York: Penguin Books.

Kerr, D. H. (1993). *Beyond education: In search of nurture.* Work in Progress Series, No. 2. Seattle, WA: Institute for Educational Inquiry.

Keyton, J., & Kalbfleisch, P. J. (1993). *Building a normative model of women's mentoring relationships.* Paper presented to the joint Central/Southern States Communication Association, Lexington, KY.

Kincheloe, J. L., & Steinberg, S. R. (1995). Introduction: The more questions we ask, the more questions we ask. In J. L. Kincheloe & S. R. Steinberg (Eds.), *Thirteen questions: Reframing education's conversation* (2nd ed., pp. 1–11). New York: Peter Lang.

Krathwohl, D. R. (1994). A slice of advice. *Educational Researcher, 23*(1), 29–32.

Lakoff, G., & Johnson, M. (1980). *Metaphors we live by.* Chicago: University of Chicago Press.

Lawrence, R. D. (1985). *Shark! Nature's masterpiece.* Shelburne, VT: Chapters Publishing.

L'Engle, M. (1962). *A wrinkle in time.* New York: Farrar, Straus & Giroux.

Little, W. J. (1989). The picture of success. In L. Shalaway (Ed.), *Learning to teach ... not just for beginners* (p. 267). New York: Scholastic Professional Books.

MacLachlan, P. (1993). *Baby.* New York: Bantam Doubleday Dell.

May, W. T. (1994). The tie that binds: Reconstructing ourselves in institutional contexts. *Studies in Art Education, 35*(3), 135–148.

Mead, M. (1972). *Blackberry winter: My early years.* New York: William Morrow.

Miezitis, S. (1994). The journey continues: From traveller to guide. In A. L. Cole & D. E. Hunt (Eds.), *The doctoral dissertation journey: Reflections from travellers and guides* (pp. 99–108). Toronto: OISE Press.

Mullen, C. A. (1994). A narrative exploration of the self I dream. *Journal of Curriculum Studies, 26*(3), 252–263.

_____. (1997a). Hispanic preservice teachers and professional development: Stories of mentorship. *Latino Studies Journal, 8*(1), 3-35.

_____. (1997b). *Imprisoned selves: An inquiry into prisons and academe.* Lanham, MD: University Press of America.

Mullen, C. A., & Dalton, J. A. (1996). Dancing with sharks: On becoming socialized teacher-educator researchers. *Taboo: The Journal of Culture and Education, I,* 55–71.

Noddings, N. (1984). *Caring: A feminine approach to ethics and moral education.* Berkeley: University of California Press.

_____. (1992). *The challenge to care in schools.* New York: Teachers College Press.

Pagano, J. (1994). Teaching women. In L. Stone (Ed.), *The education feminism reader* (pp. 252–275). New York: Routledge.

Patterson, L., & Stansell, J. (1984). Teachers and researchers: A new mutualism. *Language Arts, 64*(7), 717–721.

Potter, E. B. (1976). *Nimitz.* Annapolis, MD: Naval Institute Press.

Phillips, E. M., & Pugh, D. S. (1994). *How to get a Ph.D.: A handbook for students and dissertation supervisors.* Milton Keynes, Philadelphia: Open University Press.

Piper, W. (1990). *The little engine that could.* New York: Platt & Munk.

Pitters, M. (1994). Riding a roller coaster in a fog: Trusting the search for truth. In A. L. Cole & D. E. Hunt (Eds.), *The doctoral thesis journey: Reflections from travellers and guides* (pp. 125–134). Toronto: OISE Press.

Raymond, D., Butt, R., & Townsend, D. (1992). Context for teacher development: Insights from teachers' stories. In A. Hargreaves & M. G. Fullen (Eds.), *Understanding teacher development* (pp. 143–161). New York: Teachers College Press.

Reiman, A. J. (1988). *An intervention study of long-term mentor training: Relationships between cognitive-developmental theory and reflection.* Unpublished doctoral dissertation, North Carolina State University, Raleigh, N. C.

Reis, S. M. (1995). Talent ignored, talent diverted: The cultural context underlying giftedness in females. *Gifted Child Quarterly, 39,* 162–170.

Roberts, W. (1985). *Leadership secrets of Attila the Hun.* Salt Lake City, UT: Publishers Press.

_____. (1988). *The enculturation of battlefield leaders for the twenty-first century.* The Omar N. Bradley Lecture Series address presented at The U. S. Army Command and General Staff College, Leavenworth, KS.

Rosen, H. (1986). The importance of story. *Language Arts, 63*(3), 226–237.

Rosenblatt, L. (1969). Towards a transactional theory of reading. *Journal of Reading Behavior, 1*(1), 31–47.

_____. (1978). *The reader, the text, the poem.* Carbondale, IL: Southern Illinois University Press.

_____. (1985). Viewpoints: Transaction versus interaction–A terminological rescue operation. *Research in the Teaching of English 19,* 96–107.

Sadker, M., & Sadker, D. (1994). *Failing at fairness.* New York: Charles Scribner's Sons.

Salmon, P. (1992). *Achieving a Ph.D.–ten students' experiences.* Oakhill, Staffordshire: Trentham.

Saltzman, A. (1996, March 25). Woman versus woman: Why aren't more female executives mentoring their junior counterparts? *U.S. News & World Report,* 50–53.

Sands, R. G., Parson, L. A., & Duane, J. (1991). Faculty mentoring faculty in a public university. *Journal of Higher Education, 62*(2), 174–193.

Saunders, D. (1995, June 24). Harassment policies aim to heat up 'chilly climate.' *The Globe and Mail,* A8.

Shalaway, Linda. (1989). *Learning to teach ... not just for beginners.* New York: Scholastic Professional Books.

Showers, B., & Joyce, B. (1996). The evolution of peer coaching. *Educational Leadership, 53*(6), 12–16.

Simon, R. (1987). Empowerment as a pedagogy of possibility. *Language Arts, 64*(4), 370–382.

Skinner, B. F. (1957). *Verbal behavior.* New York: Appleton-Century-Crofts.

Smith, F. (1981). Demonstrations, engagement, and sensitivity: A revised approach to language learning. *Language Arts, 52,* 103–112.

Speare, E.G. (1958). *The witch of Blackbird Pond.* New York: Houghton Mifflin.

Steinberg, S. R. (1995). Teachers under suspicion: Is it true that teachers aren't as good as they used to be? In J. L. Kincheloe & S. R. Steinberg (Eds.), *Thirteen questions: Reframing education's conversation* (2nd ed., pp. 61–67). New York: Peter Lang.

Thompson, E. (1984). *Three letters from Teddy.* Unpublished lecture delivered at the University of Houston, Texas.

Townsend, B. L., & Patton, J. M. (1995). Three "warring souls" of African American high school students with gifts and talents. *Proceedings of the Fourth Biennial International Special Education Conference* (pp. 64–70). Brighton, UK: International Special Education Association.

U. S. Department of Education, National Center for Education Statistics. (1995). *The condition of education* (pp. 95–273). Washington, DC.

Webb-Johnson, G. C., & Young, C. Y. (1992). The utilization of doctoral students: Retention strategies for culturally diverse students in education–A futuristic look. In E. Middleton, E. Mason, E. Bickel, D. Jones, & R. Gaskins (Eds.), *Proceedings of the Sixth Annual National Conference for Recruitment and Retention of Minorities in Education* (pp. 71–77). Lexington, Kentucky.

Walker, B. A., & Mehr, M. (1992). *The courage to achieve: Why America's brightest women struggle to fulfill their promise*. New York: Simon & Schuster.

White, E. B. (1952). *Charlotte's web*. New York: Harper & Row.

Winfield, L. F., and Manning, J. B. (1992). Changing school culture to accommodate student diversity. In M. E. Dilworth (Ed.), *Diversity in teacher education: New expectations*. San Francisco, CA: Jossey-Bass.

Young, C. Y. (1994). *Effects of a retention program on culturally diverse preservice teachers*. Unpublished doctoral dissertation, Illinois State University, Normal, Illinois.

# Notes on Contributors

*Diane Sopko Adoue* is a doctoral student at Texas A&M University and teacher educator in professional development schools whose classroom teaching background is in science. She is interested in teacher education, science education, and in instituting reform that will lead to student learning and performance. Her research is in the area of the nature of science as understood by preservice teachers and professional development schools. She includes, in her approach, the influence of culture in the development of preservice teachers. Diane was a member of the Self-Study Writing Group that resulted in this book.

*Cindy King Boettcher* is a doctoral student at Texas A&M University in the College of Education. She was an elementary public school teacher for 10 years and a principal for a decade. Her interests include children's literature and its importance in the classroom. Her dissertation study is concerned with gender issues in children's literature. She is author of the recent children's book, *Anna Meagan: The Aggie Cinderella Story* (with illustrator Tammie L. Bissett). Cindy was a member of the mentoring group.

*Maggie D. Cox,* a Graduate Merit Fellow at Texas A&M University, is pursuing a doctorate with an emphasis in literacy and environmental education. She earned a B.A. and M.S. in elementary education as well as certification as a school librarian. Her involvement in mentorship has continued throughout her 30 years of public school teaching at the elementary, middle school, and college levels. Currently, Maggie is an educational consultant providing staff development in the areas of gifted education, creativity, language arts, and science instruction. She is developing a hands-on K-2 integrated curriculum for a Texas state park to use with visiting school groups. Her dissertation research will look at the influence of field-based educational experiences on young students, literacy, and environmental activity. She was a participant in our *Circle*.

*Jane B. Hughey* is currently a visiting assistant professor in the Department of Curriculum and Instruction in the College of Education at Texas A&M University. She earned a Ph.D. in educational psychology from Texas A&M University and B.A. and M.A. degrees in English from the University of Oklahoma. Her primary interests involve a specialization in writing and writing assessment, the development of creativity in instruction, and work with the gifted and talented. She is developer and director of a research-based National Diffusion Network (NDN) program under the auspices of the U.S. Department of Education. Her NDN program recently won reapproval for another six years. Over the past five years, she has been researching the effects of different approaches to teaching writing on adolescent students with low socio-economic status and limited English proficiency. Mentoring is a thread that runs through much of what she does.

*William A. Kealy* is an associate professor in the Department of Secondary Education at the University of South Florida where he teaches courses in instructional media design and production. He also serves as the Co-Director of the Florida Center for Instructional Technology. Dr. Kealy's research is in the area of learning from graphic displays used in instructional texts and has appeared in such publications as the *Journal of Educational Psychology* and *Contemporary Educational Psychology*. Prior to his current position, he was on the faculty at Florida State University and Texas A&M University. His doctorate is in learning and instructional technology from Arizona State University. Because of his mentoring experiences as a doctoral student, Dr. Kealy is especially interested in communicating the importance of mentorship as a means of enriching one's scholastic and professional development.

*April Whatley Kemp* is a doctoral student at Texas A&M University and former elementary teacher who is currently working on her dissertation. Her interests are in gender issues, children's literature, and gifted education. She has taught children's literature at the university level and worked as a consultant in gifted education. April's dissertation is a life history study of female teacher educators and how their life experiences have shaped their personal visions of education. Her interest in mentoring began while she was working with gifted students and it developed while exploring comentoring with others in the *Circle*.

*Carol A. Mullen* is faculty at the Leadership Development Department, University of South Florida. Her teaching and research interests explore the topics of leadership (mentoring theory and practice), partnership, and diversity within schools, universities, and prisons. With this self-study group of graduate students and professors, Dr. Mullen offers her redefinition of traditional mentoring theory and practice through story line, metaphor, and artwork. She has produced many guest edited issues of academic journals. She has also published numerous articles and three other books: *New Directions in Mentoring* (1999, Falmer Press), *The Postmodern Educator* (with C. T. P. Diamond, 1999, Peter Lang), and *Imprisoned Selves* (University Press of America, 1997). Dr. Mullen received her doctorate in curriculum studies and teacher development at the Ontario Institute for Studies in Education, University of Toronto, Canada, in 1994. URL: www.coedu.usf.edu/mullen. As a member of various *Circles*, Carol initiates rewarding comentoring opportunities that inspire the development of new communities of scholars.

*John C. Stansell* is a professor of educational curriculum and instruction at Texas A&M University. His teaching and research interests include literacy and literacy education, professional development schools, and the simultaneous restructuring of schools and teacher education programs to better serve the interests of a democratic society. A member of the Self-Study Writing Group on whose work this book is based, he sees mentors and mentoring as integral parts of each of his areas of interest.

*Gwendolyn Webb-Johnson* is an assistant professor in the departments of Educational Curriculum and Instruction and Special Education at Texas A&M University. She is also the Director of the Office for Culturally Diverse Student Services and Research for the College of Education. She completed her master's at Northeastern Illinois University and her doctorate at Illinois State University. Dr. Webb-Johnson teaches undergraduate courses in multicultural education, language arts, and behavior management for the teacher preparation program. She also teaches graduate foundations courses. Gwen is committed to mentoring as a way of life as evinced by her professional and research efforts in the successful retention of culturally diverse preservice teachers. She participated in our *Circle*.

*Donna L. Wiseman* has recently joined the faculty at Northern Illinois University as a professor and holds the Morgridge Endowed Chair for Teacher Education. She has served in several college administrative roles and teaches graduate and undergraduate courses in reading/language arts and teacher education. Her research interests include topics related to collaborative school-university reform, diversity and equality, and language arts. Dr. Wiseman is working on two teacher education textbooks and is writing a series of children's books based on the tales of Japanese folk toys. Donna was a member of our self-study group.

*Luana Zellner* is a fifth-generation Californian living in Texas with her husband and two grown sons. She received her B.A. from San Jose State University, her M.A. from the University of Northern Colorado, and is currently working on her Ph.D. in Educational Curriculum and Instruction at Texas A&M University. She has taught public school in California, Arizona, Colorado, and Texas. For the past eight years she has functioned as lecturer, curriculum developer and coordinator, student advisor, and university liaison. She is currently program coordinator for the School Leadership Initiative Program in the Department of Educational Administration, College of Education, Texas A&M University. Luana contributed as a participant of our mentoring group.

Photo: William A. Kealy

**Carol A. Mullen** is on the faculty at the Leadership Development Department, University of South Florida, College of Education, 4202 East Fowler Avenue, EDU 162, Tampa, Florida 33620-5650 USA. Her teaching and research interests explore the topics of leadership (mentoring theory and practice), partnership, and diversity within schools, universities, and prisons. With this self-study group of graduate students and professors, Dr. Mullen offers her redefinition of traditional mentoring theory and practice through story line, metaphor, and artwork. She has produced many guest edited issues of academic journals. She has also published numerous articles and three other books: *New Directions in Mentoring* (1999), *The Postmodern Educator* (with C. T. P. Diamond, Peter Lang, 1999), and *Imprisoned Selves* (1997). Dr. Mullen received her doctorate in curriculum studies and teacher development at the Ontario Institute for Studies in Education, University of Toronto, Canada, in 1994. Email: cmullen@tempest.coedu.usf.edu; personal URL: www.coedu.usf.edu/mullen.

Counterpoints publishes the most compelling and imaginative books being written in education today. Grounded on the theoretical advances in criticalism, feminism and postmodernism in the last two decades of the twentieth century, Counterpoints engages the meaning of these innovations in various forms of educational expression. Committed to the proposition that theoretical literature should be accessible to a variety of audiences, the series insists that its authors avoid esoteric and jargonistic languages that transform educational scholarship into an elite discourse for the initiated. Scholarly work matters only to the degree it affects consciousness and practice at multiple sites. Counterpoints' editorial policy is based on these principles and the ability of scholars to break new ground, to open new conversations, to go where educators have never gone before.

For additional information about this series or for the submission of manuscripts, please contact:

Joe L. Kincheloe & Shirley R. Steinberg
637 West Foster Avenue
State College, PA 16801